T0305904

Employee Wellbeing

Drawing on work and positive psychology, this insightful book addresses contemporary workplace challenges and analyses evidence-based interventions in the employee wellbeing domain.

Recent years have seen significant developments in the area of employee wellbeing, with many organisations becoming more interested in wellbeing at work. This book begins by contextualising employee wellbeing before and after the onset of the pandemic and demonstrates how employers are seeking advice and proactively implementing wellbeing policies and practices. It goes on to consider such issues as employee voice, employee growth mindset, burnout, quiet quitting, sleep hygiene, and psychological safety. Each chapter is supported by thought-provoking questions and activities that encourage readers to reflect on their learning and apply their understanding of the material in practice, as well as suggestions for further reading that offer resources for continued study. The book closes by analysing a range of specific interventions that organisations can employ, including potential pitfalls to avoid. In so doing, it offers clear, practical guidance for employers looking to improve employee wellbeing in their organisations.

Employee Wellbeing is an important read for stakeholders within and outside of organisations, and will also be of interest to students and academics studying work psychology, organisational behaviour, wellbeing at work and related fields.

Pooja Vishwanathan has served as a lecturer at Amity University, Dubai, passionately educating young people within the domains of psychological and health sciences and as an associate tutor at Warwick University, UK. Her undergraduate and postgraduate degrees are from the UK – majoring in Organisational Psychology. Shifting course for her PhD degree, she chose to pursue Educational and Positive Psychology for her research.

Employee Wellbeing

Contemporary Workplace Challenges and Evidence-Based Interventions

Pooja Vishwanathan

Routledge
Taylor & Francis Group

LONDON AND NEW YORK

Cover Image: © Getty Images

First published 2025

by Routledge
4 Park Square, Milton Park, Abingdon, Oxon OX14 4RN

and by Routledge
605 Third Avenue, New York, NY 10158

Routledge is an imprint of the Taylor & Francis Group, an informa business

© 2025 Pooja Vishwanathan

The right of Pooja Vishwanathan to be identified as author of this work has been asserted in accordance with sections 77 and 78 of the Copyright, Designs and Patents Act 1988.

All rights reserved. No part of this book may be reprinted or reproduced or utilised in any form or by any electronic, mechanical, or other means, now known or hereafter invented, including photocopying and recording, or in any information storage or retrieval system, without permission in writing from the publishers.

Trademark notice: Product or corporate names may be trademarks or registered trademarks, and are used only for identification and explanation without intent to infringe.

British Library Cataloguing-in-Publication Data
A catalogue record for this book is available from the British Library

Library of Congress Cataloging-in-Publication Data
Names: Vishwanathan, Pooja, author.
Title: Employee wellbeing: contemporary workplace challenges and
evidence-based interventions / Pooja Vishwanathan.
Description: Abingdon, Oxon; New York, NY: Routledge, 2025. |
Includes bibliographical references and index.
Identifiers: LCCN 2024024014 (print) | LCCN 2024024015 (ebook) |
ISBN 9781032705101 (hbk) | ISBN 9781032704524 (pbk) | ISBN 9781032705125 (ebk)
Subjects: LCSH: Employees–Psychology. | Work environment. | Well-being.
Classification: LCC HD4901 .V56 2025 (print) | LCC HD4901 (ebook) |
DDC 658.3/8–dc23/eng/20240716
LC record available at https://lccn.loc.gov/2024024014
LC ebook record available at https://lccn.loc.gov/2024024015

ISBN: 978-1-032-70510-1 (hbk)
ISBN: 978-1-032-70452-4 (pbk)
ISBN: 978-1-032-70512-5 (ebk)

DOI: 10.4324/9781032705125

Typeset in Optima
by Deanta Global Publishing Services, Chennai, India

Contents

Preface

The 'employee wellbeing' theme has been meticulously analysed within the domains of psychology and organisational/occupational psychology.

Increasing in number, well sought-after, high-impact journal articles and books highlight the findings of investigations that have examined employee wellbeing. Embracing a lucid writing style, this book aims to contextualise employee wellbeing in the context of the onset of the pandemic. It explores contemporary workplace challenges that are increasingly crippling organisations, including how organisational psychologists are able to assess the extent to which these challenges persist in their organisations. Critically analysing evidence-based interventions to address these concerns, this resource additionally appraises what the 'next normal' potentially holds for organisational stakeholders.

Although written with the objective of informing anyone who is concerned with mental health and wellbeing in the workplace, this text will serve as a useful read for undergraduate and postgraduate learners enrolled on psychological and health sciences courses, and in management studies. The book bridges the gap between research and practice by offering a wealth of examples, drawing from findings within the literature and of professional bodies such as the British Psychological Society (BPS) and the Chartered Institute of Personnel Development (CIPD).

The book, making for an interesting and beneficial read for all organisational stakeholders, urges policy-makers within governmental bodies, employers of small-, medium- and large-scale businesses, employees, educators within universities and those employed within research settings to reflect, further investigate and implement carefully designed employee wellbeing policies and practices. It makes evidence-informed recommendations for policy and practice.

Preliminary knowledge in psychology and/or organisational studies/business management will prove to be beneficial to comprehend the content. The author has employed technical language and has made earnest attempts at clarifying any technical terminology that has been used in the book. Whilst you are reading, I hope that you will be able to think and learn more deeply about employee wellbeing and subsequently analyse and implement policies and practices that foster wellbeing in the workplace with greater ease.

Acknowledgements

To my supervisors – Mr. Ian Abbott and Dr. Deborah Biggerstaff –
Thank you for all your teachings, good will and love.

To all those who believed in and added to my light! – Thank you!

About the Author

Dr. Pooja Vishwanathan has served as a lecturer at Amity University, Dubai, passionately educating young people within the domains of psychological and health sciences, and as an associate tutor for Warwick University (UK). Her undergraduate and postgraduate degrees are from the UK – majoring in Organisational Psychology. Shifting course for her PhD degree, she chose to pursue Educational and Positive Psychology for her research.

Her work experiences within human resources, particularly in recruitment, employee relations, psychometric testing and education have particularly been in the European and the Middle Eastern context. Early in her career, Pooja's research focussed on job satisfaction, employee absenteeism, performance-related pay, mental health and wellbeing. She has acquired higher education teaching qualifications from Warwick University (UK) and Harvard University (USA).

Having been certified as an Associate Member of the Chartered Institute of Personnel Development (CIPD), an Associate Fellow of the Higher Education Academy and an active member of the British Psychological Society (BPS), Dr. Pooja has been an avid contributor to *Gulf News*, one of the national newspapers in the United Arab Emirates. She writes this book for all stakeholders within organisations, researchers and learners to reflect, design and implement policies and practices that foster employee wellbeing in the workplace. Her research interests include organisational grit, the growth mindset, psychological safety in workplaces and purpose-building within organisations.

Chapter 1

Employee Wellbeing
Pre-Pandemic

1.1 The 'Employee Wellbeing' Theme

The World Health Organization (WHO) proclaim employment to be a social determinant of health and wellbeing (Mäkikangas, Kinnunen, Feldt & Schaufeli, 2016; Benach, Vives, Amable, Vanroelen, Tarafa & Muntaner, 2014; WHO, 2024). An individual's work has a significant influence on their health and wellbeing – physical, emotional, mental, financial and social – in addition to their sense of purpose and their ability to grow (Mäkikangas et al., 2016). In this light, international world organisations (such as WHO) recognise employee wellbeing (EW) as a highly subjective, multi-faceted and complex construct. This is appraised as 'an employee's ability to understand his/her own capability, manage normal stressors of life, to work productively and be able to make a contribution to his/her community' (Hati & Pradhan, 2019). Variables such as 'employee physical health', 'job satisfaction', 'employee burnout', 'employee engagement' and 'employee commitment' count as crucial 'wellbeing' markers (Hati et al., 2019; Reidhead, 2021). Guest (2017) recognises EW as enhancing 'employee experience', more than any other business outcome.

Research within the domains of 'employee health and wellbeing' has made enormous progress in the past decades (Sonnentag, Tay, & Nesher Shoshan, 2023). Scientific developments from the last 25 years have appraised three key themes. This has included i) the formulation of new theoretical frameworks and refinement of the existing ones (particularly including frameworks that demonstrate the significance of employee resources), ii) potential facilitators and barriers to employee health and wellbeing and iii) methodological approaches by which EW is analysed (this included daily diary and intervention studies). However, when contextualising EW within contemporary workplace policy-making and practice (in contrast to the domains of 'research'), it is fair to appraise this as an 'unfinished enterprise' in its infancy (Sonnentag et al., 2023).

DOI: 10.4324/9781032705125-1

1.2 The Role of Human Resources in the Employee Wellbeing Narrative and the 'Paradox Lens'

Human Resources (HR) assumes various roles – that of a business partner, change agent, administrative expert and employee champion. Nevertheless, its effectiveness must be measured in terms of its service to the business and business competitiveness, rather than 'employee comfort' (Renwick, 2002). HR teams enact two distinct roles, which are of relevance to EW – the role of a 'guardian' or that of a 'gambler' (Kelly & Gennard, 2001; Renwick, 2002).

Fostering employee welfare and acting as a 'guardian of ethics', HR adopts 'soft approaches', initiating diversity and inclusion interventions, employee championing, family friendly policies and employee counselling services on alcohol/drug use/abuse (Kelly et al., 2001). An alternative perspective holds HR assuming the role of a 'gambler', where HR often acts out of its own interests, rather than that of the employee. This perspective perceives 'wellbeing' as of little significance to HR; any initiative is assumed to be only implemented with top leaders for HR's own survival within the organisation (Kelly et al., 2001). EW propositions are or should be criticised for being of 'aesthetic appeal' and not as catering to the 'needs of the business' (Renwick, 2002).

More recent studies from the pandemic era appraise the 'paradox lens'. The perspective appraises the significance of a 'both/and' approach, in contrast to a 'binary/or' approach. This HR 'lens' is evidenced as diminishing bias and relatively more 'effective' in manoeuvring paralysing and frustrating times such as those of COVID-19 (Collings, Nyberg, Wright & McMackin, 2021). Public health emergencies are marked by the poor health of organisational stakeholders (including employees and clients) and disruptions in core HR practices – including global mobility, internal communications, leadership development and succession planning. An understanding of the 'people-profit' paradox calls HR to possess a greater awareness of how two conflicting options do not necessitate a compromise.

Organisations draw a balance between the evolving demands of organisational culture, competition and the generation of sustainable employee returns (Kelly et al., 2001). This is possible by adopting more 'active' responses in contrast to choosing 'defensive' ones, although the latter approach might temporarily decrease the perceived number and extent of contradictions or might reaffirm a false sense of order and deteriorated levels of HR anxiety. Active responses involve employing 'transcendence' ('synthesising opposing elements at a higher level and finding new ways of framing that eliminate the contradiction') and acceptance ('viewing tensions in terms of potential for creativity and opportunity, through the immersion of oneself, within the opposing forces') (Collings et al., 2021; Daubner-Siva, Vinkenburg & Jansen, 2017).

These methods foster 'paradoxical thinking', encouraging broader discussions and the building of resolutions – either by 'splitting and choosing between a tension' or by discovering synergies that accommodate opposing tensions. By building on both possibilities and resolutions, HR is able to draw a balance between long-term benefits of investing in EW and the owner's short-term financial demands (Collings et al., 2021; Daubner-Siva et al., 2017).

1.3 Challenges with Appraising and Addressing Employee Wellness

Employee Wellbeing Perceived as 'Insignificant'

Holding immense potential to foster positivity and contribute to enhanced physical health and a strengthened immune system, the 'wellbeing' theme, however, entails a high degree of complexity and subjectivity. This is often misunderstood as a 'hurray' theme and one that fosters 'easy' work. EW is much more than a 'fresh fruit Friday'. It concerns enhancing the 'joy' component, subsequently improving an employee's quality of life. This social misunderstanding has primarily contributed to the theme being taken for granted by employers, with stakeholders within organisations failing to perceive EW and investments in interventions as a priority. Leaders underestimate the number of employees and the extent to which individuals are being challenged with wellbeing concerns, globally. Also, less heed is paid to the undisputable, significant, positive correlation between EW and employee commitment, productivity and retention (Hati et al., 2019).

Solely Paying Heed to Employee Physical Health Parameters

EW is thought about 'narrowly'; 'wellness' means more than considering cholesterol levels, diet and exercise. Employee mental health experiences such as anxiety and depression significantly influence workplace productivity. The challenge, therefore, is with employers poorly gauging the scope of 'wellness'. Their tendencies of solely paying heed to physical health parameters, failing to be inclusive of employee mental health assessments and interventions inadequately serve their workforce (Baun, Berry and Mirabito, 2010; Proper, & Van Oostrom, 2019).

Suggested Activity

Reflect and discuss the extent to which your organisation pays heed to physiological health parameters versus those of employee psychological wellbeing.

Reactive, Emotional Approaches to Addressing Employee Wellness

Most organisations adopt reactive, emotional approaches to addressing challenges with EW. This approach implies the organisation taking action only after an internal or external trigger has caused and aggravated a physical or mental health incident. A lack of insight or comprehensive data around current performance (this includes recruitment, retention and presenteeism) and poor, evidence-based knowledge on 'collective practice' drives the wide-spread employment of reactive, emotional approaches to EW (Nielsen, Nielsen, Ogbonnaya, Känsälä, Saari & Isaksson, 2017).

Although most organisations express an interest in learning more about what best practice looks like, a 'collective lack of information' acts as a significant barrier to EW wellbeing initiations. Poor EW forecasting and risk assessments, inappropriate assessments of current policies, practices and interventions and ineffective decision making for future EW challenges follow as a result (Deloitte, 2017; Nielsen et al., 2017).

Employing Evidence Based Policy and Practice for Employee Wellbeing

EW is a monumental and an 'intimate' concern – employers cannot afford reactive approaches or play 'offence' rather than 'defence'. This places their relationships with their employees at stake. Investments in EW hold potential to create and sustain strong bonds with employees and consequentially with other stakeholders in the industry (Barands, Briener & Rousseau, 2014; Baun et al., 2010).

Professional, accreditation bodies such as the American Psychological Association (APA) (2021) advise how proactive, data-driven, evidence-based approaches are preventive, emphasising on quantification of wellbeing markers such as employee absenteeism and presenteeism. High-quality, data-driven decisions, wellbeing policies and effective practices are a consequence of critically appraising and analysing evidences from a wide variety of strong and credible sources. The sources include scientific evidence on personnel management, organisational evidence (including facts and figures gathered from the company), stakeholder evidence (including the perspectives and concerns of those who may be affected by any wellbeing policy, practice or intervention) and experiential evidence (taking into consideration the judgement and advice of practitioners and business leaders) (APA, 2021; CIPD, 2023a; EW, Provost & Fawcett, 2013; Zwetsloot, Leka, Kines & Jain, 2020).

When employing a data driven/evidence-based approach, any proposition is made on the basis of hard facts, rather than on obsolete information, short term wellbeing fads or natural biases. Evidences facilitate the designing, development and implementation, defending and justification of wellbeing policy and practice. A data driven/evidence-based method assembles a stronger repertoire of knowledge, is more trustworthy and is likely to succeed (Bache, 2019; Provost et al., 2013). The What Works Centre for Wellbeing, which comprises departments from within the UK government and the Economic and Social Research Council, firmly reinstates evidence-based wellbeing policy and practice as significantly contributing to early appraisal of wellbeing concerns, early intervention, consequential local economic growth and a larger social impact (Bache, 2019).

In addition to employing evidence-based methods, the CIPD (2023) appraise principles-led (decision making on the basis of principles upholding the work itself and employees within the organisation and embracing professionalism) and outcome-driven methodologies for appropriately addressing EW. This enables organisations to cautiously and systematically review their approach towards EW, take into consideration funding decisions and Return on Wellbeing Investments (ROI) and have a greater potential to influence business leaders, quality of work and workplace wellbeing (Provost et al., 2013; Nasamu, Connolly, Bryan & Bryce, 2022).

Differentiating between Basic, Intermediate and Advanced Level, Evidence-Based Initiations

Deloitte (2017) distinguishes between organisations who employ evidence-based wellbeing initiations at basic, intermediate and advanced levels.

Organisations who possess little evidence-based knowledge would place little significance on EW and operate at a 'basic' level. Their motivation to invest in an intervention is to deteriorate the likelihood of risks and health hazards and comply with legal regulations. They design and implement no (or very basic) wellbeing policies. These basic EW initiations (if any) are implemented on the basis of an individual's needs. No (or few) measures are employed to assess EW or the ROI or the effectiveness of the wellbeing intervention (Koontz & Wilcox, 2022 and Ozminkowski, Serxner, Marlo, Kichlu, Ratelis & Van de Meulebroecke, 2016).

Organisations who operate at an 'intermediate' level have reactive and case-based motivation to engage with EW. With basic policies and practices being drafted and implemented, the reach of 'wellbeing' interventions is limited to individuals in need and managers. Measuring of EW, in this light, is against the KPI. Employers who function at 'advanced' levels, develop comprehensive EW policies and practices with the intention to recruit and retain a workforce, possessing skill, talent and potential. Pro-active initiatives with formulating and reporting wellbeing business cases, wellbeing policies and practices reach the wider workforce (Koontz et al., 2022; Ozminkowski et al., 2016).

Lastly, employers functioning at 'highly advanced levels' embrace 'best practices'. This group is highly motivated to foster wellbeing, to build and invest in an inclusive workforce and to significantly enhance employee performance and productivity. Here, wellbeing policy formulation and execution is a strategic priority. The employer conducts comprehensive, cost benefit analysis, prior to administering any wellbeing proposition or intervention (Baicker, K., Cutler & Song, 2010). Continually appraising EW on the organisation's agenda, the organisation draws from statistical insights and encourages 'wellbeing' related conversations with internal and external stakeholders on a regular basis. They take initiatives to dedicate job roles to workplace wellbeing on the organisational structure chart and formulate a wellbeing framework suited to their context (Deloitte, 2017).

Suggested Activity

Reflect on the 'level' at which your organisation was operating pre-pandemic. What factors do you believe contributed to the organisation operating at this level?

Top employers, additionally, create a 'buy in' case for EW investments. The contribution and analysis EW interventions must ideally focus on 'hard-dollar' returns – i.e. money invested versus money saved – this accounts for the 'Return on Investments' (ROI). This is, however, not straight-forward; the degree of subjectivity and complexity is high (Baun et al., 2010; Bennett, Weaver, Senft & Neeper, 2017; Nasamu, Connolly, Bryan & Bryce, 2022).

EW interventions contribute subtly to the strengthening of organisational culture, organisational reputation, trust and employee commitment, which are 'hard-to-measure' nuances. Little knowledge on the most suited methodologies to measure the ROI discourages and offers a lack of incentive for employers to make appropriate investments. The lack of validity, robust research and evidence on ROI instruments limit employers from furthering wellbeing initiatives within workplaces (Berry, Mirabito & Baun, 2020). Tailored, workplace context relevant approaches possess the potential to demonstrate what the cost of getting it (EW assessments and interventions) wrong is (Bennett et al., 2017; Berry et al., 2020; Thonon, Godon-Rensonnet, Perozziello, Garsi, Dab & Emsalem, 2023).

On another note, researchers recommend employers employ the lens of assessing the 'value' (VOI) instead of the 'returns' on EW investments (Ozminkowski, Serxner, Marlo, Kichlu, Ratelis & Van de Meulebroecke, 2016). In contrast to the ROI that solely accounts for the financial metrics (the health care cost savings, for instance), the VOI perspective considers nuances such as employee food consumption, employee morale and enhanced quality of life (Melnyk & Tucker, 2019; Nasamu, Connolly, Bryan & Bryce, 2022).

Suggested Activity

What factors do you believe encourage or discourage your organisation from

   i) Considering investments in employee wellbeing?
  ii) Systematically assessing the return/value on investments?

1.4 Employing Contemporary Methods to Assess Employee Wellness

Employing Occupational Health Professionals

Organisational analysts recommend employing occupational health professionals for the assessment and fostering of employee wellness (Peckham, Baker, Camp, Kaufman & Seixas, 2017). Pursuing roles such as that of a Functional Assessor, Occupational Health Nurse, Occupational Hygienist, Occupational Physician, Occupational Psychologist, Occupational Physician and Occupational Health Technician, these professionals employ evidence-based methodologies to observe and assess how individuals, groups and organisations behave and function and work related illnesses and offer advice on adjustments to enable employers to enhance workplace productivity and retention levels. Although an expensive investment, these professionals design, assess, implement and offer advice on a diverse range of workplace challenges, promote employee physical and mental health, design and conduct employee health surveillance and protection programmes and are appropriately qualified for the designing, assessment and implementation of employee wellbeing policies, practices and methodologies (research instruments) (Peckham et al., 2017). For instance, the NHS (2024) employ occupational health practitioners for their staff and appraise how OH professionals conduct telephonic assessments, pre-employment health assessments, closely examine biological monitoring results, hold case conferences with employers, human resource teams and employees, and conduct site visits and employee stress risk assessment reviews. The initiative enables NHS (2024) to protect and retain their skilled workforce, resulting in enhancing the quality of their client (patient) services.

Implementing Employee Assistance Programmes (EAP)

Employee Assistance Programmes, or EAP, are employer sponsored programmes designed to support employees with work related, personal or health related challenges. EAP confidential face to face, telephonic and online services, including medical assessments/'fitness to work assessments', employee training and counselling services are often offered by third party providers. Clover HR Consultancy Services in the UK, for instance, conduct EAP sessions, offering their clients employee self – help sheets, ad hoc and structured telephonic stress assessments and counselling support, face to face and e- counselling services (CloverHR, 2024).

Kelloggs, a leading multi-national FMCG organisation, avails of EAP services from HelpNet (Kellogg Community College, 2024). Offered this work-life benefit, Kellogg employees receive professional advice on relationship issues, substance abuse, stress and anger management, family concerns, supervisor relationship management and work life balance concerns. On a similar note, the free and confidential EAP services at Jaguar Land Rover offer employees with advice on money management, house moving, legal issues, illnesses and injuries (JaguarLandRover, 2024). Evidences affirm how EAP implementation enables timely appraisal and assessment of stressors and influences wellbeing markers, reducing tendencies of employee absenteeism, presenteeism, quiet quitting behaviours and overall business expenses, enhancing levels of retention and boosting organisational reputation (Mark, 2019).

Conducting Employee Stress Audits or 'Stress Risk' Assessments

The Health and Safety Executive (HSE) Body in the UK (2024) advice employers to conduct employee stress audits and risk assessments. The audits examine what employee physiological or psychological triggers/hazards are prevalent, which employees are likely to be harmed/affected, what specific actions the employer is able to take, to control the trigger, the consequential physiological and psychological harm, who is responsible to carry out this action and when this needs to be carried out (HSE, 2024). These nuances can potentially be explored on staff surveys, employee focus group interviews and/or stress management training workshops.

'Stress talking' toolkits, in addition, are collated and implemented to assist managers in conversing effectively with employees, supporting with preventing and managing employee stress. The manager-employee conversation toolkit appraises statements pertaining to themes of work demands, control, support, relationships, role and change. The toolkit is available on the Health and Safety Executive website (2024).

Analysing the Uptake of Flexible Working and other Wellbeing Interventions

The uptake of or the degree to which employees choose flexible working options, participation on employee assistance programmes, return to work times, sickness absence rates and incidences of physical/mental ill health account as some of the many methods to assess employee wellbeing and psychological commitment. The analysis of employee engagement levels, participation on health and wellbeing initiatives, ill health versus healthy retirement rates within the organisation may be employed to gauge wellness (Berkery, Morley, Tiernan, Purtill & Parry, 2017).

Employing 'People Analytics' to Assess Employee Wellbeing

People analytics (PA) accounts for a number of processes that employ descriptive, visual and statistical methods, aided by technology, to make meaning of employee data and HR processes (Marler & Boudreau, 2017). These analytical processes pertain to key themes such as human capital, HR systems and processes, and organisational performance and external benchmarking data (Marler & Boudreau, 2017). PA is objective, rational and a relatively less error-prone domain of study (Giermindl, Strich, Christ, Leicht-Deobald, and Redzepi, 2022). Drawing from historical data, it predicts future possibilities and behaviours. Its large processing capacity enables the analysis of an immense depth and breadth of information, thus fostering an accurate detection of patterns and correlations. It additionally allows for bias-free decision-making. This is in contrast to human decision-makers, who are only able to manage a limited amount of input (Falletta & Combs, 2020; Giermindl et al., 2022).

Three types of analytics are employed for the analysis of EW. Within descriptive analytics (for instance, HR metrics, HR reporting, HR benchmarking and the HR score card), during which employee data is summarised into meaningful charts and reports. This is in contrast to predictive analytics, which employs employee data from the past (for instance, employee intention to resign, predicted sick days) or predict future performance; i.e. it offers trend analysis and forecasting. Prescriptive analytics seeks to combine product turnover data, pricing strategy and employee rota to design an optimal opportunity for successful sales (Tursunbayeva, Di Lauro, & Pagliari, 2018).

Contemporary workplace literature confirms the widespread implementation and effectiveness of people analytics for EW. On this note, Lathabhavan (2023) affirmed how the domain of study offered evidence and insights on the performance of specific departments, enabling HR teams to gauge person-job role fit, employee engagement, intent to resign, workforce promotion, engagement and turnover forecasting. It consequently assisted with determining and forecasting employee strain and the likelihood of experiencing physical health (such as cardiovascular diseases) and mental health (such as anxiety) challenges, designing and implementation of workplace wellbeing interventions (Lathabhavan, 2023).

However, for PA systems to positively contribute to EW, HR professionals had to demonstrate strategic alignment and engagement with the use of people data. They had to positively perceive the system (Tursunbayeva et al., 2018). In this light, the literature appraises a number of successful 'people analytic' propositions initiated to foster EW. These are discussed in the following sections.

Google's 'People Analytic' Initiatives

The People and Innovation Laboratory (the 'PiLab')

Patil and Afza (2023) elucidate the example of PA systems and propositions at Google, one of the largest and most successful technology companies in the world. The organisation is appraised as a 'front runner' when considering the implementation of people analytics. Google significantly benefitted from this, fostering wellness and achieving superior employee performance and business outcomes. 'The People Innovation Laboratory', or 'the PiLab', accounts for one of the many propositions of the organisation to foster data-driven decision-making (Shrivastava et al., 2018). The lab, whilst employing psychologists, decision scientists and researchers, aims to use academic research, science and data to inform HR policies and practices. It conducts experimental studies to recognise and appraise the most effective methods for managing talent and maintaining a productive environment (including the type of incentive that enhances employee happiness). For instance, on the basis of experimental data findings, the organisation improved employee physiological health by reducing employee calorie intake, offering them smaller plates at their eating facilities (Patil et al., 2023).

Project Oxygen

Project Oxygen, Google's multi-year, evidence-based project, is aimed to identify eight behaviours of good leaders/managers. The project has comprehensively analysed qualitative interview findings from employee surveys, employee expectations from their complaints/feedback, and appreciation phrases from performance reviews and top manager awards. Their study offers clarity on what employees expect from their managers. Researchers appraise six key themes: i) being a good coach and empowering teams, ii) not micro-managing, iii) expressing an interest in EW, iv) being productive and result-oriented, v) assisting the team with career development and vi) demonstrating key technical skills that help advise the team. These findings have been incorporated in line manager training and development programmes at Google (Knaflic, 2015). The themes are particularly considered for performance review meetings and promotions. The initiative fosters team cohesiveness, enhances the quality of relationships shared between leaders and team members and, enhances levels of psychological safety and positive affect (Davidson, Brin & Page, 2017; Knaflic, 2015).

Algorithm-Based People Management Practices

Algorithm-based people management practices at Google have been evidenced as beneficial to EW and consequentially to business outcomes. The mathematical algorithms employ statistical methodologies to map employee attitudes, behaviours, personality details, etc., to the organisation's knowledge and skill specifications, by asking candidates to complete elaborate online surveys. Points are assigned to candidates using mathematical formulas; candidate-organisation fit is then predicted. The intervention has deteriorated tendencies of employees experiencing frustration and angst whilst on the job and has enhanced their perceived levels of satisfaction (Shrivastava, Nagdev & Rajesh, 2018).

'Retention Algorithm'

'Retention algorithm' employs past employee data such as employee compensation, performance reviews and promotions to identify employees who are likely to leave the organisation. This permits Google to adopt proactive measures before it is too late, whilst assisting the employer to personalise retention solutions (Shrivastava et al., 2018). The multinational organisation employed to recognise that extraordinary innovation is a consequence of an amalgamation of three distinct factors – discovery (new learning), teamwork and fun. Workplace practices have been drafted and implemented by taking these factors into account. Leaders foster collaboration whilst employing analytics. At Google headquarters, employees are intentionally required to wait in long queues for their meals and are encouraged to discuss new ideas and projects with their colleagues; this time invested on collaborations is tracked. Emphasising on the subtle powers of the collective, group collaboration and cohesiveness, the organisation fuels innovation, employee sense of belongingness and consequentially psychosocial wellness (Shrivastava et al., 2018).

Challenges with Employing 'People Analytics' for Employee Wellbeing

HR teams, in most contemporary workplaces, across the globe, lack the knowledge and skills to successfully implement employee people analytics within their workplaces. There persists a significant gap in the knowledge repertoire and application of the data sciences, statistical and numerical skills. When implemented inappropriately, HR makes analytics an excuse for treating employees as 'interchangeable widgets' (Lathabhavan, 2023).

A lack of HR's esteem in their abilities to conduct sophisticated and advanced levels of analysis of any people data is an additional challenge. 'Unlocked skills' prevent people professionals from employing contemporary, progressive methodologies. This resulted in employees failing to continually, statistically track organisational changes and employ obsolete and/or irrelevant wellbeing practices and interventions (Marler et al., 2017). Grant (2019) on another note, explicates how 'resistance to data-driven insights' ('that's not what our experience has taught us'), 'resistance to change' ('but that's the way we've always done it') and 'organisational uniqueness bias' ('that will never work here') act as barriers to effectively employing people analytics (Grant, 2019).

Also, few individuals from statistical and numerical disciplines are attracted to human resources as a career (Giermindl et al., 2022). Potential HR candidates claim they are a 'people person' and not a 'numbers person'. This philosophical barrier of failing to recognise the significance of quantitative methodologies in HR is cumbersome. It curbs employee skill development and the implementation of modern methods to solve large-scaled, people challenges, resulting in ineffective organisational decision-making for EW (CIPD, 2023a; 2023b; Giermindl et al., 2022).

Suggested Activity

Have a think and make note of what factors encourage or discourage your organisation from employing people analytics for EW assessment, intervention implementation and evaluation. From your research and reading, what strategies could leaders potentially employ to encourage stakeholders to invest in people analytics for employee wellness?

1.5 Drafting the Business Case for Employee Wellbeing

The UK government (2013) has launched a comprehensive 'workplace wellbeing tool'. The instrument recommends employers to determine the length of time (in years), during the course of which HR departments wish to assess the EW project and expect to see returns for the organisation's EW investment, costs of injuries, sickness absence, absenteeism, presenteeism, labour turnover and total costs (including start-up costs, running costs, staff and business costs), prior and post a wellbeing intervention/initiative. Alternatively, analysing the benefit-cost ratio is useful. The workplace wellbeing tool for the drafting of a business case can be accessed on the UK government's website (Department of Work and Pensions, 2013; UK Government, 2013).

Before drafting a business case for EW, it is crucial for employers and human resource teams to build on a strong, people centric culture (Chandra, 2020). Engaging in the knowing more of who employees are as people and, more importantly, recognising their needs to foster appropriate and effective social, emotional, informational and financial support are imperative to the initiation of the process. By engaging in active listening and initiating few informal conversations, employers are able to select, administer and assess wellbeing interventions appropriately for the business case (Balta, Soon & Morton, 2020; Chandra, 2020).

Secondly, HR analysts must appraise and address 'business pain points'. For instance, HR teams may wish to address employee benefits and claim costs (metrics that are easily tracked and monetised). These pain points or costs may include medical claims, employee compensation claims, hardship loans, costs of errors and mistakes, which may result from high levels of stress/chronic illness. These points account for indicators of employee distress and make for useful information for the drafting of an EW business case (Schaltegger, Hörisch, & Freeman, 2019; Warr, 1990).

Other leaders may choose to draft and implement cases, policies and practices on the basis of HR metrics – addressing challenges with the average time to hire, employee engagement – absenteeism, quiet quitting and presenteeism, employee promotion and retention.

For instance, local talent challenges such as skilled employees being challenged with extenuating circumstances, failing to turn up consistently to work, employees unable to hold employment due to poor and failing health, may cripple the functioning of the organisation (Cooper & Dewe, 2008; Scott et al., 2019). Employers may find it challenging to collate quantifiable evidence to report on EW business cases. Drawing from the findings of employee engagement surveys and conducting periodic reviews to track EW intervention usage, addresses this challenge (Sivapragasam & Raya, 2018).

The collated data enables critical evaluation of the 'actual uptake' of any EW intervention. Whilst reporting the 'employee demand' for the intervention, the business case must address how the demand of the proposition varies between the 'type of employee', 'geographical location', age, marital/familial status, etc.

The Role of Human Resources in the EW Business Case Formulation

When drafting a business case for EW and analysing the 'actual uptake', HR knowledge and skills to propagate, administer and continually assess EW interventions must be realistically evaluated. Employers may offer a diverse range of EW incentives; if HR departments, however, lack knowledgeable and skilled employees, 'employee uptake' may deteriorate. On another note, HR may have tendencies to gather personal information about their employees, in order to assess and provide for employee needs, when formulating a business case. This increases the likelihood of the employer being accused of 'breach in privacy', opening them up to law suits and other legal challenges. Adhering to ethical norms and practices and refraining from high-risk practices, talent data must be gathered by location/region, job title or store – protecting employee privacy and rights, employee and organisational reputation and dignity (Pirson, 2019).

Lastly, employee needs vary between individuals and these needs keep changing every day. In this light, HR must assess the 'uptake' based not on the needs of all employees but on who 'needs' the intervention/provision most and for whom EW investments are likely to yield the maximum benefits for the business (Deloitte, 2017; Scott & Spievack, 2019; Sigblad, Savela & Okenwa Emegwa, 2020). Including employees in the drafting of the business case is, therefore, recommended. Being receivers of EW interventions, employees are best positioned to offer additional advice on the selection and implementation of an intervention, appropriate communication and marketing strategies for wellbeing interventions (Sakka & Ahammad, 2020).

The Role of Third-Party Wellbeing Benefit Providers

HR and third-party wellbeing benefit providers (large-scaled organisations, particularly, outsource the provision of voluntary benefits to third party vendors that specialise in services related to EW), although distinct, possess important roles to play. Both stakeholders offer diverse responses, collating evidence with separate but complementary data and methods (Ott-Holland, Shepherd & Ryan, 2019). Third party wellbeing benefit providers possess a comprehensive understanding of the realistic significance of their own EW proposition, articulate their value to a client, justifiably allocate EW analytic resources and engage in evaluating the value of a wellbeing intervention for an organisation. They offer a confidential space within which research is conducted. They administer employee surveys with proper consent and are able to gather data about participating employees, without any restrictions, other than those that would be appropriate for an employer (Ott-Holland et al., 2019). Thus, third party wellbeing providers significantly benefit the drafting of the business case for EW.

Key Challenges with Effective Formulation of EW Business Cases

Few organisations make well-intentioned efforts to build evidence in the public sphere by drawing from or referring to or appraising their own experiences of EW benefits or interventions -

i) 'Proprietary knowledge' accounts for one of the most significant challenges to enhancing the quality of public research and analysis for the formulation of appropriate and effective EW assessments and interventions. Both stakeholders – HR departments and third-party benefit providers – may choose to refrain from disclosing their intervention findings with competitors, perceiving any disclosure as placing the organisation at a competitive disadvantage (Khoreva & Wechtler, 2020).

ii) Both stakeholders are 'risk averse' – i.e. vehemently protecting their company from any data that may pose a potential risk to their reputation. This includes data from failed wellbeing experiments or interventions. On occasional instances when employers and third-party providers choose to release, 'perceptions of bias' may plague the release of their findings – the public may perceive them as unreliable or biased, given that their analysis is not independently conducted or reviewed (Scottet al., 2019).

Choosing to work with multiple stakeholders including business consultant experts, practicing professionals, researchers/scientists from within the domains of HR and social sciences, with third party benefit providers and employers/HR departments, risks to an organisation's reputation are limited. Adhering to ethical practices and respecting the privacy of individuals ensures that the reputation of the organisation, third-party benefit provider and employee is protected.

Additionally, pooling individual level data from across establishments within businesses, varied sectors and industries, age groups, etc., subsequently 'deidentifying' any business or individual related data is recommended. Investigators further appraise the testing of generalised models or packages of benefits. Testing or an analysis do not only approve or disapprove of a specific service provider, but inform the broader workplace literature of 'generalisable knowledge' that can potentially help inform the design of future wellbeing interventions and practices (Khoreva & Wechtler, 2020; Sabesan & Vasanth, 2023; Scott et al., 2019).

1.6 Contextualising Employee Wellbeing Pre-Pandemic

A Surge in the Number of Employees Experiencing Clinical Anxiety and Depression.

Deloitte (2017) reported that approximately 4,88,000 employees had experienced high levels of anxiety or depression; 77% of employees claimed that work-related stressors were deteriorating their performance and quality of life. More than 72% of employers in the UK drafted no wellbeing policy, in the UK specifically. Subsequently, during the course of employee recruitment and retention, 56% of employers reported how they were unlikely to recruit an individual who were battling depression (even if they were the most suitable candidate, otherwise). In this light, more than 90% of employees reported how being challenged with a mental health condition acted as detrimental to their career progression. More recent pre-pandemic evidence from the CIPD 'health and wellbeing' report (2019) appraised 55% of employees as 'feeling exhausted', 'miserable at work' and 'experiencing excessive workload/work pressure'.

Mental health and wellbeing challenges have consequentially costed the UK economy approximately £15.1 billion per annum (Henderson, Potts & Robinson, 2020; Van Stolk, 2021). In the United States, Derr (2016) appraised how small-, medium- and large-scale organisations were increasingly discussing the pace of their businesses and recognising the need to care for their 'overwhelmed' employees.

EW challenges were also found to plague developing countries such as India – findings demonstrated increasing trends in employee absenteeism/presenteeism and chronic illness resulting from psychological distress. An increasing number of employee deaths due to hypertension and cardiovascular diseases leading to death between the ages of 34 and 65 were evidenced; these numbers are expected to surge in future. This has significantly burdened national and global healthcare and economic systems. Globally, although, most countries have recognised the significance of EW, reactive approaches (in contrast to proactive methods) have commonly been found to be employed.

An Increase in Conversations Pertaining to Employee Wellbeing

The National Academy of medicine and the Occupational Safety and Health Administration (USA) appraised EW as of global significance in 2019. In UK, EW conversations were marked by an increasing trend from less than 60% in 2018 to more than 70% in 2019. Employee physical and mental health was high on the government's agenda, with targeted funding being channelised for wellbeing initiatives. There was an increasing awareness regarding physical and mental health inequalities, propagating the significance of inclusion and 'patient empowerment' and 'challenging health and wellbeing stigma' during public awareness discourses (Passey, Brown, Hammerback, Harris & Hannon, 2018; Hastuti & Timming, 2021).

A Louder Call for Employee Wellbeing Initiatives

Pre-pandemic surveys appraised how 'millennials from 19 out of 30 countries did not expect to be "happier" employees than their parents' (McCleary, Goetzel, Roemer, Berko, Kent & De La Torre, 2017). There was a noteworthy difference in what employees valued versus what employers were offering (McCleary et al., 2017). In attempts to 'call louder' for EW interventions, well-advertised campaigns such as 'time to change' were initiated by mental health charities such as 'Mind' and 'Rethink Mental Illness'. Receiving financial aid from the Department of Health, the Comic Relief Fund and the Big Lottery Fund, the campaign aimed to end the stigma and discrimination that people with mental health and wellbeing challenges face. There have been increasing initiatives by Governments in the USA, the UK and Canada to build and foster new mental health and wellbeing networks and alliances (particularly those involved in active campaigning and public awareness). These groups have offered support to individuals willing to share their mental health concerns or advice to support other individuals, seeking assistance.

Lastly, public figures endorsing the significance of EW have further increased the number of public conversations and enhanced the attention the theme has been receiving – this has fostered social support structures for EW (Abraham, Easow, Ravichandren, Mushtaq, Butterworth, & Luty, 2010; Deloitte, 2017).

In the Indian context, Vohra, Chari, Mathur, Sudarshan, Verma, Mathur and Gandhi (2015) appraised initiatives of large-scale organisations such as *Wipro*, that initiated a 'diversity and inclusion programme' in 2008. The organisation made attempts at being more inclusive of women, employees with disabilities and those hailing from underprivileged/disadvantaged communities. Making attempts at fostering inclusion, the proposition was a 'call' for employers to be sensitive and respectful of diversity, deteriorate tendencies of incivility, bullying and abusive behaviours in the workplace, and consequentially enhance levels of esteem and wellbeing (Vohra et al., 2015).

Globally, in analysing the impact of well-advertised campaigns, the creation of employee health and wellbeing networks and an increasing number of public figure endorsements for wellbeing campaigns, organisational analysts confirmed that 2.5 million people developed an improved attitude towards EW between the years 2011 and 2015. Additionally, there was a 7% rise in the willingness to continue a friendship and work with an employee challenged with wellbeing concerns. Finally, 91% of the surveyed employees agreed that society needed to embrace greater inclusivity and tolerance of people challenged with wellbeing concerns (Deloitte, 2017; Hamilton, Pinfold, Cotney, Couperthwaite, Matthews, Barret, & Henderson, 2016).

Increased Openness for Employee Mental Health

According to the CIPD (2019) in the UK and studies such as Etuknwa, Daniels, Nayani, and Eib (2023) more than 50% of the surveyed, public-sector organisations were reported to invest in an insurance policy that covered mental health. They adopted approaches such as offering 'phased return to work' options and/or making reasonable adjustments at work, offering workplace mental health aid services and related training, provision to the services offered by 'mental health/wellbeing champions', counsellors and employee assistance programmes.

On another note, James (2019) reported many organisations in the Indian context as having formulated and implemented employee assistance programmes for mental health. Employers across the country recognised the significance of appraising and proactively addressing employee mental health challenges; companies such as Capgemini India, Mahindra and Mahindra, Uber India and Google India offered free counselling services to employees and their families. Michael Page India, more specifically, emphasised on fostering an organisational culture that urges employees to speak freely about mental health, normalising conversations about EW (James, 2019).

Similarly, Deloitte (2019) and Peters (2018) highlight how organisations in the Canadian context such as Bell (a telecommunications company offering advanced broadband communications networks and services to consumers and business customers across the country) initiated 'Bell, Let's Talk' – the largest corporate initiative fostering Canadian mental health, in 2010. The proposition aimed to combat stigma pertaining to employee mental health and improve access to psychological care and resources, support research initiatives and lead by example in workplace mental health.

More broadly, evidences suggested an increasing trend (in the years 2016, 2017 and 2018) in the provision of psychological care benefits within Canadian workplaces, increasing employee engagement in mental health campaigns and employee workplace mental health events and investments in training for employees and leaders (Deloitte, 2019; Peters, 2018).

Appraising Key Employer Concerns – Employee Presenteeism and Leavism

Habermann and Lohaus (2019) recognised employee presenteeism and leavism a widespread global phenomenon – its prevalence has been increasingly documented amongst evidences from the United States, Denmark, Sweden, Sri Lanka and the Middle-East. Deteriorating employee physical and mental health (evidenced as causes of poor employee productivity) has been appraised as associated with presenteeism and leavism tendencies. Supporting evidences appraise the role of personality and individual differences in the perception of their health and choices to engage in presenteeism, leavism or 'quiet quitting' work behaviours (Johns, 2010).

Thriving Innovations within the Corporate Wellness Industry

The workplace literature, pre-pandemic, appraised thriving innovations within the corporate wellness (including employee wellbeing programmes, employee food subscription services, fitness club memberships) and digital wellbeing industries (offering food tracking application subscription services, employee wearable devices, access to mindfulness applications, for instance) (Carolan, Harris & Cavanagh, 2017).

Jaguar Land Rover (JLR), in the UK, for instance, propagated the NHS approved digital proactive prevention tool to address employee stress and anxiety. Free access to the mobile application offered employees with proactive CBT programme services, meditation, deep muscle relaxation, applied relaxation, calm breathing, mood journal, progress tracking, goal setting, early detection of wellbeing challenges, educational content and in-app therapy services. The JLR employee, additionally, has free access to 'Aviva Digicare + Workplace' medical and wellbeing support services. This included 3 virtual GP appointments, 6 mental health appointments, Bereavement support, 6 nutritionist appointments, 2 second medical opinions and annual health check-up (JaguarLandRover, 2024). Organisational stakeholders, in the pre-pandemic era, therefore, did demonstrate an increasing awareness of EW not accounting merely as an employee benefit but as an employer's responsibility (Carolan et al., 2017).

1.7 Summary

This chapter aimed to briefly explore the EW theme and examined the role of HR in the EW narrative. Traditional workplace literature appraised two faces of HR – the 'guardian' versus the 'gambler'. More recent literature, post the onset of the pandemic, however, affirmed the significance of employing the paradox lens/people-profit lens. Employing 'transcendence' ('synthesising opposing elements at a higher level and finding new ways of framing that eliminate the contradiction') and acceptance ('viewing tensions in terms of potential for creativity and opportunity, through the immersion of oneself, within the opposing forces') could enable HR teams to build on both possibilities and resolutions to effectively tackle challenges pertaining to EW (Collings, et al., 2021). Organisational stakeholders can potentially build resolutions building resolutions by splitting and choosing between tensions or by discovering synergies that accommodate opposing tensions.

In addition to the complex role that HR played in the EW narrative, other challenges with addressing EW within workplaces were identified. This included EW being perceived as 'insignificant' stakeholders often placing significance on physical health parameters or adopting a reactive, emotional approach to poor levels of wellbeing

In the next sections, various contemporary methods by which EW can be assessed within workplaces were explored. Professional bodies recommend employing occupational health professionals, designing and implementing Employee Assistance Programmes, conducting employee stress audits, analysing the uptake of flexible working and assessing the prevalence of sickness absence, presenteeism, quiet quitting behaviours and labour turnover, to gauge wellness. Modern day workplaces, such as Google, were found to benefit from employing people analytic practices for the assessment and intervention designing and implementation of EW. Most human resource teams, across the globe, however, lack the knowledge, numerical skills and esteem to employ people analytic practices effectively to enhance levels of EW. Given the significance and usefulness of people analytic sciences in the analysis of wellbeing, professional accreditation bodies could continue to build an evidence base for the domain, propagate and offer advice on effectively employing this within workplaces. Employers will benefit from employing individuals with honed numerical skills in their HR teams, upskilling and reskilling their workforce; stakeholders are advised to invest continually in research, training and development.

Later, the author draws the reader's attention to the drafting of a business case of employee wellbeing, for which the workplace wellbeing tool proposed by the UK government in 2013 is highly recommended. The tool enables employers and HR teams to systematically calculate the various business costs, whilst analysing the benefits or 'value for money' nuance of an investment. To conclude, Chapter 1 contextualised EW during the pre-pandemic era, appraising key themes – including a surge in employees experiencing clinical anxiety and depression, an increase in conversations pertaining to EW, a louder call for EW interventions, an increased openness about employee mental health challenges, employee presenteeism and leavism behaviours and the thriving of the corporate wellness industry. In the next chapter, the author explores EW, given the onset of the pandemic. The sections contextualize theoretical frameworks, statistical insights reflecting employee physical and mental health whilst critically analyzing evidence based interventions, relevant to the public health emergency.

1.8 Further Readings

Barling, J., & Frone, M. R. (2017). If only my leader would just do something! Passive leadership undermines employee well-being through role stressors and psychological resource depletion. Stress and Health, 33(3), 211–222.

Baun, W. B., Berry, L., & Mirabito, A. M. (2020) What's the hard return on employee wellness programs. Harvard Business Review. Accessed on: 13 November 2023

Collings, D. G., Nyberg, A. J., Wright, P. M., & McMackin, J. (2021). Leading through paradox in a COVID-19 world: Human resources comes of age. Human Resource Management Journal, 31(4), 819–833.

Isson, J. P., & Harriott, J. S. (2016). People Analytics in the Era of Big Data: Changing the Way You Attract, Acquire, Develop, and Retain Talent. New Jersey: John Wiley & Sons.

Khoreva, V., & Wechtler, H. (2020). Exploring the consequences of knowledge hiding: an agency theory perspective. Journal of Managerial Psychology, 35(2), 71–84

Probst, T. M., Goldenhar, L. M., Byrd, J. L., & Betit, E. (2019). The Safety Climate Assessment Tool (S-CAT): A rubric-based approach to measuring construction safety climate. Journal of Safety Research, 69, 43–51

Sabesan, S., & Vasanth, M. A. S. (2023). Preserving employees' well-being: An organization's post-pandemic imperative. In Chakraborty, Mishra, Ganguly & Chaterjee

(Eds.), Human Resource Management in a Post-Epidemic Global Environment: Roles, Strategies, and Implementation. New York: Apple Academic Press

Schulte, P., & Vainio, H. (2010). Well-being at work–overview and perspective. Scandinavian Journal of Work, Environment & Health, 36(5), 422–429.

Shanafelt, T., Goh, J., & Sinsky, C. (2017). The business case for investing in physician well-being. JAMA Internal Medicine, 177(12), 1826–1832.

Wright, T. A., & Huang, C. C. (2012). The many benefits of employee well-being in organizational research. Journal of Organizational Behavior, 33(8), 1188–1192.

Zheng, X., Zhu, W., Zhao, H., & Zhang, C. (2015). Employee well-being in organizations: Theoretical model, scale development, and cross-cultural validation. Journal of Organizational Behavior, 36(5), 621–644.

1.9 Suggested Websites

American Psychological Association (2023). Available at: https://www.apa.org/topics /healthy-workplaces Accessed on: 5 November 2023

International Labour Organisation & World Health Organization (2023). Mental health at work: Policy brief. Available at: https://iris.who.int/ Accessed on: 5 November 2023

NHS Employers (2023). Evidence-based approaches to workforce wellbeing. Available at: https://www.nhsemployers.org/articles/evidence-based-approaches-workforce -wellbeing Accessed on: 5 November 2023

NHS Employers (2023). Health and wellbeing. Available at: https://www.nhsemployers .org/health-and-wellbeing Accessed on: 5 November 2023

World Health Organization (2023). Mental health at work. Available at: https://www .who.int//news-room/fact-sheets/detail/mental-health-at-work/ Accessed on: 5 November 2023

World Health Organization (2023). Guidelines on mental health at work. Available at: https://www.who.int/publications Accessed on: 5 November 2023

1.10 Reflective Questions – for Learners

From your reading and research:

1. Conduct a Psychinfo/EBSCOhost search covering literature published in the past using the term 'employee wellbeing'. Identify a study that resonates with your interests and that is feasible to replicate and extend. Conduct the replication.
2. Reflect on your understanding of the 'employee wellbeing' theme.
3. What factors do you believe potentially contribute to employee wellness?
4. Explicate your understanding of 'people analytics' and its significance within contemporary workplaces.

1.11 Reflective Questions – for Researchers/Practitioners

From your reading and research:

1. What were the specific wellbeing policies, practices or interventions that were employed by your organisation pre-pandemic? Discuss the extent to which these were deemed effective.
2. Does your organisation employ an emotional/reactive approach to addressing employee wellbeing? If yes, what are the factors that prevent stakeholders from employing an evidence-based, data-driven methodology?
3. Elucidate some of the 'business pain points' that your organisation's employee wellbeing interventions must address.
4. Conduct a Psychinfo/EBSCOhost search covering literature published in the past using the terms 'people analytics' and 'employee wellbeing'. Identify a study that resonates with your interests and that is feasible to replicate and extend. Conduct the replication.
5. Conduct a Psychinfo/EBSCOhost search covering literature published in the past analysing any instrument/proposition from the corporate wellness industry. Identify a study that resonates with your interests and that is feasible to replicate and extend. Conduct a replication to further test the effectiveness of the instrument/proposition.

References

Abraham, A., Easow, J. M., Ravichandren, P., Mushtaq, S., Butterworth, L., & Luty, J. (2010). Effectiveness and confusion of the time to change anti-stigma campaign. *The Psychiatrist, 34*(6), 230–233.

Adams, J. M. (2019). The value of worker well-being. *Public Health Reports, 134*(6), 583–586.

Alghamdi, M. A. A., Ng, S., Ho, J. A., Ramachandran, S., & Abdulsamad, A. (2021). Employee well-being and knowledge sharing behavior among employees of Saudi Aramco. *Advances in Social Sciences Research Journal, 8*(8), 261–284.

APA. (2021). APA Guidelines on evidence-based psychological practice in health care. Available at: https://www.apa.org/about/policy/psychological-practice -health-care. Accessed on: 30 May 2024.

Bache, I. (2019). How does evidence matter? Understanding 'what works' for wellbeing. *Social Indicators Research, 142*(3), 1153–1173.

Baicker, K., Cutler, D., & Song, Z. (2010). Workplace wellness programs can generate savings. *Health Affairs, 29*(2), 304–311.

Balta, A., Soon, J., & Morton, R. (2020). Person-centred healthcare versus patient centricity-what is the difference and how are pharmaceutical companies aiming to secure internal representation of the patient voice. *European Journal for Person Centered Healthcare, 8*(3), 277–281.

Barands, E., Briener, R. B., & Rousseau, D. M. (2014). *Evidence Based Management: The Basic Principles.* Amsterdam: The Center for Evidence Based Management.

Baun, W. B., Berry, L. L., & Mirabito, A. M. (2010). What's the hard return on employee wellness programs? Available at: www.hbr.org, Accessed on: 14 July 2024.

Benach, J., Vives, A., Amable, M., Vanroelen, C., Tarafa, G., & Muntaner, C. (2014). Precarious employment: understanding an emerging social determinant of health. *Annual Review of Public Health, 35*(1), 229–253.

Bennett, J. B., Weaver, J., Senft, M., & Neeper, M. (2017). Creating workplace well-being: Time for practical wisdom. In C. L. Cooper & J. C. Quick (Eds.), *The handbook of stress and health: A guide to research and practice* (pp. 570–604). Sussex: Wiley Blackwell.

Berkery, E., Morley, M. J., Tiernan, S., Purtill, H., & Parry, E. (2017). On the uptake of flexible working arrangements and the association with human resource and organizational performance outcomes. *European Management Review, 14*(2), 165–183.

Bostock, S., Crosswell, A. D., Prather, A. A., & Steptoe, A. (2019). Mindfulness on-the-go: Effects of a mindfulness meditation app on work stress and well-being. *Journal of Occupational Health Psychology, 24*(1), 127.

Brdar, I. (2022). Positive and negative affect schedule (PANAS). In *Encyclopedia of Quality of Life and Well-Being Research* (pp. 1–4). Cham: Springer International Publishing.

Brooks, A. C. (2023). Harvard's Arthur C. Brooks on the secrets to happiness at work. *Harvard Business Review.* Available at: https://hbr.org/2023/09/harvards-arthur-c-brooks-on-the-secrets-to-happiness-at-work Accessed on: 3 November 2023.

Bryson, A., Forth, J., & Stokes, L. (2017). Does employees' subjective well-being affect workplace performance?. *Human Relations, 70*(8), 1017–1037.

Callaghan, S., Losch, M., Medalsy, J., Pione, A., & Teichner, W. (2022). Still feeling good: The US wellness market continues to boom. Available at: https://www.mckinsey.com/industries/consumer-packaged-goods/our-insights/still-feeling-good-the-us-wellness-market-continues-to-boom Accessed on: 24 March 2024

Carr, A. (2011). *Positive Psychology: The Science of Happiness and Human Strengths.* London: Routledge.

Carretta, R. (2022). Workplace health and wellness program: Enhancing employee morale via incentives, gym memberships, and fitness trackers: A secondary review. *College of Health Sciences Posters, 11.* Available at: https://digitalcommons.odu.edu/gradposters2022_healthsciences/11

Carolan, S., Harris, P. R., & Cavanagh, K. (2017). Improving employee well-being and effectiveness: Systematic review and meta-analysis of web-based psychological interventions delivered in the workplace. *Journal of Medical Internet Research, 19*(7), e271.

Chandra, Y. (2020). A psychology of building healthy employee-employer relationships: Corporate social responsibility, a people-centric approach. *Tathapi, 19*(43), 185–195.

Chetty, L. (2017). An evaluation of the health and wellbeing needs of employees: An organizational case study. *Journal of Occupational Health, 59*(1), 88–90.

CIPD (2019). *Health and Wellbeing at Work.* London: Chartered Institute of Personnel and Development.

CIPD (2023a). Evidence based practice for decision making. Available at: https://www.cipd.org/en/knowledge/factsheets/evidence-based-practice-factsheet/ Accessed on: 22 October 2023

CIPD (2023b). People analytics. Available at: https://www.cipd.org/en/views-and-insights/cipd-viewpoint/people-analytics/ Accessed on: 25 October 2023

Cooper, C., & Dewe, P. (2008). Well-being—Absenteeism, presenteeism, costs and challenges. *Occupational Medicine, 58*(8), 522–524.

Dall'Ora, C., Ball, J., Recio-Saucedo, A., & Griffiths, P. (2016). Characteristics of shift work and their impact on employee performance and wellbeing: A literature review. *International Journal of Nursing Studies, 57*, 12–27.

Daubner-Siva, D., Vinkenburg, C. J., & Jansen, P. G. (2017). Dovetailing talent management and diversity management: The exclusion-inclusion paradox. *Journal of Organizational Effectiveness: People and Performance, 4*(4), 315–331.

Davidson, C. N., Brin, S., & Page, L. (2017). The surprising thing Google learned about its employees—and what it means for today's students. *The Washington Post, 20.*

Day, A., & Penney, S. A. (2017). Essential elements of organizational initiatives to improve workplace wellbeing. In C. Cooper & M. Leiter (Eds.), *The Routledge Companion to Wellbeing at Work* (pp. 314–331). New York: Routledge.

Deloitte (2017). *At a Tipping Point: Workplace Mental Health and Wellbeing.* United Kingdom: Deloitte Centre for Health Solutions

Deloitte (2019). *The ROI in Workplace Mental Health Programs: Good for People, Good for Business; A Blueprint for Workplace Mental Health Programs.* Deloitte Insights. Available at: https://www2.deloitte.com/in/en.html Accessed on: 14 November 2023

Department for Work and Pensions (2013). Workplace wellbeing tool. Available at: https://www.gov.uk/government/publications/workplace-wellbeing-tool Accessed on: 5 November 2023

Derr, A. S. (2016). Mental health service use among immigrants in the United States: A systematic review. *Psychiatric Services, 67*(3), 265–274.

Dunn, L. B., Iglewicz, A., & Moutier, C. (2008). A conceptual model of medical student well-being: Promoting resilience and preventing burnout. *Academic Psychiatry, 32*, 44–53.

Ernst Kossek, E., Kalliath, T., & Kalliath, P. (2012). Achieving employee wellbeing in a changing work environment: An expert commentary on current scholarship. *International Journal of Manpower, 33*(7), 738–753.

Etuknwa, A., Daniels, K., Nayani, R., & Eib, C. (2023). Sustainable return to work for workers with mental health and musculoskeletal conditions. *International Journal of Environmental Research and Public Health, 20*(2), 1057.

Falletta, S. V. & Combs, W. L. (2020). The HR analytics cycle: A seven step process for building evidence based and ethical HR analytics and capabilities. *Journal of Work – Applied Management, 31*(1), 162–187.

Fitzsimons, L. (2020). The role of champions in promoting family focused practice across adult mental health and children's services. *Advances in Mental Health, 18*(3), 251–260.

Fort, T. L., Raymond, A. H., & Shackelford, S. J. (2016). The angel on your shoulder: Prompting employees to do the right thing through the use of wearables. *Northwestern Journal of Technology and Intellectual Property, 14*, 139.

Fox, K. E., Johnson, S. T., Berkman, L. F., Sianoja, M., Soh, Y., Kubzansky, L. D., & Kelly, E. L. (2022). Organisational-and group-level workplace interventions and their effect on multiple domains of worker well-being: A systematic review. *Work & Stress, 36*(1), 30–59.

Giermindl, L. M., Strich, F., Christ, O., Leicht-Deobald, U., & Redzepi, A. (2022). The dark sides of people analytics: Reviewing the perils for organisations and employees. *European Journal of Information Systems, 31*(3), 410–435.

Goergen, C. J., Tweardy, M. J., Steinhubl, S. R., Wegerich, S. W., Singh, K., Mieloszyk, R. J., & Dunn, J. (2022). Detection and monitoring of viral infections via wearable devices and biometric data. *Annual review of Biomedical Engineering, 24*, 1–27.

Grant, A. (2019). The surprising value of obvious insights. *MIT Sloan Management Review, 60*(3), 8–10.

Guest, D. E. (2017). Human resource management and employee well-being: Towards a new analytic framework. *Human Resource Management Journal, 27*(1), 22–38.

Habermann, W., & Lohaus, D (2019). Presenteeism: A review and research directions. *Human Resource Management Review, 29*(1), 43–58.

Hamilton, S., Pinfold, V., Cotney, J., Couperthwaite, L., Matthews, J., Barret, K., & Henderson, C. (2016). Qualitative analysis of mental health service users' reported experiences of discrimination. *Acta Psychiatrica Scandinavica, 134*, 14–22.

Hastuti, R., & Timming, A. R. (2021). An inter-disciplinary review of the literature on mental illness disclosure in the workplace: Implications for human resource management. *The International Journal of Human Resource Management, 32*(15), 3302–3338.

Hati, L., & Pradhan, R. K. (2019). The measurement of employee wellbeing: Development and validation of a scale. *Global Business Review*, 1–23.

Henderson, C., Potts, L., & Robinson, E. J. (2020). Mental illness stigma after a decade of Time to Change England: Inequalities as targets for further improvement. *European Journal of Public Health, 30*(3), 497–503.

JaguarLandRover. (2024). Support services. Available at: https://wellbeing.jaguarlandrover.com/support%20services. Accessed on: 31 May 2024.

James, N. (2019). Mental health: The elephant in the rooms of corporate India. Available at: https://www.thehindubusinessline.com/blink/cover/mental-health-the-elephant-in-the-rooms-of-corporate-india/article30211327.ece. Accessed on: 14 November 2023

Johns, G. (2010). Presenteeism in the workplace: A review and research agenda. *Journal of Organizational Behavior, 31*(4), 519–542.

Karasneh, R. A., Al-Azzam, S. I., Alzoubi, K. H., Hawamdeh, S., Jarab, A. S., & Nusair, M. B. (2022). Smartphone applications for sleep tracking: Rating and perceptions about behavioral change among users. *Sleep Science, 15*(S1), 65–73.

Kelly, J., & Gennard, J. (2001). *Power and Influence in the Boardroom: The Role of the Personnel/HR Director*. London: Routledge.

Khoreva, V., & Wechtler, H. (2020). Exploring the consequences of knowledge hiding: An agency theory perspective. *Journal of Managerial Psychology, 35*(2), 71–84.

Knaflic, C. N. (2015). *Storytelling with Data: A Data Visualization Guide for Business Professionals*. New Jersey: John Wiley & Sons.

Wilcox, A., & Koontz, A. (2022). Workplace well-being: Shifting from an individual to an organizational framework. *Sociology Compass, 16*(10), e13035.

Kun, Á., Balogh, P., & Krasz, K. G. (2017). Development of the work-related well-being questionnaire based on Seligman's PERMA model. *Periodica Polytechnica Social and Management Sciences, 25*(1), 56–63.

Lathabhavan, R. (2023). Mental wellbeing through HR analytics. *Personnel Review*, 0048–0386.

Lewis, L., & Ferguson, D. (2010). Using the connected reporting framework as a driver of change within EDF energy. In A. Hopwood, J. Unerman & J. Fries (Eds.), *Accounting for Sustainability: Practical Insights* (pp. 73–89). London: Earthscan.

Mäkikangas, A., Kinnunen, U., Feldt, T., & Schaufeli, W. (2016). The longitudinal development of employee well-being: A systematic review. *Work & Stress, 30*(1), 46–70.

Marler, J. H., & Boudreau, J. W. (2017). An evidence-based review of HR analytics. *The International Journal of Human Resource Management, 28*(1), 3–26.

McCleary, K., Goetzel, R. Z., Roemer, E. C., Berko, J., Kent, K., & De La Torre, H. (2017). Employer and employee opinions about workplace health promotion (Wellness) programs. *Journal of Occupational and Environmental Medicine, 59*(3), 256–263.

Mehta, D. (2021). Motivation: Maslow's hierarchy of needs. *International Journal of Law, Management and Humanities, 4*(3), 913–919.

Melnyk, B. M., & Tucker, S. (2019). Leading organizational change and building wellness cultures for maximum ROI and VOI. In B. Melnyk & T. Raderstorf (Eds.), *Evidence-Based Leadership, Innovation, and Entrepreneurship in Nursing and Healthcare: A Practical Guide to Success* (pp. 107–124). Springer.

Mitrofanova, E. A., & Mitrofanova, A. E. (2019). Analysis of perspectives and risks of the corporate well-being programes. *European Proceedings of Social and Behavioural Sciences, 1*, 1330–2357.

Nasamu, E., Connolly, S., Bryan, M., & Bryce, A. (2022). Workplace well-being initiatives: evaluating the costs and benefits. In P. Brough, E. Gardiner, & K. Daniels (Eds.), *Handbook on management and employment practices* (pp. 1–18). Cham: Springer International Publishing.

Nielsen, K., Nielsen, M. B., Ogbonnaya, C., Känsälä, M., Saari, E., & Isaksson, K. (2017). Workplace resources to improve both employee well-being and performance: A systematic review and meta-analysis. *Work & Stress, 31*(2), 101–120.

NHS. (2024) Occupational health for NHS staff. Available at: https://www.nhsemployers.org/articles/occupational-health-nhs-staff. Accessed on: 31 May 2024.

Ott-Holland, C. J., Shepherd, W. J., & Ryan, A. M. (2019). Examining wellness programs over time: Predicting participation and workplace outcomes. *Journal of Occupational Health Psychology, 24*(1), 163.

Ozminkowski, R. J., Serxner, S., Marlo, K., Kichlu, R., Ratelis, E., & Van de Meulebroecke, J. (2016). Beyond ROI: Using value of investment to measure employee health and wellness. *Population Health Management, 19*(4), 227–229.

Page, K. M., & Vella-Brodrick, D. A. (2009). The 'what', 'why' and 'how' of employee well-being: A new model. *Social Indicators Research, 90*, 441–458.

Passey, D. G., Brown, M. C., Hammerback, K., Harris, J. R., & Hannon, P. A. (2018). Managers' support for employee wellness programs: An integrative review. *American Journal of Health Promotion, 32*(8), 1789–1799.

Patil, P. S. & Afza, N. (2023). How HR analytics can manage HR during uncertainty?-A case study on Google. *Journal of Informatics Education and Research, 3*(2).

Peckham, T. K., Baker, M. G., Camp, J. E., Kaufman, J. D., & Seixas, N. S. (2017). Creating a future for occupational health. *Annals of Work Exposures and Health, 61*(1), 3–15.

Peters, M. (2018). How Bell Canada capitalises on the millennial: Affective labour, intersectional identity, and mental health. *Open Cultural Studies, 1*(1), 395–405.

Pirson, M. (2019). A humanistic perspective for management theory: Protecting dignity and promoting well-being. *Journal of Business Ethics, 159*, 39–57.

Proper, K. I., & van Oostrom, S. H. (2019). The effectiveness of workplace health promotion interventions on physical and mental health outcomes–a systematic review of reviews. *Scandinavian Journal of Work, Environment & Health, 45*(6), 546–559.

Provost, F., & Fawcett, T. (2013). Data science and its relationship to big data and data-driven decision making. *Big Data, 1*(1), 51–59. https://doi.org/10.1089/big.2013.1508

Reidhead, C. (2021). Employee well-being becomes top priority. *Journal of Economics, Finance and Management Studies, 4*(11), 2268–2274.

Renwick, D. (2002). HR managers: Guardians of employee wellbeing. *Personnel Review, 32*(3), 341–359.

Roslender, R., Monk, L., & Murray, N. (2020). Promoting greater levels of employee health and well-being in the UK: How much worse do the problems have to get?. In R. Aguado & A. Eizaguirre (Eds.), *Virtuous Cycles in Humanistic Management: From the Classroom to the Corporation* (pp. 135–149). Springer Verlag. https://doi.org/10.1007/978-3-030-29426-7_8.

Sakka, G., & Ahammad, M. F. (2020). Unpacking the relationship between employee brand ambassadorship and employee social media usage through employee wellbeing in workplace: A theoretical contribution. *Journal of Business Research, 119*, 354–363.

Schaltegger, S., Hörisch, J., & Freeman, R. E. (2019). Business cases for sustainability: A stakeholder theory perspective. *Organization & Environment, 32*(3), 191–212.

Scott, M. M., & Spievack, N. (2019). *Making the Business Case for Employee Well-Being*. Washington, DC: Urban Institute.

Shrivastava, S., Nagdev, K., & Rajesh, A. (2018). Redefining HR using people analytics: The case of Google. *Human Resource Management International Digest, 26*(2), 3–6.

Sigblad, F., Savela, M., & Okenwa Emegwa, L. (2020). Managers' perceptions of factors affecting employees' uptake of workplace health promotion (WHP) offers. *Frontiers in Public Health, 8*, 145.

Silcox, S. (2016). Building an employee wellbeing programme. *Occupational Health & Wellbeing, 68*(2), 12.

Šimunjak, M., & Menke, M. (2022). Workplace well-being and support systems in journalism: Comparative analysis of Germany and the United Kingdom. *Journalism, 24*(1), 2474–2492.

Sivapragasam, P., & Raya, R. P. (2018). HRM and employee engagement link: Mediating role of employee well-being. *Global Business Review, 19*(1), 147–161.

Sonnentag, S., Tay, L., & Nesher Shoshan, H. (2023). A review on health and well-being at work: More than stressors and strains. *Personnel Psychology. 76*(1), 473–510

Sorensen, G., Sparer, E., Williams, J. A. R., Gundersen, D., Boden, L. I., Dennerlein, J. T., & Wagner, G. R. (2018). Measuring best practices for workplace safety, health and wellbeing: The workplace integrated safety and health assessment. *Journal of Occupational and Environmental Medicine, 60*(5), 430.

Taormina, R., & Gao, J. (2013). Maslow and the motivation hierarchy: Measuring satisfaction of the needs. *The American Journal of Psychology, 126*(2), 156–160.

Tennant, R., Hiller, L., Fishwick, R., Platt, S., Joseph, S., Weich, S., & Stewart-Brown, S. (2007). The Warwick-Edinburgh mental well-being scale (WEMWBS): Development and UK validation. *Health and Quality of life Outcomes, 5*(1), 1–13.

Tursunbayeva, A., Di Lauro, S., & Pagliari, C. (2018). People analytics—A scoping review of conceptual boundaries and value propositions. *International Journal of Information Management, 43*, 224–247.

UK Government (2013). Workplace wellbeing tool. Available at: https://www.gov.uk /government/publications/workplace-wellbeing-tool Accessed on: 14 November 2023

Van Beukering, I. E., Smits, S. J. C., Janssens, K. M. E., Bogaers, R. I., Joosen, M. C. W., Bakker, M. & Brouwers, E. P. M. (2021). In what ways does health related stigma affect sustainable employment and well-being at work? A systematic review. *Journal of Occupational Rehabilitation, 32*(3), 1–15.

Van Stolk, C. (2021). The cost of stress to UK employers and employees. In E. K. Kelloway & S. C. Cooper (Eds.), *A Research Agenda for Workplace Stress and Wellbeing* (p. 33). Cheltenham, MA: Edward Elgar Publishing.

Vohra, N., Chari, V., Mathur, P., Sudarshan, P., Verma, N., Mathur, N., & Gandhi, H. K. (2015). Inclusive workplaces: Lessons from theory and practice. *Vikalpa, 40*(3), 324–362.

Warr, P. (1990). The measurement of well-being and other aspects of mental health. *Journal of Occupational Psychology, 63*(3), 193–210.

World Health Organisation. (2024). World Health Organisation. Available at: https:// www.who.int/activities/promoting-healthy-safe-and-resilient-workplaces-for-all. Accessed on: 30 May 2024.

Yildiz, E. P. (2021). Academist perceptions on the use of web 2.0 tools through Maslow's needs hierarchy: A case study. *Education Quarterly Reviews, 4*(1), 173–188.

Zwetsloot, G., Leka, S., Kines, P., & Jain, A. (2020). Vision zero: Developing proactive leading indicators for safety, health and wellbeing at work. *Safety Science, 130*, 104890.

Chapter 2

The Dawn of a New Era for Employee Wellbeing Post-Pandemic

2.1 Employee Wellbeing: The Onset of COVID-19

The pandemic was marked by the rapidly spreading virus, challenging individuals with respiratory and other health ailments, crippling the global health care systems, a 'lockdown' – 'restricted movements that mandated the temporary closure of non-essential businesses' (Al-Jubari, Mosbah & Salem, 2022; Richter, 2020). It may be fair to suggest that almost all employees benefitted during the pandemic – not having rush hour commutes and being able to spend more quality time with family. Many employers across the globe reported positive performance outcomes and greater productivity from 'home working' or 'work from anywhere' methodologies (Richter, 2020).

The crisis was, however, marked by sharp economic and financial challenges, long-term unemployment, closure of businesses, educational and cultural activities, and severe travel constraints (Rashid & Zarowsky, 2023). Social venues like restaurants were closed. This had a significant influence on labour markets, forcing many to work from home and altering the dynamics of physical and psychological health, work and workplace relationships.

Co-worker/supervisor absenteeism, poor health and high volumes of work/workloads were a leading source of stress. Pandemic-related anxieties, commute fatigue and frustrations, new work-related demands as a consequence of home working and pressures to meet deadlines further altered EW parameters (Rashid & Zarowsky, 2023; Richter, 2020). According to reports from *Deloitte,* the UK, specifically, fell five places (from 13th to 18th) on the UN's World Happiness Report as a consequence of illness, grief, social distancing, isolation, furloughing, job loss and pandemic-related anxieties in 2021 (Belloni, Carrino & Meschi, 2022). Levels of happiness, quality of life and wellbeing were found to similarly deteriorate in other countries (Belloni et al., 2022; Northwood, Siskind, Suetani, & McArdle, 2021; Robertson, Maposa, Somaroo, & Johnson, 2020). EW was not anymore considered an 'add on' or 'nice to have' nuance to the organisation's business objectives and day-to-day operations – this had now become a necessity (Richter, 2020).

DOI: 10.4324/9781032705125-2

The physical, mental, social and financial health impact, however, varied between individuals. Critics argue how personality, individual differences and perceived levels of stress moderated anxiety levels and the subsequent experience of the pandemic (Liu, Lithopoulos, Zhang, Garcia-Barrera, & Rhodes, 2021). For instance, employees who scored high on neuroticism were more likely to appraise work stressors as crippling, did not believe they were supported adequately, emotionally, socially and financially within the organisation, and reported experiencing psychological strain – ranging from mild irritation to drastic dysfunction (Belloni et al., 2022). Individuals scoring high on 'adaptability' were likely to embrace uncertain and challenging times with greater ease (Liu et al., 2021).

In response to this, seven out of ten employers considered 'wellbeing' as a 'boardroom' issue – on the agenda list of senior leaders, according to the CIPD (2022). Thirty-three percent employers drafted a budget to accommodate wellbeing interventions and more than 81% of employers tailored work to support employee concerns, mental health and wellbeing. Employers were found to offer part-time days and monetary allowances for vaccinations, eye tests, health screening and dietary advice. A surge in the implementation of complementary therapies, employee counselling services, on-site relaxation services and wellbeing days at work was reported. Categorising this as a 'shelter in place' phase, reports from the Harvard Business Review (2020) established how home working policies and practices, continual sanitisation of workspaces and adoption of contactless payments for deliveries, for instance, counted as ways in which workplace operating models shifted. Business leaders and the human resource community, globally, put tremendous effort into continually fostering EW (Claxton, Rae, Damico, Young, Kurani, & Whitmore, 2021).

2.2 The Theoretical Approaches

Embracing the perspective that an employee's goal in life is to experience the maximum amount of pleasure, the hedonic stance appraises what makes life and its experience pleasant/unpleasant, free from problems and 'happy' (Ryan & Deci, 2001). Researchers analysing hedonic wellbeing appraise how individuals equipped with adequate resources (informational, financial resources) at work experience higher levels of vitality and job satisfaction, and lower levels of fatigue and/or burnout, in contrast to employees lacking organisational resources (Carr, 2011; Sonnentag et al., 2023). 'Challenge stressors' (such as employee workload and time pressure) and 'hindrance stressors' (such as hassles and role ambiguity) significantly increased affective distress, subsequently impairing hedonic EW (Grant & McGhee, 2021; Sonnentag et al., 2023).

On another note, the eudaimonic stance, according to Aristotle, perceived 'wellbeing' to be 'less vulgar of an ideal', not presenting employees as 'slavish followers of desires' (Ryan et al., 2001). The philosophy called upon employees who strive and exert effort, engaged in activities that resonated with their true selves, deeply held values and were holistically and fully engaged (Grant & McGhee, 2021; Ryan et al., 2001). When challenged, employees were intensely alive and authentic. The concept primarily revolved around the employee's experience of meaning, self-determination, self-expressiveness and the pursuit of goals aligned with one's values (Grant et al., 2021; Sonnentag et al., 2023). Variables such as task identity, skill variety and task significance were strongly correlated to the eudaimonic principles of 'meaningfulness' or experiencing 'purpose'. Contradictorily, role conflict and role ambiguity were strongly negatively correlated (Monnot & Beehr, 2014).

Harvard University Professor and best-selling author Arthur C. Brooks (2023) concluded how an employee's sense of 'wellbeing at work' is primarily dependant on two key factors – i) the earning of any success and ii) experiencing a 'sense of purpose'. This was heavily compromised during COVID-19. Employees across the globe, experienced illness or were caregiving for the ill, being furloughed, experienced changes in their work responsibilities, were challenged with unemployment and restricted socialising. Employees seldom felt that achievements and progresses were earned – there was a need to socialise and feel appreciated in front of other people (Brooks, 2023).

On a more generic note, Brooks (2023) added how an individual's 'quality of life' is determined by, first, the quality of relationships they share with family, second, the quality of relationships they share with friends, third, the extent and the quality of engagement with work that serves society and, fourth, the faith that they choose to follow.

In order to foster authentic happiness, fulfilment and wellbeing at work, in the post-pandemic era or the 'next normal', employers will need to invest in the principles of eudaimonia and the four crucial ingredients to enhancing employee quality of life: appropriately investing in (employees), incentivising and building 'meaningful work' policies and practices.

What Does 'Maslow's Hierarchy of Needs' Mean for Employee Wellbeing?

Abraham Maslow in 1943 proposed systematic ways in which human needs and consequential wellbeing may be addressed within workplaces (Durmu-, 2024). Chetty (2017) establishes how it is only after an employee's fundamental 'psycho-physiological needs' (including quality air, mobility, access to quality food or workplace catering services, water and sanitation, quality sleep, occupational healthcare services, health and fitness checks) are met that the next levels on the hierarchy hold significance.

However, the application of Maslow's hierarchy of needs has evolved with the advancements in digital technology. Digital tools such as computers, smart phones (making provisions for employees to make/receive video and audio calls) and internet connection (enabling employees to send/receive emails, shop online and run a search on the web) additionally account for employee primary needs and hold equal relevance and significance as traditional primary employee needs (particularly during the pandemic) (Taormina & Gao, 2013).

The pyramid, further, demonstrates the upward 'wellbeing' stairs to employee 'safety' needs (including safety from physical tremors, loud noises, harmful chemical substances, biological exposures to microbes, bacteria, mould and viruses, and the organisation's appropriate compliance with the law). In technologically advanced workplaces, employee safety needs are fostered by employers offering data safety backup and information safety. Cyber security and network security concerns are proactively addressed (Yildiz, 2021).

Employee 'belongingness' needs (including acceptance of and respect for individual differences, sense of healthy, high-quality social connections, friendships and intimacy) and 'self-esteem' needs (sense of respect, strength, freedom, status and recognition) for the experience of 'wellness' have been interestingly explored in studies published by Taormina et al. (2013) and Yildiz (2021).

Granting access and permission to sustain an active social life on applications such as Facebook, WhatsApp, Skype and Instagram offers opportunities for employees to build and invest in friendships, opportunities to love and be loved by their community, gain social identity and social status, and improve self-esteem (Yildiz, 2021). Contemporary workplaces equipped employees with resources to navigate 'fake relationships established in virtual environments' and 'distrust' from social connections on Web 2.0 tools (Chetty, 2017).

Lastly, employee 'self-actualisation' needs (including competence management, individual and workplace morality, expressing and honing creativity, purpose, the maximisation of one's potential and innovation) have been placed at the peak of the 'wellbeing' pyramid (Alghamdi, Ng, Ho, Ramachandran, & Abdulsamad, 2021). Organisations that encouraged employees to 'teach and learn' on platforms such as YouTube and LinkedIn enabled the breaking down of stereotypes and prejudices, honing creativity and saving time accessing useful resources (Tariq, Khan & Araci, 2020).

Google's Implementation of Maslow's Hierarchy of Needs for Employee Wellness

Google, one of the world's largest and most well-known IT corporations, employing the 'lens' of the pyramid, implemented its propositions to address EW needs. Making provisions for free, healthy meals in their cafeteria, discount coupons for employees to avail of reduced rates at selected stores, providing a nutritionist and a free gym trainer, the organisation made earnest attempts at addressing employee primary and safety needs. Company policies and practices further support the care of children and the elderly, offering six weeks of paid leave to new fathers and 18 weeks of paid leave to new mothers (Mehta, 2021).

During the pandemic, Google, in the United States, offered free, weekly COVID tests at home, where employees could request a test to occur within 48 hours at the expense of the company. In addition to this, employees were offered $1,000 each to invest in equipment for the customisation of their workplace. Employees were encouraged to engage in the innumerable fitness classes that were conducted online and were urged to have regular interactions with peers and subordinates to check in on each other's physical and mental health, fostering a sense of belongingness during unprecedented times (Mehta, 2021).

Despite the pyramid's practical usefulness in systematic EW assessment and intervention implementation, critics to Maslow's needs proposition argue how there is limited research that explores the significance and implications of Maslow's hierarchy within collectivistic work contexts. In India, for instance, the fundamental need is for an employee to experience a sense of belongingness; physical, psychological, financial, self-esteem and self-actualisation needs follow, consequentially. EW policies, practices and interventions, in this light, must be designed to address and appraise employee social needs to a greater extent within these contexts (Alghamdi et al., 2021).

The Coping Reservoir Model

Drawing from within the domains of educational psychology, the author of this book additionally draws from and employs the lens of the 'coping reservoir'/'coping reserve tank' model proposed by Dunn, Iglewicz and Moutier (2008). The proposition suggests that employee physical and psychological 'replenishers' (such as access to and quality of psychosocial support, mentorship, social recognition and appreciation, opportunities for intellectual stimulation, and access to physical health services) must be significantly greater than employee physical and psychological 'depleters' (time and energy demands, caregiving responsibilities, emotionally/financially draining relationships). This would enhance employee resilience, physical and mental health. When depleters are significantly more than replenishers, employees are challenged with burnout and cynicism (Dunn et al., 2008).

The model can be useful for comprehending, drafting and implementing EW business cases and wellbeing interventions. Its implementation enables employers to inculcate, enhance and demonstrate ideal characteristics, such as empathy, integrity, commitment to service and life-long learning. In addition to employers, governmental stakeholders and practitioners can potentially employ the model as a reference point for policy-making and wellbeing practice within workplaces.

The appraisal of artificial intelligence (AI), gamification methodologies, advancements in technology and the thriving of the corporate wellness industry is likely to alter the dynamics of six increasingly sought-after domains of EW in future: employee health, fitness, nutrition, appearance, sleep and mindfulness. Organisational analysts expect to witness significant changes in the determining of which EW interventions, incentives, products and services constitute or act as a basic/fundamental, safety, 'belongingness', esteem or growth/developmental need for wellbeing on the pyramid hierarchy or as an effective 'replenisher' for employee wellness.

Reports from at McKinsey and Company, for instance, appraise how employees in future will be more likely to value over the-counter medicines, vitamins and personal hygiene products and services (Callaghan, Losch, Medalsy, Pione and Teichner, 2022). Further, fitness club memberships, at-home fitness equipment and fitness wearables are likely to be highly sought-after (Callaghan et al., 2022; Carretta, 2022). From within the domains of employee mindfulness and sleep, employee meditation studios, meditation apps, sleep supplements, app-enabled sleep trackers and other employee sleep-enhancing interventions, products and services are expected to witness an increased uptake (Bostock, Crosswell, Prather, & Steptoe, 2019; Karasneh, Al-Azzam, Alzoubi, Hawamdeh, Jarab, & Nusair, 2022). These nuances are explored in greater detail in the chapters to follow.

Suggested Activity

Reflect on your life at work. Which factors do you believe act as physical and psychological depleters? Which factors do you believe replenish you, physically and psychologically?

If your depleters are more than your replenishers, what steps are you particularly going to take to foster physical and psychological replenishment?

2.3 Contextualising Employee Physical Health and Wellbeing

Poor Air Quality, Uptake of Air Purifiers and Employee 'Stop Smoking' Support

COVID-19 investigations affirmed poor quality air significantly deteriorating EW, performance and productivity. Coronavirus death rates and respiratory illnesses were triggered by the inhalation of infected droplets in the environment. The absence of medical interventions necessitated the need to invest architectural nuances to curb the spread of the virus (Richter, 2020).

Vertical Greening of Portable Walls and Nature Based Interventions

A research study conducted by the World Green Building Council in 2019 recorded an 11% difference in productivity and overall health as a consequence of increasing fresh, quality air and reducing the prevalence of pollutants in the workplace with the implementation of vertical greening of walls (or growing plants on vertical walls or outside office buildings) (Helman, Yungstein, Mulero & Michael, 2022; Kamarulzaman, Saleh, Hashim, & Abdul-Ghani, 2011). Investing in indoor nature considering nuances of thermal comfort, acoustics and lighting, psychologically resonated with an individual's innate desire to connect with nature. Employing portable (which could be a potential option), 'vertical green walls' reduced heat transfer significantly, fostering indoor thermal comfort. The technique deteriorated tendencies of experiencing the 'sick building' syndrome and was evidenced as an effective air cleaning methodology, curbing the spread of infectious diseases, enhancing levels of employee performance and fostering a sense of psychological 'calm' (Navaratnam, Nguyen, Selvaranjan, Zhang, Mendis & Aye, 2022; Sadick & Kamardeen, 2020).

Contexts which employ knowledge workers more specifically were found to similarly benefit from 'nature' interventions; participants reported greater clarity in thought, enabling effective problem solving, decision making and evaluation (Sadick & Kamardeen, 2020).

Although serving as a 'smart', 'green' city solution for the future, analysts caution of how the challenge to spatially, continually monitor green living walls may prove to be expensive. Precision in agricultural tools and sensors and advancements in artificial intelligence hold the potential to offer spatially, real time, continuous pictures of green walls within workplaces, offering insights on nuances such as ergonomic furnishing, room ventilation rate and plant disease. Policy makers, stakeholders within organisations and organisational analysts could consider investing further in investigating the realities and effectiveness of low costs, architectural sensors and the employment of AI for the designing of 'green' workplaces and its influences on EW (Halman et al., 2022; Navaratnam et al., 2022).

Increased Uptake of Air Purifiers

Agarwal, Meena, Raj, Saini, Kumar, Gopalakrishnan and Aggarwal (2021) demonstrated how employing air quality indexing, air quality indexing forecasting, air purifiers and cleaners within workspaces and subsequent investments in ventilation decreased the likelihood of being affected by the virus. Installing portable, low-noise air purifiers proved to be a cost-effective methodology; this particularly benefitted pregnant and immuno-compromised employees (Shrikrishna, Karan and Dhillon, 2023).

'Stop Smoking' Support

The pandemic also witnessed the emergence of 'quit smoking' support groups and interventions, urging employees to stop using cigarettes, preventing contamination of the air. Given that smoking tobacco counts as a leading cause of preventable physical and mental illness and consequential death, some organisations chose to employ 'stop smoking' advisors (Agarwal et al., 2021; Jackson, Cox, Shahab, & Brown, 2022). Comprehensively analysing the causes and the prevalence of smoking behaviours within the concerned organisation, 'stop smoking' specialists drafted a business case for implementing 'stop smoking' interventions whilst additionally assessing employee knowledge, self-efficacy, optimism, environmental context and resources available to support tobacco cessation behaviours (Taylor, Sawyer, Kessler, Munafò, Aveyard, & Shaw, 2021; Vogt, Hall, & Marteau, 2010).

Song, English and Whitman (2017), Tabuchi, Hoshin and Nakayama (2016) reinstate the significance of drafting evidence-based policies that demonstrate a commitment to quality air within workplaces. The propagation of the benefits of 'smoke-free' or high-quality air workplaces (whilst adhering to the national laws and international guidelines for health and safety) and monitoring of workplace smoke-free policies and practices was suggested; ensuring the effective implementation of these initiations was crucial (Jackson, Cox, Shahab & Brown, 2022; Song et al., 2017). Employers were advised to design stop smoking interventions to combat low employee self-efficacy, pessimism and perceived stigma reported by availing of 'stop smoking' support services (Vogt et al., 2010)

Post-pandemic, although there is a relative decline in perceived significance, 'employee quit smoking' and 'quality air' interventions, policies and practices will continue to be considered as crucial for EW. In addition to air filters and purifiers, environmental and organisational psychologists contemplate potential propagation and investments in the use of 'medical robots, unmanned aerial vehicles and smart city design models' to foster indoor and outdoor organisational air quality and, consequentially, employee physical health and wellbeing (Agarwal et al., 2021).

Mikus, Rieger and Grant-Smith (2022), whilst integrating findings from the pre-pandemic era and from the onset of the pandemic, advise the eudaimonic design of contemporary workplaces. Drawing from the principles of eudaimonia, a 'health-based architectural design' has been evidenced as beneficial, fostering a balance between employee physical (workplace air quality, tracked employee diets and goal driven exercise schedules, etc.), mental (psychological resilience, toughness) and social (stable, social relationships, sense of belongingness and connection) needs (Mikus et al., 2022). For instance, the implementation of this design could potentially include making provisions for 'quiet library zones' for noise-sensitive employees, preventing an increase in blood pressure levels, or the provision of a 'social hub'.

The Lock-Down and 'At-Home' Testing Kits

'At home testing' kit intervention entailed 'sampling and rapidly interpreting test results for various health conditions, from the comfort of one's home. Pre-pandemic, individuals across the globe were found to employ kits for blood glucose monitoring for diabetes, oral HIV tests and pregnancy testing. Everlywell, Texas for instance, offers its clients with more than 30 at-home testing kits, enabling employees to test for food sensitives, sexually transmitted diseases, thyroid function conditions, etc. The 'lockdown' circumstances increased the uptake of 'at-home' testing kits; these were of significant interest to a larger population, in attempts to substitute in-person health care appointments. The proposition facilitated quick contact tracing during a public health emergency enabled the quick delivery and sharing of test results.

According to a survey conducted by McKinsey and Company in 2024, 26% of US consumers were interested in testing for vitamin and mineral deficiencies at home, 24% for cold and flu symptoms and 23% for cholesterol levels. Organisations were found to invest in determining the costs of these kits and create employee feedback loops for the fostering of wellbeing and employee incentivisation. Employees from JP Morgan Chase, for instance, were able to order at-home testing kits, from the company's internal website. Lee and Lim (2023) discuss workplace regulations, public health campaigns, mass media influence and trust in authorised kits to moderate the administration of user-friendly testing kits.

The discomfort associated with self-testing, the uncertainties associated with employing methods with disputable reliability and validity and continually changing testing requirements accounted as some of the many drawbacks of at-home testing kits during the time. Additionally, COVID tests and/or at-home testing kits were seldom covered by company medical insurance policies; this made testing expensive for organisational stakeholders and less accessible to employees hailing from poorer economic backgrounds.

Forecasting an increasing trend for 'at-home' kits, future employers and researchers are advised to draft evidence-based business cases for the provision of employee at home testing kits; prioritising physiologically vulnerable employees and those who travel often. Employee incentivisation policies, health insurances, benefits, and EW products and services will need to adapt to the changing preferences of the workforce, who are increasingly expected to opt for at home testing and hospital services, over-the-counter accessible medication, multi-vitamins and personal hygiene products. Investing in generative AI, to assist with the analysis and delivering of personalised results, is expected to benefit stakeholders. Organisations in future are expected to draw from public health data captured by drones and the services of these unmanned, pilotless, aerial vehicles, during public health emergencies. Featuring infrared camera systems, camera scanner mechanisms, detection sensor units and signal generators, drones can broadcast useful public health information, disinfect common areas, temperature-based detection of illnesses, monitor population movements, especially during a public health crisis and deliver food and medical aid (Balasingham 2017; Kumar, Elsersy, Darwsih, Hassanien, 2021).

Suggested Activity

Reflect on and discuss the factors that potentially influenced your organisation from encouraging/discouraging its employees from administering at-home testing kits.

Employee Beauty Care and the Onset of the Pandemic

The onset of COVID significantly changed the dynamics within the global beauty industry and altered employee consumption of beauty care services such as skin care, colour cosmetics, hair care, fragrances and personal care. The pandemic necessitated face mask wearing and subsequently witnessed soaring sales of eye-make up for women. Some organisations offered employees free sanitisers and cleaning agents. Health care service providers, in some countries, offered free beauty services to their front-line workers (Gerstell, Marchessou, Schmidt and Spagnuolo, 2020; Ścieszko, Budny, Rotsztejn and Erkiert-Polguj, 2021).

Given the lockdown and physical restrictions, the pandemic ushered in trends such as 'at-home' grooming and beauty care services or 'in home' salon services, 'do-it-yourself', 'self-care' products (such as body washes, soap and lotions), grooming kits for men and 'skinmalism' (the minimal use of cosmetics that allows for the skin to breathe and restore its natural glow) (Gerstell et al., 2020). Researchers observed a surge in the demand for natural and 'clean' products. This was crucial for employee 'zoom' faces (for the increasing number of 'zoom' meetings that employees were needed to attend during the pandemic), social and self-esteem and implied that organisations offering discounts or beauty care vouchers for in-person beauty care visits, had to alter or cease this employee incentive. Employers had to switch to exploring and investing in e-commerce and shoppable social media platforms (Gulnaz Banu, Mondal & Gautam, 2022).

Analysts predict employee concerns about safety and hygiene to continue and/or surge in the future. In this light, the exploration, analysis and employing of artificial intelligence for employee testing, discovery, customisation and investments in natural products to foster EW and employee incentivisation could prove to benefit the future workforce (Gerstell, et al., 2020; Gulnaz et al., 2022).

The Implementation of Choice Architecture and the 'Nudge' Theory

Rooted in behavioural economics, 'choice architecture' is coined as the 'design of the diverse ways in which choices are presented to decision makers and the consequence of that presentation on decision making'. A 'choice architect' has the 'responsibility of organizing the context in which people make decisions', setting default options, product ranking and information framing (Balz, Sunstein & Thaler, 2012). Employing 'nudges' (an aspect of design employed to change employee behaviours, in a predictable manner, without forbidding any options or significantly altering their financial incentives) enables this (Selinger & Whyte, 2011). Choice architecture can be used to help nudge people, to make better choices (Balz et al., 2012).

Thorndike, Riis, Sonnenberg and Levy (2014) demonstrated how the use of traffic light labels (such as a 'green label' for 'healthy', 'yellow label' for 'less healthy' and 'red label' for 'unhealthy' food and drinks) in workplace cafeterias promoted healthier choices, made these options more visible and accessible, altered employee eating behaviours, deteriorated cardio-vascular symptoms and ill health.

In similar light, Google has created job roles for employee food architecture, nutrition and physiological health. Their 'food choice architecture' team has recently initiated the 'food choice architecture' programme that makes 'the healthiest choice, the easiest choice' within the company. Drawing from nutrition science programming, behavioural sciences and the various wellbeing approaches, the team creates meaningful experiences for employees. They design spaces which offer healthy snack and meal options, employing 'plant forward' approaches to eating (encouraging an intentional and mindful consumption of fruits, vegetables, beans, legumes, nuts and seeds). The organisation appraises their focus on creating a 'water-forward' experience, ensuring healthy beverages such as water are more accessible, in contrast to high in sugar and aerated drinks. These carefully designed spaces are created to foster employee collaboration, energise and enhance the quality of employee working relationships. During the public health emergency, choice architecture and nudging methodologies were particularly effective for organising vaccination camps and encouraging employees towards the COVID-19 vaccination (Sinha & Jain, 2022).

These theories from behavioural economics can further be employed to enhance not only employee physical health but employee mental health and wellbeing, too. For instance, Google nudges its employees to participate on mindfulness programmes and encourages restful breaks during their work day.

Health-Related Technological Advancements and Employee Wellness

With the lockdown and social distancing significantly altering employee physical, mental and financial wellbeing, Carolan, Harris and Cavanagh (2017) discuss how improvements within occupational health care systems, health risk assessment tools, wearable devices and bio-digital marker apps were being endorsed and propagated within corporate wellness industries. Employees were increasingly found to engage in mobile/online wellbeing applications – they were able to report their moods, record their voice as a means to gauge their own emotional state or use their smart watch to check their heart rate, skin temperature and electrodermal activity to assess their wellbeing (Carolan et al., 2017; Brassey, Gunter, Issak & Silberzahn, 2021). Soma Analytics, for instance, developed an application that measured work related stress. Employing sensors in employee smart phones, the application tracked behavioural changes such as 'sleep quality', 'emotion in the voice' and 'physical activity' that indicated the extent to which they were vulnerable to work related ill health. The intervention enabled both individual employees and HR teams to monitor EW and enhance levels of employee resilience – individually and through a dashboard function (Haynes, 2017). 'Workplace health related technology' such as EW platforms, trackers, workforce monitoring, coaching and consultation, occupational health and safety measures were evidenced as rehabilitative in nature.

Analysts are witnessing employees to be increasingly engaging and investing in health 'tracking' behaviours – this plays an imperative role in motivation, guidance and coaching for health and wellness (Chung, Gorm, Shklovski & Munson, 2017). Health tracking behaviours and interventions foster employee experience, affordability, access and health and wellbeing outcomes. More than 850 organisations holding membership on the McKinsey Health Tech Network confirmed how employee anonymous data from wearables and digital marker apps demonstrate employee physiological data such as heart rate and electrodermal activity and employee moods to assess wellbeing. The aggregate data is analysed and informed EW wellbeing strategies and policies.

Moreover, virtual office visits addressing primary care (such as chronic condition checks, colds and minor skin conditions), behavioural health such as virtual psychotherapy sessions and some speciality care such as virtual cardiac rehabilitation were highly recommended by contemporary employees and researchers. In essence, there are effective evidence-based, e-interventions that can be employed to integrate technology driven EW interventions/ practices (Khakurel, Melkas & Porras, 2018). Critics argue that in the age of corporate wellness, advancements in technology may act detrimental to the employee's right to privacy and data protection. Employees may unwillingly or unknowingly share information about his/her heart ailment or insomnia.

Equipping and upskilling employees with cyber and technological knowledge is critical.

In future, analysts expect an increase in the uptake of employee personal health trackers, including applications that monitor employee fitness and calorie intake in the post-pandemic or 'next normal' phase. App enabled sleep trackers and meditation focussed applications are also expected to be in high demand (Du Plessis, 2022). Employee devices are expected to be increasingly connected to foster and enhance health and wellbeing. For instance, an employee's fridge is likely to make suggestions on what he/she must consume based on their sleep hygiene, exercise regimen and calorie intake on the day. This is possible since the employee's fridge is expected to be connected to sleep sensors under their mattress, to their wearable fitness tracker, and to their mindfulness applications (Du Plessis, 2022; McKinsey and Company, 2023).

Reports from McKinsey and Company appraise how most employees are expected to rarely visit health care service providers, investing in a doctor only when it is necessary. This could alter employer investments in employee health insurances, virtual/digital health care services, 'at-home' kits and employee self-care (physical and mental health care) resources and services.

Suggested Activity

Download a 'health and wellbeing' application from Google Play Store. Reflect and discuss your experiences of using the application.

Online Physiotherapy and Display Screen Equipment Assessments

Champion Health, one of UK's healthtech EW platforms, posts 12-minute workplace health and wellbeing podcasts (which offer insights from leading wellbeing experts, actionable advice on enhancing levels of wellbeing and bite sized episodes to fit around an employee's busy day), online physiotherapy and Display Screen Equipment Assessments (Championhealthplus, 2023). The latter is particularly evidenced as useful for high-intensity workplaces.

Offering employees the benefits of increased accessibility and anonymity (in contrast to face-to-face sessions), online physiotherapy interventions encourage less formal attendance. The flexibility of digital sessions and lack of monitoring deteriorate intervention engagement. Employees find it challenging to receive supervisor permission to access or attend a virtual physiotherapy intervention. An 'open plan' office or sharing of computers/laptops cause employees to feel emotionally exposed. Workplaces may not be appropriate for employees to demonstrate or share health and wellbeing vulnerabilities (Carolan et al., 2017; Claxton, Rae, Damico, Young, Kurani & Whitmore, 2021). Employees have increasingly reported continual scepticism about safety, security and confidentiality. In addition to technological knowledge/cyber safety interventions, organisational stakeholders could benefit from investing in health-based architectural designs.

Employee Treadmill Desks

Modern-day workplaces require employees to spend long hours at a computer desk, which has a detrimental effect on cardiovascular health, mood and over all physiological and mental health. In this light, contemporary researchers propagate the use of cycling stations, 'bike desks' and 'treadmill desks' (Koepp, Manohar, McCrady-Spitzer, Ben-Ner, Hamann, Runge, & Levine, 2013). Enabling an employee to walk on a treadmill whilst continuing daily work activities, the 'treadmill desk' encompasses a 'quiet motor' meant for a 'slow speed' (MacEwen, MacDonald, & Burr, 2015). The so-called 'work-walker' can burn an estimated 100–130 calories an hour at speeds slower than two miles an hour (Giumetti, O'Connor, Weissner, Keegan, Feinn, & Bulger, 2021; MacEwen et al., 2015).

Giumetti et al. (2021) tested the effectiveness of treadmill desks in enhancing occupational health outcomes. Experimenting with 25 university employees who completed 4,500 steps a day on average at their desk, post intervention findings affirmed significant improvements in work-related constructs and outcomes such as job satisfaction and perceived employee performance. Employees demonstrated enhanced energy levels, physical and cognitive vigour, mood and mental toughness at work. More willing to persevere when faced with challenges, fewer employees reported poor physical, emotional and mental health symptoms. Tendencies of experiencing headaches, musculoskeletal disorders, insomnia and dizziness were found to decrease significantly. Employees were less emotionally exhausted or fatigued (Giumetti et al., 2021; Slitar & Yuwan, 2015).

Some critics argue that using treadmill desks decreased motor speed and control when working and increased the number of errors and impaired cognitive function. Most findings in the literature, however, report no errors or deterioration in concentration and engagement when employees cycle between 40 and 80 watts, specifically (Podrekar, Kozinc, Šarabon, 2020; Giumetti et al., 2021).

Hewitt, Whyte, Moreton, Van Someren and Levine (2008), in addition to treadmill and cycle desks, propagate the initiation of workplace exercise regimes. They piloted the implementation of a progressive aerobic exercise programme (with those in the intervention group assigned to regular aerobic exercise classes for an eight-week period) using a randomised controlled trial. The analysts reinstated significant improvements in participant's oxygen consumption, heart rate and body mass index (BMI), Making individuals less susceptible to cardiovascular conditions (Hewitt et al., 2008).

Blake, Zhou and Batt (2013), on a similar note, found how increased access to gym equipment and physical trainers was marked by significant, positive improvements in wellbeing and general health of participants in the intervention group. Blake et al. (2013) designed a multi-model intervention. The researchers increased the provision of exercise classes, staff gym facilities, dedicated exercise and wellbeing rooms, cycle storage and showers and dietary interventions. The model entailed regular health campaigns, health education, health screening checks and relaxation therapies. Administered amongst more than 1,000 healthcare employees, the intervention was found to significantly decrease employee levels of absenteeism and marked improvements in employee job satisfaction and physical activity levels (Blake et al., 2013).

During the pandemic, the provision of treadmill desks, bike desks or cycling stations was proven to be beneficial within workplaces and employee homes. Work from home necessitated working at desks, on computers, for long periods of time. In this light, few organisations such as Google, for instance, offered their employees the working from home option, with coupon codes to order for treadmill desks during the time.

2.4 Contextualising Employee Mental Health and Wellbeing

Psychological Distancing and Re-Interpretation

COVID-19, whilst witnessing the changing nature of work and social distancing, observed a large number of employees on furlough and mass lay-offs, changing work relationships, deteriorating trust and psychological safety. Challenged with suffering from severe symptoms of the virus, witnessing the anguish and/or death of loved ones, employees were engulfed with grief. The prevalence of physiological and psychological consequences such as generalised and social anxiety, depression and insomnia appraised the signficance of adopting effective emotion regulation strategies (Dicker, Jones and Denny, 2022).

Denny and Ochsner (2014) recognised the use of 'psychological distancing' to foster emotional coping and wellbeing. 'Psychological distancing, a form of cognitive reappraisal, involves taking on the perspective of an impartial and objective observer and/or increasing perceived physical/temporal distance or adopting objectivity, in the face of a stress inducing stimulus or situation' (Denny & Ochsner, 2014). For instance, when experiencing emotional hurt after being criticised by a colleague, an individual (employing psychological distancing) might attempt to minimise the impact of the incident by imagining how a neutral, objective observer would perceive the situation. The psychological distancing re-appraisal strategy focusses on 'transforming the viewpoint from which the stimulus is considered' (Labar & Powers, 2018).

Shahane and Denny (2019) further investigating employee emotional health indicators illustrated how psychological distancing and employing 'linguistic distancing' positively influenced employee emotional regulation. For instance, when using non-first person pro-nouns or non-first person language, in general, participants appraised future stressors as less threatening. The implementation of objective language significantly deteriorated negative affect (stress and depressive symptoms) and risks to physiological conditions such as blood pressure and cardio-vascular diseases (Shahane & Denny, 2019).

This is in contrast to 're-interpretation' – an alternative cognitive reappraisal strategy, which emphasises on the transformation of content or meaning of any traumatic event/experience. Employees may reframe a circumstance as less intimidating or gain a renewed perspective that alleviates its emotional impact. Reinterpretation mobilises the brain areas responsible for the selecting and inhibiting of a stimulus, necessitating an individual to psychologically choose alternative meanings. Considering the previously elucidated example, when employing re-interpretation, the individual may change their emotional response by imagining that a colleague is not simply engaging in criticism but trying to help (Labar & Powers, 2018). Psychological distancing and re-interpretation cognitive reappraisal strategies were found to benefit employees significantly, fostering emotional coping. This was, however, more advantageous for health care workers, given their increased exposure to pandemic stressors (Zhu, 2023).

Zhu (2023) analysed writings on social media over 12 weeks from people who self-reported having tested positive for COVID-19. Over a period of time, people employed fewer words reflecting anxiety and psychological distancing. Relatively a greater number of words indicating reinterpretation were evidenced. In the face of the pandemic and during any future crisis, analysts appraise how 'distancing' and 'reinterpretation' strategies unfold differently. Psychological distancing can be employed more quickly. Reinterpretation is 'cognitively effortful'; it demands that 'employees work through emotional situations and construct alternative meanings about their emotional experiences' (Zhu, 2023). In this light, any reinterpretation, lasted for a longer period of time, given the cognitive effort needed to comprehend the changing circumstance (Dicker, et al., 2022).

Overcoming Pandemic Fatigue and Managing Employee Disillusionment

The pandemic appraised conflicting personal interests, heightened fear, inappropriately evaluating the severity of the pandemic, isolation, misinformation, unequal distribution of resources, and governments being poorly equipped with knowledge, skills and resources, and the propagation of contradictory information fostered ideal conditions for frustration and fatigue (Taylor, 2022). In this light, 'pandemic fatigue' was coined by WHO as an 'individual's demotivation to follow recommended protective behaviors, emerging gradually over time and affected by a number of emotions, experiences and emotions' (Haktanir, Can, Seki, Kurnaz & Dilmac, 2022). Manifesting itself by a significant number of individuals' decreasing effort to stay updated and make efforts to follow recommendations and guidelines, the 'pandemic fatigue' theme was comprehensively analysed by psychologists at the time (Haktanir et al., 2022; Taylor, 2020).

Employee burnout and 'employee disillusionment' were consequences of pandemic fatigue. Disillusionment referred to the 'shattering of belief systems and work values individuals held' and, in this light, was distinct from employee sadness or disappointment. Psychologically altering several employees and organisations, across the globe, in terms of their motivation, mental health and energy, employee disillusionment has, unfortunately, received little attention within the workplace literature. This is despite organisations continuing to be challenged with physically and psychologically re-energising their workforce (Gee, Weston, Harshman, & Kelly, 2022).

Suggested Activity

Reflect on experiences within your workplace – what were the specific ways in which your employer addressed the pandemic fatigue?

Bounded Optimism

Employing 'bounded optimism' acts as an antidote to crisis fatigue and employee disillusionment, particularly (Dhoopar & Sihag, 2023). It integrates confidence and hope with a sense of realism. The 'bounded optimism' theme urges employees and leadership, more specifically, to demonstrate inspiration and hope, tempered by reality. Stakeholders are encouraged to exhibit 'authentic confidence' – refraining from displaying pessimism or blind optimism, in the face of a crisis. The strategy, for instance, endorses the communicating of hopeful messages that are seldom about returning to normal and more about acceptance of the new normal (Sufi, 2021).

Employing this antidote enabled the individual to cope with the consequential sense of grief with greater 'psychological steadiness' and grace, in contrast to when leaders reimagined and constructed a new normal or responded with over confidence, in the face of the challenge (Dhoopar & Sihag, 2023). Continually engaging in 'meaning making', leaders practising bounded optimism fostered a 'sense of purpose', employee confidence and efficacy. By enabling followers perceive meaning in their new reality, employees demonstrated greater engagement, psychological stability and wellbeing (Smet, Tegelberg, Theunissen & Vogel, 2020).

The challenge, however, during the pandemic or when faced with similar unprecedented challenges was the lack of awareness of the theme, its significance and the effective ways in which it could be implemented within organisations. This, consequentially, heightened anxiety and psychological unrest (Smet et al., 2020, Sufi, 2021).

The future offers organisational stakeholders an opportunity to build on learnings from the pandemic, to effectively combat 'crisis fatigue' and tackle 'employee disillusionment'. This meant investing further in innovative working models, implementing new technological interventions within days, rather than in months or years, empowering teams whilst subsequently enhancing levels of employee experience and engagement, 'stripping down unnecessary bureaucracy' – making faster decisions in the face of uncertainty (Smet et al., 2020; Dhoopar et al., 2023).

Psychological Flexibility

Pandemic related uncertainties induced and heightened levels of fear. In this light, analysts recommend the re-working of stress appraisals through psychological flexibility (Rashid & Zarowsky, 2023). Psychological flexibility refers to an individual's tendency to modify their own behaviours, to be more functionally adaptive, in the face of challenges. Research evidences elucidate how employees with high psychological flexibility employed 'acceptance' and 'positive framing'; they were more resilient, possessed better coping resources to respond to adverse circumstances and seldom experienced anxiety, depression and insomnia during the pandemic (Rashid & Zarowsky, 2023). These individuals experienced pandemic fatigue relatively less frequently or with lesser intensity.

Puolakanaho, Tolvanen, Kinnunen and Lappalainen (2020) investigating further, recommend the implementation of acceptance commitment therapeutic (ACT) practices and behavioural commitment interventions for enhancing levels of employee psychological flexibility. The investigators, in this light, drew from Williams and Penman (2011) and administered an 8 week programme, combining elements of ACT and 'mindfulness'. Encouraging participants to engage in formal mindfulness practices (such as breathing meditation, body scanning and loving kindness meditations) and informal practices that incorporated skills related to psychological flexibility into their everyday life, the intervention additionally included written resources pertaining to psychological flexibility and burnout, recorded metaphors and videos. The intervention was evidenced as significantly alleviating individuals from crisis fatigue, burnout and psychological distress, improving employee 'workability' (Puolakanaho et al., 2020).

Employing the Lens of 'Chronic Illness'

Frank (1995) during the course of research distinguished between three archetypical responses to being 'chronically ill'. Individuals who perceived chronic illness as a 'quest' embraced their challenging, unchangeable circumstances head on, gracefully accepted and incorporated them as part of their identity and experienced in their journey a greater wellness in contrast to those who engaged in 'restitution' (individuals who often spoke about how their lives were better before the crisis) or to those who referred to their circumstance as 'chaotic' (individuals who lived in the present, lost sight of the past and could not imagine who they would be in the future) (Nowakowski, 2023; Whitehead, 2006).

Employing this lens of a chronic illness to the experience of a pandemic or crisis has been evidenced as beneficial. In this light, in a capability building survey employing 1,200 global leaders and teams identified 'adaptability' – the ability to embrace change gracefully and resilience – the ability to 'bounce back', grow and develop after being faced with adversity as crucial for recovery from a crisis.

'Quest' Interventions or Capacity-Building Sessions

Designing and implementing 'quest' interventions or capacity-building sessions that seek to hone employee learning, adaptability and resilience skills (in managing virtual work, particularly) enhanced employee creativity, capacity to innovate, employee engagement, wellbeing, and overall organisational speed and performance (Nowakowski, 2023; Whitehead, 2006).

2.5 Employee Wellbeing and the Workplace

The 'Great Re-Think', the 'Great Resignation' or the 'Great Reimagination'

The occupational and psychological distress as a consequence of the pandemic resulted in more than 3.9 million employees quitting their jobs in the United States. Recorded as the highest resignation rate in 30 years, the emergence of the 'great resignation' raised serious concerns about EW and confirmed it as a significant challenge for recovering businesses (Del Rio-Chanona, Hermida-Carrillo, Sepahpour-Fard, Sun, Topinkova, & Nedelkoska, 2023).

Organisational analysts argue that this is pessimistically painted, a 'short-lived trend', amplified by the media (Jiskrova, 2022). The changing nature of work marked the pandemic as a period of 'great renewal' and 'great resilience', giving stakeholders within organisations to 'build back better' – 'opportunities in new forms of working for all employees and advantages and disadvantages for all employers' (Ng & Stanton, 2023). It meant a fundamental shift in the ways in which people perceived work, their employer and life, in general. Presenting an opportunity to find 'great joy', i.e. to rediscover joy at work, re-evaluate what employees wanted from their work and possibly reinvent where, who and what employees wanted to work on, the phase altered employee attitudes to identify and maximise joy at work. For instance, employees, during the period, significantly saved on 'costs of work' (such as meals and transit) and time taken to commute and had better control over their work environment (Jiskrova, 2022).

Researchers such as Nowell (2022), investigating this amongst the nursing population, claimed that whilst perceiving work as 'meaningful' was crucial to professional motivation, commitment and wellbeing, possessing a high degree of self-awareness was crucial to perceiving the 'resignation' phase as an opportunity to 're-imagine'. Engaging in professional learning and development opportunities, including formal and/or informal activities, interactions and reflective practices, career planning resources and organisational support, and enhancing 'purpose', enabled employees to alter the lens with which they perceived and managed work.

Mouton (2023) concluded how 'hope' was a necessary ingredient to perceive the 'great resignation' as a 'great reimagination'. With businesses shutting down, several employees losing or changing jobs, battling the virus and grieving the loss of a loved one, generating hope, 'a goal-directed thinking coupled with agency ("willpower") and the generation of multiple pathways to one's goal ("waypower")', fostered resilience, enabled employees to thrive and contributed to wellbeing.

Virtual 'Teaching and Learning' within Contemporary Workplaces

With organisations across the globe carrying out business activities to a limited extent whilst adhering to health guidelines and restrictions, 'work from home' or 'online-based, remote work' practices gained momentum. Leaders postponed and cancelled in-person meetings and face-to-face teaching and learning workshops, training and development sessions within workplaces (Shahriar, Arafat, Islam, Nur, Rahman, Khan, & Alam, 2023). Massive, global, open, online course platforms such as Course-era, Udemy, LinkedIn Learning, Mindtools and EdX offered fundamental skill courses, free of charge, whilst additionally offering financial aid to learners. Availing of this, employers were found to invest in courses, webinars and virtual classrooms, learning about management systems and open education resources for employee upskilling and reskilling. Other teaching and learning methods included conducting webinars and virtual classrooms, employing PowerPoint presentations, e-case study-based questions, e-puzzles, instructive games with level-up options, online peer review and interactions, online assignments, short e-quizzes and exams. Employers used job aids (infographics and checklists), bite-sized films/videos, podcasts and vlogs, mobile apps and learner-generated content (Newman & Ford, 2021).

Blake, Bermingham, Johnson and Tabner (2020) designed and recommended the implementation of a digital learning package that offered interventions to foster psychological safety, reduce social stigmatisation (challenged with those infected with the virus) and employ psychological first aid practices within their workplaces. Specific steps to propagate self-care practices such as sleep hygiene, work breaks, fatigue and healthy life-style behaviours were also recommended.

The e-package equipped individuals with advice from mental health practitioners and front-line workers, and made signposts for public mental health guidelines more easily accessible. Evidence-based suggestions on managing emotions (such as moral injury, coping, guilt, grief, fear, anxiety, depression, prevention of burnout and psychological trauma) were additionally offered in the package. Accessed 17,633 times, healthcare providers confirmed having immediately adopted and implemented the e-learning package. Further research confirmed high user satisfaction with content, usability and utility. Free to use, the resource was proven to be meaningful and useful in the UK context specifically (Blake et al., 2020).

Multi-national and large-scale organisations, banks and non-bank financial institutions designed and implemented their own e-teaching, learning platforms and digital content libraries (with open education resources) for upskilling, reskilling, multi-skilling and cross-functional skilling to retain talented employees and create future-ready leaders (Shahriar et al., 2023).

Also, animation and gaming interventions, virtual reality, chatbots, curation through supporting technologies and augmented reality were found to be initiated and useful during the pandemic (Manuti, Pastore, Scardigno, Giancaspro, & Morciano, 2015). E-learning cultures enabled organisations to gracefully cope with the pandemic, secure sustainable continuity of organisational development and ensure decent work and growth within and across organisations (Manuti et al., 2015). This addressed an employee's self-actualisation needs or needs for 'growth', maximising one's potential on Maslow's pyramid and acted as an effective intellectual replenisher.

Loréal's Virtual Teaching and Learning Interventions

Loréal designed a 'learning never stops' programme and a 'My Learning' platform, engaging its employees in continuous learning. The initiation entailed a variety of short learning modules and live webinars from experts, with regularly updated content. The organisation demarcated four distinct roles within their learning and development team: this included architects (to create learning paths); curators (to find and create the best content for individual employees); producers (to develop online learning events); and activators (to engage employees in the content) (CIPD, 2021; Collin & Taillard, 2021). The intervention made possible the reskilling and upskilling of the workforce, deteriorating tendencies of errors, workplace conflict, role ambiguity and anxiety and increasing the probabilities of effective problem solving and decision making.

The 'SPARK' Application

Furthering this initiative, L'Oréal in China developed and propagated an application named 'SPARK', on which virtual classrooms and a wide range of learning resources were made available to the organisation's employees on their mobile phones. Stakeholders were additionally able to 'like', 'comment', 'share' and/or 'create' their own learning content with their colleagues. The intervention was awarded a Gold Medal at the Global Brandon Hall Awards for the best use of learning technology, and a silver medal at the APAC Stevie Awards for the best innovative learning application.

Virtual teaching and learning applications on mobile phones, however, expose employees to a number of threats including cyber bullying and harassment, data leakage, direct hacker attacks, intercepting communication, phishing and social engineering. In this light, analysts advise making user authentication the highest priority (with biometric or personal identification number (PIN) screen locks) (Li, 2020).

Blended/Hybrid Teaching and Learning Methods Employed by Lloyds

Employing both synchronous and asynchronous methods, blended/hybrid methods enhanced the quality of peer-to-peer and educator-to-employee instructions and subsequently their relationship. Higher levels of employee engagement and improved employee learning outcomes were additionally reported (Nguyen, 2015).

A mixed model approach, for instance, was employed by *Lloyds Banking Group*, UK, in 2018. Whilst identifying ten employee core skill needs (such as agile project management, artificial intelligence, customer service, relationship management and leadership skills), the bank employed 'Discover Learning' – a learning management system, which made learning easier to find and increased 'take up'. Further, by giving employees the benefit of learning at their own pace, evidence has highlighted how employees report requiring less time to learn and upskill and improved retention of new knowledge and skills when using e-teaching and learning practices in contrast to when engaging in face-to-face sessions.

Taking this into consideration, the US insurer *'Nationwide'* launched a five-year programme to upskill and reskill its staff through its 'Future of Work' centre. Every year, employees were offered a personalised curriculum, placing significance on the knowledge and skills the employee needed for the future. Moreover, they were monetarily incentivised for their participation (Daniel, Cano, & Cervera, 2015). These interventions, whilst keeping employees invested in their work, prevented employee fatigue, learning angst and frustration, consequentially, fostering wellbeing (Daniel et al., 2015).

The Challenges

Hawkins (2022) argued how reducing headcounts, rapidly evolving organisations (and subsequent changes in organisational structures), the increasing need for employee agility, 'learner demand for personalisation of content' and the demand for 'learning on the go' content drives and continually challenges virtual teaching and learning practices within workplaces. Technological barriers, such as disparities of access to technological devices (such as a computer, laptop or mobile), a lack of technological support and poor user-friendliness of technological intervention, low-quality technological devices, bandwidth and connectivity issues, can interfere with the employer's technological initiation and heighten angst and frustration amongst employees (Amankwah-Amoah, Khan, Wood, & Knight, 2021). Instructional barriers, such as poor instructor digital competence, 'instructor's behaviour and attitudes', continual designing of 'engaging and user-friendly learning content', lack of employee accountability to enhance their own knowledge and skills, lack of training and support offered and inappropriateness of the learning topic for virtual training and development needs, accounted as additional challenges faced by organisational stakeholders (Chanana & Sangeeta, 2021).

Other evidences in the literature, lastly, appraise learning barriers (such as employee perceived loneliness, lack of motivation, poor employee time management skills, unfamiliarity or lack of experience with the digital learning platform, inability to avoid personal, and familial and social distractions during virtual training sessions), as deteriorating the quality of virtual teaching and learning (Chanana & Sangeeta, 2021; CIPD, 2021).

In essence, i) poor fit of the virtual intervention with the learning needs of the employees; ii) the financial costs associated with engaging on a virtual teaching and learning platform; iii) the inability to access resources and attend virtual workshops in a timely manner when faced with a technological challenge; iv) low employee academic attainment and confidence levels; and v) employees from lower-income and under-represented backgrounds (Hawkins, 2022; Nguyen, 2015).

Suggested Activity

Reflect, discuss and make note of the various teaching and learning methods your organisation adopts.

1. What are the key differences between the various methods the employer chooses to adopt?
2. List the advantages of each of the teaching and learning methods.
3. List the disadvantages of each of the teaching and learning methods.
4. Which method did you find most useful during the pandemic? Why was this the case?

In order to support and effectively implement virtual teaching and learning practices, employers will need to formulate robust virtual employee teaching and learning policies. Research studies appraise evidence-based practices/interventions, such as making provision for 'reverse mentoring' practices – particularly beneficial for older people, which address technological advancements within the organisation as useful. Critically assessing the organisational context, its goals and objectives, employee learning preferences and the available digital tools, refraining from being blinded by technological advancements in the industry and continually placing people ('such as learners, instructors, corporate learning and development leaders and senior management') at the core of virtual teaching and learning practices is key (Manuti, Pastore, Scardigno, Giancaspro & Morciano, 2015).

Policy makers/governments must increasingly invest in analysing and addressing the social divide in the access and availability of technological infrastructure. Lower income groups and unemployed individuals must be particularly prioritised to allow for upskilling and reskilling. Researchers further propose the initiation of a free or heavily subsidised, digital or blended learning skills wallet, monitoring an employee's individual skill learning account (Sousa & Rocha, 2019). Financial incentives can generously be offered to knowledge and skill providers, rapidly building capacity of those developing new quality digital learning opportunities (Sousa & Rocha, 2019).

Post-pandemic, online education programmes (such as LinkedIn, Mindtools, etc.), job aids (such as infographics and checklists) and bite-sized film videos continued to be highly sought after by employers. Workplaces will continue to successfully employ social learning methodologies, digital tools to address learning, coaching and mentoring. Learning experience platforms, podcasts/vlogs, mobile apps, learning embedded systems, learner generated content, animation and gaming methodologies although, relatively minimally employed, have been evidenced as useful by employers. Still fewer organisations have reported virtual reality, chat bots, curation through supporting technologies and augmented reality methodologies, as employed and of value, within contemporary workplaces (CIPD, 2020; Newman & Ford, 2021; Swartz, Barbosa, Crawford & Luck, 2021).

Professional bodies over the next 5 years, believe artificial intelligence or machine learning is likely to drive more active personalisation in employee e-training and development initiatives. Further, virtual or augmented reality, social learning and the drawing on and compilation of data on employee learn-ing habits and preferences are likely to be further propagated, implemented and appreciated amongst the contemporary workforce. Live streaming/live videos, teaching and learning embedded within business applications, more accurate industry data on essential employee skills and chatbots are foreseen to significantly influence organisational teaching and learning methods in the near future (Newman & Ford, 2021; Swartz et al., 2021).

An Increased Uptake of Flexible/Hybrid Working

Flexible working practices or 'working arrangements that offer flexibility on how long, where, when and what times employees work' have increas-ingly been contemplated within workplaces and the domains of study and research. Given the onset of the pandemic, more than 50% of employers have reported allowing staff to work from home on a regular and/or ad hoc basis, informal flexibility (i.e. the ability to change hours or location on an as-need basis, informally agreed with the line manager) and part-time hours. Flexitime options (i.e. a system of working a set number of hours, with the starting and finishing chosen with agreed limits by the employee), home working (always working from home) and career breaks have additionally been offered within contemporary workplaces. Relatively fewer organisa-tions have evidenced implementing compressed working hours, a four-day week, job sharing, term-time working, annualised hours (i.e. a set number of contracted hours in a year) and zero hour contract (i.e. no guaranteed minimum working hours) policies and practices (Au, Dong, & Tremblay, 2021; Austin-Egole, Iheriohanma, & Nwokorie, 2020; Ramakrishnan & Arokiasamy, 2019).

Why Pay Heed to 'Flexible Working Hours?'

Employers are witnessing more than 40% of employees requesting flexible working hours. Employing the 'happy to talk flexible working' on their job adverts, organisational psychologists recommend the formulation and imple-mentation of evidence-based, flexible working hour policies and practices, clearly stating whether, how often and in which circumstances employees can request flexible working hours. Choosing to highlight options for flexible working (if applicable) whilst advertising for vacancies has assisted in attract-ing a wider pool of candidates who are looking for flexible roles.

More than 80% of the surveyed employees by CIPD (2020) reported that this workplace benefit was crucial to addressing work-life balance needs. Further, flexible working hours have made the 'commute to work' more manageable, making it relatively easier to save money. In addition, invest-ing time, money and energy in pursuing interests/hobbies and/or any volun-teering opportunities, managing childcare or caregiving responsibilities (i.e.

older parents with disabilities or long-term support health conditions and support) became more feasible, physiologically and psychologically causing less strain on the employee (Au et al., 2021; Bainbridge & Townsend, 2020).

Line manager attitudes, lack of senior-level support, concerns about meeting operational and customer requirements and the nature of the work people do, however, account as some of the many challenges to flexible working implementation. Analysts recommend that employers invest in employee knowledge and skill evaluation, job re-designing, and training and development workshops that reinstate the significance and methods by which flexible working can potentially be embraced (Au et al., 2021). This consequentially addresses employee physiological and psychological symptoms of work stress (Ciarniene & Vienazindiene, 2018; CIPD, 2020; Cheese, 2020).

Flex-from-First

Professional accreditation bodies within the UK have been campaigning for 'flexfrom1st', in order to make the 'right to request flexible working', a day 1 right, rather than after 26 weeks of employment. The policy/practice held the potential for employees to invest in physiological and psychological replenishers. In this light, they suggest administering a checklist for effectively implementing 'flexible working hour' policy and practices (CIPD, 2020; Dale, 2020; Teasdale, 2020).

'The Flexible Work' Checklist

The checklist firstly addresses the 'facilitators of flexible working'. These include assessing whether the organisation possesses a healthy organisational culture. It is additionally useful to assess whether senior leaders act as champions and sponsors for flexible working - supporting and demonstrating flexible working. The organisation must explicitly make a commitment to health and wellbeing, and actively promote flexible working as an option for those employees who are also carers or parents. Moreover, the provision of IT support (technology and IT infrastructure that supports and enables flexible working), practical tools (whether the organisation helps enable flexible working by providing managers and employees with readily available guidance and tools), proactive assistance from HR (assessing if the HR function is supportive, providing managers and employees with guidance and advice on flexible working) and career progression (evaluating whether the organisation engages in developing and sharing testimonies, using examples of senior stakeholders who work flexibly to show that progression is possible whilst working flexibly) must be evaluated. The 'flexible working' checklist further addresses the 'barriers to flexible working'. Urging the employer to evaluate their organisation for i) the challenging nature of job design, ii) organisational demands and iii) problematic policies, the checklist accounts for a comprehensive methodology for examining workplace flexible working barriers (Brewer, 2000; Chen, Rossi, Chevalier, & Oehlsen, 2019; CIPD, 2020).

'Time and Place Management' Intervention

The work psychology literature appraises flexible work initiatives that focus on the changes of 'where' (spatial boundaries) and 'when' (temporal boundaries) employees work. There, however, needs to be more concrete evidence on the influences of tele-working (spatial flexibility), compressed workweeks (temporal flexibility) and flexible elements of new ways of working (time-spatial flexibility) on EW (De Ruiters & Peters, 2022). As an alternative, Morelock, McNamara and James (2017), tested a 'time and place' management intervention with 437 healthcare workers. Findings indicated the proposition to be particularly effective with older employees. Whilst flexible working options offered employees more choice and control over the time and place of their work, a time and place management intervention emphasised the processes and the regulations imperative for the successful management of choice and control, rather than the options alone. This consequentially fostered employee productivity, physiological and psychological ease when managing work and life (Morelock et al., 2017).

Policy-makers are encouraged to propagate the flexible working methodology, working with employers on 'myth busting' around flexible working to dispel the notion that this may not be workable for certain job roles or employees. Further, building on a 'challenge fund' to test the implementation of flexible working practices for front-line workers, whilst assessing the impact on employee and business metrics, is recommended. Designing, assessing and implementing resources for workplaces transitioning to and embracing flexible cultures proves to be beneficial – this, however, must be in resonance with employee inclusion and wellbeing policies (Choi, 2020; CIPD, 2020, 2023).

Forward versus Legacy Thinking

The onset of the pandemic necessitated a 'mindset shift' for the understanding and fostering of EW. Employing a 'forward thinking' mindset whilst embracing an 'ambition for human sustainability' was imperative. This implied perceiving work as a determinant of wellbeing, as a shared responsibility of all stakeholders within the organisation and as being significantly moderated by organisational structures and the norms to which work is adhered and carried out. This is in contrast to adopting a 'legacy thinking' – perceiving wellbeing as a result of balancing two distinct aspects, work and life, perceiving 'wellbeing' as the responsibility of the individual and as being moderated by organisational perks and benefits (Bordeaux et al., 2023; Deloitte, 2017).

The 'Cost of Living' Crisis and Employer Financial Wellbeing Interventions

Defined as 'an expression of the overall financial health of an individual', 'employee financial wellbeing', in recent years, has increasingly been reported as a cause of concern. Highlighting a lack of control over finances, researchers illustrate how an increase in employee withdrawals from the hardship fund and/or requests for loans has been evidence of this (Bayer, Bernheim, & Scholz, 2009). Salaries have failed to compete with inflation, and 'rising job insecurities and health care costs'. Consequentially, several employees have failed to manage their finances effectively, making them more vulnerable to financial shocks and unanticipated expenses (Bayer et al., 2009). These heightened levels of stress deteriorated employee physical and mental health.

Studies demonstrate the 'average annual cost' of absenteeism and presenteeism, due to financial stressors to account for approximately £4,000 within small organisations, £22,000 within medium-sized organisations and £300,000 within large-scale organisations (De-la-Calle-Durán & Rodríguez-Sánchez, 2021). Financial wellbeing, in essence, was marked as crucial to human resource objectives such as personnel planning, employee selection, engagement and retention, in addition to significantly contributing to EW (De-la-calle-duran, et al., 2021; Sabri, Wijekoon & Rahim, 2020).

Employee financial health is moderated by individual differences, financial circumstances, financial literacy and financial behaviours (managing finances, 'planning ahead', 'proactively seeking advice') (Bayer et al., 2009; Sabri et al., 2020). Financial numeracy abilities, 'an understanding of financial concepts and knowledge of where to access this', additionally, impacted employee financial wellbeing. Given the onset of pandemic, amplified financial inequalities within societies, the 'cost of living crisis', the challenge with coping with sharply rising prices and an array of unforeseen circumstances and challenges, research studies explicate the significance of propagating, investing in and availing of legal and financial wellbeing tools and interventions.

The Drafting of Organisational Financial Policies

The drafting of financial wellbeing policies, in this light, has been perceived as a 'reputation enhancer' by employees and customers. Supporting evidence, for instance, has identified that a significant 76% of employees were more attracted to an organisation that cares about their financial wellness. Financial wellbeing policies enabled employers to reduce in-work poverty by more than 35%. Consequentially, this has also proven to enhance the quality of relationships within families and societal wellbeing (Castro-González, Fernández-López, Rey-Ares, & Rodeiro-Pazos, 2020; Mahendru, Sharma & Hawkins, 2022).

Critics argue that employee financial health is moderated by individual differences, financial circumstances, financial literacy and financial behaviours (managing finances, 'planning ahead', 'proactively seeking advice') (Bayer et al., 2009; Sabri et al., 2020). Financial numeracy abilities, 'an understanding of financial concepts and knowledge of where to access this', additionally, impacted employee financial wellbeing (Lusardi, 2019). Employee 'age' is an additional factor influencing the financial wellbeing narrative – the onset of the pandemic witnessed deteriorating job security and increasing unemployment, particularly amongst older employees on account of ill health (Vieira, Potrich, Bressan, & Klein, 2021). Given the pandemic, however, proactive formulation of a business case that accommodates employee financial wellness and the employment of psychometrically robust research instruments is necessary.

Assessing Employee Financial Wellbeing

Financial wellbeing surveys can seek to acquire information concerning demographic characteristics (such as age, gender, marital status, work region, work grade and work status –full-time or part-time). The CIPD (2023) formulated and recommends using the 'Financial Wellbeing' survey, consisting of statements such as 'how do you predict your financial wellbeing will be in the next 12 months?', 'apart from increasing your pay, what would you like your employer to do to improve your financial wellbeing?'.

As an alternative methodology, Prawitz and Cohart (2014) suggest employing the 'Personal Financial Wellness Scale', which consists of statements such as 'how often do you worry about being able to meet your monthly expenses?', 'how frequently do you find yourself living paycheck to paycheck?' and 'how confident are you that you could find the money to pay for a financial emergency that costs more than $1000?'. The scale has been proven to possess strong psychometric properties. Critics argue that the scale may not always capture wellness appropriately; the findings are subject to how the employee 'feels' about their finances during that time. However, the instrument has proven to be useful for research and administration and can be further developed to enhance the reliability and validity of psychometric properties (Prawitz & Cohart, 2014).

Lastly, interviews or informal conversations with employees additionally enable the employer to assess employee needs, explore possible options and determine appropriate interventions that resonate with their needs (Vieira et al., 2021).

Interventions to Foster Employee Financial Wellbeing

The drafting, communicating and implementing of clear employee financial wellbeing policies (especially concerning bonuses, promotion structures, benefits and retirement plans) and interventions that accommodate and assure strict confidentiality are crucial. Detailing this comprehensively and in advance enables employees to plan and manage their finances effectively (Tangka, Subramanian, Jones, Edwards, Flanigan, Kaganova, & Guy, 2020).

Further, line managers discussing work-related money mistakes such as engaging in careless purchasing, mounting debt and poor attention to credit card balances can result in more savings and greater security (Prawitz & Cohart, 2014). Recommending cost-effective commuting options, economical meals, ways to adhere to a dress code without having to invest in new attire and expressing a general interest in how employee spend their earnings during work can urge employees to reflect on their relationship with money, seek financial advice if necessary and enhance their financial wellness (Bruggen et al., 2017).

Employee Financial Wellness Programmes (EFWPs) and Financial Counselling

Employers are choosing to embrace a comprehensive and relatively expensive approach to fostering employee financial wellness. Employee Financial Wellness Programmes (EFWPs), for instance, extend a range of financial products and services (Prakash, Alagarsamy, & Hawaldar, 2022). Often characterised as workplace-based financial education interventions, EFWP interventions offer financial literacy benefits including instruction on investing, training in the fundamentals of finance and budgeting (Prakash et al., 2022).

Moreover, Hannon, Covington, Despard, Frank-Miller and Grinstein-Weiss (2017) report how findings from a survey conducted by Alliant Credit Union demonstrate how 52% of employers offer medical or health care cost planning programmes, and more than 30% of workplaces offer confidential employee self-assessments of their finances, tools for tracking progress towards financial goals and targeted or customised financial education (Mahendru et al., 2022; Hannon et al., 2017). These methods have proven to enhance employee financial wellness.

Other financial workplace interventions such as debt management, investment planning and financial counselling, furthermore, have been highly sought-after by employees (Bruggen et al., 2017; Prakash et al., 2022). *Google,* for instance, offers its employees one-to-one financial coaching services and student loan reimbursements, and conducts annual cross-company pay equity pay and analysis.

'Lunch and Learn' Sessions

'Lunch and learn' sessions on financial topics such as property planning, 'business entity formation', 'stock market funds', 'real estate investments', 'leasing or purchasing of vehicles' and 'money saving methods' can prove to be beneficial to employee financial wellness (Mahendru et al., 2022).

The implementation of these initiatives improved the use of existing employee financial wellbeing benefits, improved employee recruitment, and enhanced financial wellness markers (Hannon et al., 2017). Employing interventions that are irrelevant to employee needs and decision-making, poorly presented content, quality and delivery of financial education act as detrimental to the employer's intent of contributing to employee financial wellness (Prakash et al., 2022).

The 'Rule of Thumb' Intervention

Drexler, Fischer and Schoar (2014) advice employers to appraise the 'rule of thumb' intervention as an effective methodology to initiate financial wellness. The proposition gives employees

> a physical rule to keep their money in two separate drawers (or purses) and to only transfer money from one drawer to the other with an explicit 'IOU' note between the business and the household. At the end of the month they could then count how much money was in the business drawer and know what their profits were.

Supporting evidences from Fernandes (2023) further affirm the use of 'planning prompts' and appraise the influence of peers in saving and spending behaviours.

The Challenges

Part-time employees, 'single parent' families, employees living in rented homes, those living with a disabled or chronically ill family member or those employee households with three or more children, who are headed by a member from an ethnic minority group, are more susceptible to in-work poverty (Tangka et al., 2020; Vieira et al., 2021). Business cases, when drafted in most organisations, fail to consider these vulnerable groups with appropriate consideration.

On another note, all employers may be able to informationally and financially invest in the implementation of assessments and interventions (Prawitz & Cohart, 2014). Further, the complexity involved in choosing an appropriate intervention demotivates employers from investing in a financial proposition. Lastly, a lack of interest amongst employees, data and privacy concerns, and legal and/or regulatory hurdles account for some of the other challenges to employing financial wellbeing assessments and tools (Brüggen, Hogreve, Holmlund, Kabadayi, & Löfgren, 2017).

Social media trends on TikTok and newspaper publications have appraised trends such as 'soft savings'. This trend operates under the 'soft life' approach to working and living life, implying employees as working within their contracted hours, opting for less demanding careers, investing relatively more in the present than hoarding significant amounts of money for the future. This post pandemic, sustainable, financial wellness trend, rooted in the affordability crisis and deteriorating levels of wellness, involves making minor changes, being flexible or making gradual shifts in spending habits. This is in contrast to punishing oneself with significant lifestyle cuts, deprivation of minor comforts and strict budget slashing.

The post pandemic era has also witnessed the appraisal of the 'doom spending' (a phenomenon in which individuals choose to spend excessive amounts of money on luxury items, travel or experiences in response to their anxieties of not holding the potential of achieving their financial goals – an approach that debatably results in the 'short-term gratification and long term pain') and 'loud budgeting' (a financial wellbeing, social approach wherein' individuals choose to be 'financially transparent', not feeling ashamed and sharing their financial aspirations, directly and 'not so quietly' with the people in their lives, reminding oneself and others to not spend more than what is earned) phenomenon (The Guardian, 2024). There has, however, been little scientific literature published on these nuances of employee financial wellness.

The Health Care Sectors

The global pandemic in 2019 crippled health care systems across the globe. Recent studies that investigated the wellbeing and coping strategies of healthcare workers elucidated how the unpreparedness of the healthcare sector and its subsequent inability to offer effective healthcare solutions and treatments for a large number of patients was a 'shock' to the sector, and heightened anger and frustration amongst employees (McFadden, Ross, Moriarty, Mallett, Schroder, Ravalier, & Gillen, 2021). Because of the anxiety of contracting the virus, managing social stigma, and being challenged with a lack of protective equipment, a shortage of skilled workers, subsequent work overload, and high levels of burnout, employees in this sector were categorised as at 'high risk' (Bennet, Noble, Johnston, Jones, & Hunter, 2020; McFadden et al., 2021).

Similar findings from 37 hospitals in China highlighted the widespread prevalence of depression, anxiety, insomnia and distress among healthcare workers. Frequently witnessing an increasing number of affected patients and fatalities, employees were prone to and reported symptoms of experiencing post-traumatic stress (Zhou, Zhou, Song, Ren, Ng, Xiang, & Tang, 2021).

Health Care Sector Interventions During COVID-19

A number of interventions were designed and tested by analysts to foster effective physiological and psychological coping.

Psychosocial Pandemic Committees, Offline and Online Resilience Training

On an additional note, organisations which invested in a psychosocial pandemic committee, computer-based and on-site resilience training, sleep interventions and battle buddies were evidenced to be less challenged with EW during the pandemic (Lai, Ma, Wang, Cai, Hu, Wei, Wu, Du, Chen, & Li, 2020). For instance, the Mount Sinai Hospital in Toronto employed an internal committee held regular meetings to disseminate information regarding the principles of psychosocial resilience, and facilitated communication of employee concerns and suggestions (Scerri & Grech, 2021).

Frequently revisiting how organisational informational and financial resources were distributed, the medical compensation and reimbursement models were designed, and accounted for additional wellbeing initiatives within the health care sector (Lai et al., 2020).

Self-Care Practices

Healthcare professionals who continually invested in self-care practices (exercise, sleep and a strong social support system), perceived meaning in their work and life (particularly by engaging in 'small group discussions' and 'reflective counselling') and managed their emotional health by investing time and resources in 'mindfulness' practices demonstrated greater levels of wellbeing during the course of the crisis (Heath, Sommerfield, & Von, 2020).

Suggested Activity

Interview a couple of employees working in the healthcare sector. If you were employed within the industry, reflect on your experiences too.

i) What policies/practices/interventions did the organisation employ to foster employee physiological wellbeing?

ii) What policies/practices/interventions did the organisation employ to foster psychological, social, financial and familial wellbeing at the time?

iii) What advice/support did vulnerable and/or older employees, in particular, receive when faced with the pandemic?

The Givers, Takers and Matchers – The Unforeseen Changing Dynamics of Workplace Relationships

The idea of 'the givers, takers and matchers' was conceptualised by the renowned organisational psychologist Adam Grant in an attempt to analyse workplace relationships and employee motivation. People typically have one of the three dominant motivations when interacting with others (Grant, 2019). 'Givers' or those who are 'others-oriented', help others with no strings attached; they enjoy engaging in pro-social behaviours. This is in contrast to 'takers' or those who are 'self-serving', who draw from other's resources (informational, emotional, social or financial) and invest little in return. Lastly, with the objective of keeping a fair, even balance between giving and taking, 'matchers' opt for a safe way to operate within the workplace.

In this light, the pandemic, whilst altering the modes and methods of working – embracing remote and hybrid approaches – fiercely propelled changes in the quality of workplace relationships, knowledge sharing tendencies and frequencies, reciprocity styles and the extent to which workplace relationships were transactional (Siemsen, Roth, Balasubramanian & Anand, 2009; Grant, 2019).

Evidence from Tannenbaum, Traylor, Thomas and Salas (2021) highlighted how ill health of the employees themselves, or familial and social ill health, as well as changing employee roles, pay cuts and mass lay-offs, heightened job insecurity amongst employees. Further, insufficient information about employee priorities, roles and responsibilities contributed to deteriorating self and collective efficacy (a weak belief in the ability of the team to succeed). Subsequently, an increasing attention on oneself, discomfort with speaking up or deteriorating psychological safety significantly altered the extent to which employees were motivated to help others (Siemsen, et al., 2009; Grant, 2019).

2.6 Summary

In summary, this chapter aimed to explore the specific ways in which EW evolved during the pandemic. The author begins with appraising two key theoretical approaches or 'lenses' – Maslow's 'needs' theory and the coping reservoir model, through which EW was analysed in this and the following chapters. Brooks (2023) affirmed how EW was primarily dependant on the earning of success and an employee's sense of purpose. Further, an employee's quality of life was dependant on the quality of relationships they shared with family and friends, the extent and the quality of engagement with work that served society and the faith that they chose to follow. These nuances were particularly compromised during the public health emergency.

The increasing number of respiratory and other serious health ailments, the consequential physiological, psychological, occupational, social and financial distress resulted in the 'great resignation'. The pandemic witnessed over 3.9 million employees resigning from their jobs in the United States. A deterioration or altering of quality of life led to the period being marked by a 'great renewal' and 'great resilience', urging stakeholders to build back better.

Investing and availing of EW interventions were not 'add-ons' or a 'luxury' – this was a necessity for all organisational stakeholders. It was crucial for leaders not to solely engage in EW conversations but to employ proactive, evidence-based methods to address EW challenges. The pandemic witnessed the crippling of healthcare sectors across the globe, given the industry's unpreparedness to offer healthcare solutions and services for a significantly large number of patients. Employers encouraged at-home testing kits, the use of portable, low-noise air purifiers, initiate 'quit smoking' support groups and employ 'stop smoking' specialists. Given employee preferences for 'clean', 'natural' and 'clinical' as a result of the pandemic, analysts were found to recommend health-based architectural designs for the future of employee wellness.

The chapter moved on to appraising employee at home grooming and skinmalisim trends, the potential benefits of 'plant forward' approaches and 'water forward' experiences within workplaces and the thriving of health-related technologies during the public health emergency. Later, the author informed readers of how unmanned aerial vehicles, medical robots, app-enabled sleep trackers and other connected digital technologies are likely to dominate the domains of EW. The potential powers of employee psychological distancing, reinterpretation, bounded optimism and psychological flexibility in alleviating psychological stressors and fostering better mental health, were explored.

Authors such as Blake and colleagues (2020) critically analysed virtual teaching and learning package. The section appraised initiations by Loréal and the Discover Learning management system implemented by Lloyds Banking Group. These interventions were found to foster reskilling and upskilling of employees, foster engagement and deteriorate levels of learning angst. Lastly, the chapter acquaints readers with the 'cost of living' crisis that significantly increased employee stress, absenteeism, presenteeism and quiet quitting tendencies. The author recommended the drafting of evidence based financial policies and practices, the administration of regular employee financial wellbeing surveys, employee financial wellness programmes, 'lunch and learn' workshops, personal financial counselling and the 'rule of thumb' interventions. Ethnic minority groups were identified as being relatively more prone to in-work poverty. Stronger diversity and inclusion policies that accommodate vulnerable sections of the employee population, have been evidenced as beneficial. The next chapter moves on to exploring the nuances of employee voice, appraising pre- and post-pandemic policies, practices and interventions.

2.7 Further Readings

Brynjolfsson, E., & Mcafee (2017). Artificial Intelligence, For Real. Harvard Business Review, *1*, 1–31.
Delizonna, L. (2017). High-performing teams need psychological safety. Here's how to create it. Harvard Business Review, *8*, 1–5.
Edmondson (2013). Teaming to Innovate. San Fransisco: Wiley.
Hull, L., & Radecki, D. (2018). Psychological Safety: The Key to Happy, High Performing People and Teams. Orange, CA: Academy of Brain Based Leadership.
Palomäki, L. M. (2019). Does it matter how you retire? Old-age retirement routes and subjective economic well-being. Social Indicators Research, *142*(2), 733–751.
Vlaev, I., & Elliott, A. (2014). Financial well-being components. Social Indicators Research, *118*, 1103–1123.

2.8 Suggested Websites

American Psychological Society (2023). Increase employee's options for where, when and how they work. Available at: https://www.apa.org/topics/healthy-workplaces/mental-health/flexible-work Accessed on: 6 November 2023
CIPD (2023). Technology. Available at: https://www.cipd.org/en/topics/technology/ Accessed on: 6 November 2023
NHS Employers (2023). Financial education and wellbeing. Available at: https://www.nhsemployers.org/articles/financial-education-and-wellbeing Accessed on: 6 November 2023

2.9 Reflective Questions – For Learners

From your reading and research,

1. How do you believe employees of healthcare sectors across the globe could have been better supported with their physical and mental health during the pandemic?
2. What challenges could employers potentially be faced with when implementing employee financial wellbeing interventions?
3. Explain the concept of 'psychological distancing' and its wellbeing benefits when faced with unprecedented times such as the pandemic.

2.10 Reflective Questions – For Researchers/Practitioners

From your reading and research

1. How did COVID-19 impact EW within your organisation?
2. Which specific interventions do you think could have been introduced and would have benefitted your organisation during the pandemic? What are the pros and cons of implementing these interventions?

3. Whilst employing the lens of Maslow's Hierarchy of Needs, what are the specific ways in which your organisation addressed employee needs (consequentially fostering wellbeing), during the pandemic?
4. Do you consider yourself a 'giver', 'taker' or a 'matcher' within your workplace? Did you find your role changing post-pandemic? Think about the influence your role has on

    i)   Your performance and wellbeing.
    ii) The performance of others and their wellbeing.

5. Conduct a Psychinfo/EBSCOhost search covering literature published in the past using the term 'employee wellbeing' and 'pandemic' or 'COVID-19'. Identify an intervention that resonates with your interests. Replicate, conduct the study and extend on the findings.

References

Agarwal, N., Meena, C. S., Raj, B. P., Saini, L., Kumar, A., Gopalakrishnan, N., ... Aggarwal, V. (2021). Indoor air quality improvement in COVID-19 pandemic. *Sustainable Cities and Society, 70*, 102942.

Al-Jubari, I., Mosbah, A., & Salem, S. F. (2022). Employee well-being during COVID-19 pandemic: The role of adaptability, work-family conflict, and organizational response. *SAGE Open, 12*(3), 21582440221096142.

Amankwah-Amoah, J., Khan, Z., Wood, G., & Knight, G. (2021). COVID-19 and digitalization: The great acceleration. *Journal of Business Research, 136*, 602–611.

Au, S. Y., Dong, M., & Tremblay, A. (2021). Employee flexibility, exogenous risk, and firm value. *Journal of Financial and Quantitative Analysis, 56*(3), 853–884.

Austin-Egole, I. S., Iheriohanma, E. B., & Nwokorie, C. (2020). Flexible working arrangements and organizational performance: An overview. *IOSR Journal of Humanities and Social Science (IOSR-JHSS), 25*(5), 50–59.

Bainbridge, H. T., & Townsend, K. (2020). The effects of offering flexible work practices to employees with unpaid caregiving responsibilities for elderly or disabled family members. *Human Resource Management, 59*(5), 483–495.

Balasingam, M. (2017). Drones in medicine—the rise of the machines. *International Journal of Clinical Practice, 71*(9), e12989.

Balz, J. P., Sunstein, C. R., & Thaler, R. H. (2012). *The Behavioural Foundations of Public Policy*. Princeton: Princeton University Press.

Bayer, P. J., Bernheim, B. D., & Scholz, J. K. (2009). The effects of financial education in the workplace: Evidence from a survey of employers. *Economic Inquiry, 47*(4), 605–624.

Belloni, M., Carrino, L., & Meschi, E. (2022). The impact of working conditions on mental health: Novel evidence from the UK. *Labour Economics, 76*, 102-176.

Bennett, P., Noble, S., Johnston, S., Jones, D., & Hunter, R. (2020). COVID-19 confessions: A qualitative exploration of healthcare workers experiences of working with COVID-19. *BMJ Open, 10*(12), 1–7.

Bhatt, J., Bordeaux, C., & Fisher, J. (2023). The workforce wellbeing imperative. Available at: https://www2.deloitte.com/xe/en/insights/topics/talent/employee -wellbeing.html. Accessed on: 25 May 2024.

Blake, H., Zhou, D., & Batt, M. E. (2013). Five-year workplace wellness intervention in the NHS. *Perspectives in Public Health, 133*(5), 262–271.

Blake, H., Bermingham, F., Johnson, G., & Tabner, A. (2020). Mitigating the psychological impact of COVID-19 on healthcare workers: A digital learning package. *International Journal of Environmental Research and Public Health, 17*(9), 2997.

Brassey, J., Gunter, A., Issak, K., & Silberzahn, T. (2021). *Using Digital Tech to Support Employees' Mental Health and Resilience*. Mckinsey and Company. Available at: https://www.mckinsey.com/industries/life-sciences/our-insights/using-digital-tech-to -support-employees-mental-health-and-resilience Accessed on: 15 November 2023

Brewer, A. M. (2000). Work design for flexible work scheduling: Barriers and gender implications. *Gender, Work and Organization, 7*(1), 33–44.

Brüggen, E. C., Hogreve, J., Holmlund, M., Kabadayi, S., & Löfgren, M. (2017). Financial well-being: A conceptualization and research agenda. *Journal of Business Research, 79*, 228–237.

Büchi, M. (2021). Digital well-being theory and research. *New Media and Society*. https://doi.org/10.1177/14614448211056851.

Carolan, S., Harris, P. R., & Cavanagh, K. (2017). Improving employee well-being and effectiveness: Systematic review and meta-analysis of web-based psychological interventions delivered in the workplace. *Journal of Medical Internet Research, 19*(7), e271.

Castro-González, S., Fernández-López, S., Rey-Ares, L., & Rodeiro-Pazos, D. (2020). The influence of attitude to money on individuals' financial well-being. *Social Indicators Research, 148*(3), 747–764.

Cave, D., Pearson, H., Whitehead, P., & Rahim-Jamal, S. (2016). CENTRE: Creating psychological safety in groups. *The Clinical Teacher, 13*(6), 427–431.

Chakma, T., Thomas, B. E., Kohli, S., Moral, R., Menon, G. R., Periyasamy, M., ... Panda, S. (2021). Psychosocial impact of COVID-19 pandemic on healthcare workers in India & their perceptions on the way forward-A qualitative study. *The Indian Journal of Medical Research, 153*(5–6), 637.

Championhealthplus (2023). Solutions for individuals. Available at: https://www .championhealthplus.co.uk/for-individuals Accessed on: 15 November 2023

Chanana, N., & Sangeeta (2021). Employee engagement practices during COVID-19 lockdown. *Journal of Public Affairs, 21*(4), e2508.

Cheese (2020). *A Flexible Working Future - The Opportunities and Challenges. Norgate & Cooper. Flexible Work: Designing our Healthier Future Lives*. London: Routledge, pp. 1–268.

Chen, M. Keith, Rossi, Peter E., Chevalier, Judith A., & Oehlsen, Emily. (2019). The value of flexible work: Evidence from Uber drivers. *Journal of Political Economy, 127*(6), 2735–2794.

Chiva, R. & Guinot, J. (2021). Well-being, happiness, satisfaction, burnout and the future of work. In M. Santana & R. Valle-Cabrera (Eds.), *New Directions in the Future of Work* (pp. 163–182). Leeds: Emerald Publishing Limited.

Choi, S. (2020). Flexible work arrangements and employee retention: A longitudinal analysis of the federal workforces. *Public Personnel Management, 49*(3), 470–495.

Chung, C. F., Gorm, N., Shklovski, I. A., & Munson, S. (2017). Finding the right fit: Understanding health tracking in workplace wellness programs. In G. Mark & S. R. Fussel (Eds.), *Proceedings of the 2017 CHI Conference on Human Factors in Computing Systems* (pp. 4875–4886). New York: Association for Computing Machinery.

Ciarniene, R., & Vienazindiene, M. (2018). Flexible work arrangements from generation and gender perspectives: Evidence from Lithuania. *Engineering Economics, 29*(1), 84–92.

CIPD (2020). CIPD good work index 2020: UK working lives survey. Available at: www.cipd.org Accessed on: 16 July 2024.

CIPD (2021). *Health and Wellbeing at Work Survey 2021*. London: Chartered Institute of Personnel and Development.

CIPD (2022). Health and wellbeing at work 2022. Available at: www.cipd.org Accessed on: 16 July 2024.

CIPD (2023). *Workplace Support for Employees Experiencing Fertility Challenges, Investigations or Treatment*. London: Chartered Institute of Personnel and Development.

CIPD (2024). Flexible working practices. Available at: www.cipd.org Accessed on: 16 July 2024.

Claxton, G., Rae, M., Damico, A., Young, G., Kurani, N., & Whitmore, H. (2021). Health benefits in 2021: Employer programs evolving in response to the COVID-19 Pandemic: Study examines employer-sponsored health benefits programs evolving in response to the COVID-19 pandemic. *Health Affairs, 40*(12), 1961–1971.

Collin, B., & Taillard, M. (2021). *Digital Makeover: How L'Oréal Put People First to Build a Beauty Tech Powerhouse*. New Jersey: John Wiley & Sons.

Dale, G. (2020). *Flexible Working: How to Implement Flexibility in the Workplace to Improve Employee and Business Performance*. London: Kogan Page Publishers.

Daniel, J., Cano, E. V., & Cervera, M. G. (2015). The future of MOOCs: Adaptive learning or business model? *RUSC. Universities and Knowledge Society Journal, 12*(1), 64–73.

De-la-Calle-Durán, M. C., & Rodríguez-Sánchez, J. L. (2021). Employee engagement and wellbeing in times of COVID-19: A proposal of the 5Cs model. *International Journal of Environmental Research and Public Health, 18*(10), 5470.

Del Rio-Chanona, R. M., Hermida-Carrillo, A., Sepahpour-Fard, M., Sun, L., Topinkova, R., & Nedelkoska, L. (2023). Mental health concerns precede quits: Shifts in the work discourse during the Covid-19 pandemic and great resignation. *EPJ Data Science, 12*(1), 49.

Deloitte. (2017). Rewriting the rules for the digital age. Available at: https://www2.deloitte.com/us/en/insights/focus/human-capital-trends/2017.html. Accessed on: 25 May 2024.

Dunn, L. B., Iglewicz, A., & Moutier, C. (2008). A conceptual model of medical student well-being: promoting resilience and preventing burnout. *Academic Psychiatry, 32*, 44–53.

Denny, B. T., & Ochsner, K. N. (2014). Behavioral effects of longitudinal training in cognitive reappraisal. *Emotion, 14*(2), 425.

Dhoopar, A., & Sihag, P. (2023). Managing organisational effectiveness during a pandemic: A conceptual framework. *International Journal of Business Continuity and Risk Management, 13*(2), 188–203.

Dicker, E. E., Jones, J. S., & Denny, B. T. (2022). Psychological distancing usage uniquely predicts reduced perceived stress during the COVID-19 pandemic. *Frontiers in Psychology, 13*, 838507.

Drexler, A., Fischer, G., & Schoar, A. (2014). Keeping it simple: Financial literacy and rules of thumb. *American Economic Journal: Applied Economics, 6*(2), 1–31.

Du Plessis, M. (2022). Working remotely in the new normal: Towards a conceptual framework for managing employee well-being. In I. L. Potgeiterer & N. Ferreira (Eds.), *Managing Human Resources the New Normal* (pp. 165–191). Cham: Springer International Publishing.

Durmuş, İ. (2024). Organizational overview of Maslow and management research. *Turkish Psychological Counseling and Guidance Journal, 14*(72), 137–152.

Fernandes (2023). 17 Evidence based interventions for financial wellbeing. In N. Mazar & D. Soman (Eds.), *Behavioural Science in the Wild*. Toronto: University of Toronto Press.

Frank, A. W. (1995). *The wounded storyteller: Body, illness & ethics*. London: University of Chicago Press.

Gee, P. M., Weston, M. J., Harshman, T., & Kelly, L. A. (2022). Beyond burnout and resilience: The disillusionment phase of COVID-19. *AACN Advanced Critical Care, 33*(2), 134–142.

Gerstell, E., Marchessou, S., Schmidt, J., & Spagnuolo, E. (2020). How COVID 19 is changing the world of beauty. Available at: https://www.mckinsey.com/industries/consumer-packaged-goods/our-insights/how-covid-19-is-changing-the-world-of-beauty Accessed on: 17 March 2024

Giumetti, G. W., O'Connor, S. A., Weissner, B. N., Keegan, N. R., Feinn, R. S., & Bulger, C. A. (2021). Walk your way to well-being at work: impact of a treadmill workstation on employee occupational health outcomes. *Occupational Health Science, 5*(3), 345–360.

Grant, A. M. (2019). Writing a book for real people: On giving the psychology of giving away. *Perspectives on Psychological Science, 14*(1), 91–95.

Grant, P., & McGhee, P. (2021). Hedonic versus (true) eudaimonic well-being in organizations. In S. Dhiman (Ed.), *The Palgrave Handbook of Workplace Well-Being* (pp. 925–943). Palgrave Macmillan/Springer Nature. https://doi.org/10.1007/978-3-030-30025-8_37.

Gulnaz Banu, P., Mondal, D., & Gautam, P. (2022). Study of beauty and makeup trends for Indian millennials amidst the COVID-19 pandemic. *NIFT Journal of Fashion, 107*.

Haktanir, A., Can, N., Seki, T., Kurnaz, M. F., & Dilmaç, B. (2022). Do we experience pandemic fatigue? current state, predictors, and prevention. *Current Psychology, 41*(10), 7314–7325.

Hannon, G., Covington, M., Despard, M., Frank-Miller, E., & Grinstein-Weiss, M. (2017). *Employee Financial Wellness Programs: A Review of the Literature and Directions for Future Research*. St. Louis: Washington University, Center for Social Development.

Hawkins, M. (2022). Virtual employee training and skill development, workplace technologies, and deep learning computer vision algorithms in the immersive metaverse environment. *Psychosociological Issues in Human Resource Management, 10*(1), 106–120.

Haynes, S. (2017). Guide to wellbeing technology in the workplace. *Occupational Health & Wellbeing, 69*(9), 12.

Heath, C., Sommerfield, A., & von Ungern-Sternberg, B. S. (2020). Resilience strategies to manage psychological distress among healthcare workers during the COVID-19 pandemic: A narrative review. *Anaesthesia, 75*(10), 1364–1371.

Helman, D., Yungstein, Y., Mulero, G. & Michael, Y. (2022). High through-put remote sensing of Vertical Green Living Walls (VGWs) in workplaces. *Remote Sensing, 14*(14), 34–85.

Hewitt, J. A., Whyte, G. P., Moreton, M., Van Someren, K. A., & Levine, T. S. (2008). The effects of a graduated aerobic exercise programme on cardiovascular disease risk factors in the NHS workplace: a randomised controlled trial. *Journal of Occupational Medicine and Toxicology, 3*, 1–10.

Jackson, S. E., Cox, S., Shahab, L., & Brown, J. (2022). Prevalence of use and real-world effectiveness of smoking cessation aids during the COVID-19 pandemic: A representative study of smokers in England. *Addiction, 117*(9), 2504–2514.

Jiskrova, G. K. (2022). Impact of COVID 19 pandemic on the workforce: From psychological distress to the great resignation. *Journal of Epidemiology and Community Health, 76*(6), 525–526.

Kamarulzaman, N., Saleh, A. A., Hashim, S. Z., Hashim, H., & Abdul-Ghani, A. A. (2011). An overview of the influence of physical office environments towards employee. *Procedia Engineering, 20*, 262–268.

Khakurel, J., Melkas, H., & Porras, J. (2018). Tapping into the wearable device revolution in the work environment: A systematic review. *Information Technology & People, 31*(3), 791–818.

Koepp, G. A., Manohar, C. U., McCrady-Spitzer, S. K., Ben-Ner, A., Hamann, D. J., Runge, C. F., & Levine, J. A. (2013). Treadmill desks: A 1-year prospective trial. *Obesity, 21*(4), 705–711.

Kolbe, M., Grande, B., & Spahn, D. R. (2015). Briefing and debriefing during simulation-based training and beyond: Content, structure, attitude and setting. *Best Practice and Research: Clinical Anaesthesiology, 29*(1), 87–96.

Kolbe, M., Weiss, M., Grote, G., Knauth, A., Dambach, M., Spahn, D. R., & Grande, B. (2013). TeamGAINS: A tool for structured debriefings for simulation-based team trainings. *BMJ Quality and Safety, 22*(7), 541–553.

Kumar, A., Elsersy, M., Darwsih, A., & Hassanien, A. E. (2021). Drones combat COVID-19 epidemic: Innovating and monitoring approach. In A. E. Hassanien & A. Darwish (Eds.), *Digital transformation and emerging technologies for fighting COVID-19 pandemic: Innovative approaches*. Studies in Systems, Decision and Control (pp. 175–188). Cham: Springer.

Labar, K., & Powers, J. P. (2018). Regulating emotion through distancing: A taxonomy, neurocognitive model, and supporting meta-analysis. *Neuroscience Bio Behavioural Review, 173*, 96–155.

Lai, J., Ma, S., Wang, Y., Cai, Z., Hu, J., Wei, N., ... Hu, S. (2020). Factors associated with mental health outcomes among health care workers exposed to coronavirus disease 2019. *JAMA Network Open, 3*(3), e203976–e203976.

Edmon, H. (2021). Changes in workplace practices during the COVID-19 pandemic: The roles of emotion, psychological safety and organisation support. *Journal of Organizational Effectiveness: People and Performance*, 8(1), 97–128.

Lee, G. Y. & Lim, R. B. (2023). Are self-test kits still relevant post COVID-19 pandemic? Qualitative study on working adults' perceptions. *Infection, Disease & Health*, 29(2), 73–80.

Li, Q. (2020). Mobile security: Threats and best practices. *Mobile Information Systems*, 2020, 1–15.

Liu, S., Lithopoulos, A., Zhang, C. Q., Garcia-Barrera, M. A., & Rhodes, R. E. (2021). Personality and perceived stress during COVID-19 pandemic: Testing the mediating role of perceived threat and efficacy. *Personality and Individual Differences*, 168, 110351.

MacEwen, B. T., MacDonald, D. J., & Burr, J. F. (2015). A systematic review of standing and treadmill desks in the workplace. *Preventive Medicine*, 70, 50–58.

Mahendru, M., Sharma, G. D., & Hawkins, M. (2022). Toward a new conceptualization of financial well-being. *Journal of Public Affairs*, 22(2), e2505.

Manuti, A., Pastore, S., Scardigno, A. F., Giancaspro, M. L., & Morciano, D. (2015). Formal and informal learning in the workplace: A research review. *International Journal of Training and Development*, 19(1), 1–17.

Mayer, I. S. (2018). Assessment of teams in a digital game environment. *Simulation and Gaming*, 49, 1–18.

McFadden, P., Ross, J., Moriarty, J., Mallett, J., Schroder, H., Ravalier, J., & Gillen, P. (2021). The role of coping in the wellbeing and work-related quality of life of UK health and social care workers during COVID-19. *International Journal of Environmental Research and Public Health*, 18(2), 815.

McKinsey and Company (2023). Could this be a glimpse into life in the 2030s? Available at: https://www.mckinsey.com/featured-insights/the-next-normal/2030s Accessed on: 15 November 2023

Mehta, D. (2021). Motivation Maslow's hierarchy of needs. *Issue 3 International Journal of Law, Management and Humanities*, 4, 913–919.

Microsoft (2019). Microsoft teams adoption strategy prepares employees for a new culture of work. Available at: https://www.microsoft.com/insidetrack/blog/microsoft-teams-adoption-strategy-prepares-employees-for-a-new-culture-of-work/ Accessed on: 16 March 2024

Mikus, J., Rieger, J., & Grant-Smith, D. (2022). Eudaemonic design to achieve well-being at work, wherever that may be. In *Ergonomics and Business Policies for the Promotion of Well-Being in the Workplace* (pp. 1–32). IGI Global.

Monnot, M. J., & Beehr, T. A. (2014). Subjective well-being at work: Disentangling source effects of stress and support on enthusiasm, contentment, and meaningfulness. *Journal of Vocational Behavior*, 85(2), 204–218.

Morelock, J. C., McNamara, T. K., & James, J. B. (2017). Workability and requests for flexible work arrangements among older adults: The role of a time and place management intervention. *Journal of Applied Gerontology*, 36(11), 1370–1392.

Mouton, A. (2023). Hope and work: From the pandemic to possibility, purpose and resilience. *Current Opinion in Psychology*, 49, 101–550.

Navaratnam, S., Nguyen, K., Selvaranjan, K., Zhang, G., Mendis, P., & Aye, L. (2022). Designing post COVID-19 buildings: Approaches for achieving healthy buildings. *Buildings*, 12(1), 74.

Newman, S. A., & Ford, R. C. (2021). Five steps to leading your team in the virtual COVID-19 workplace. *Organizational Dynamics, 50*(1), 100802.

Ng, S., & Stanton, P. (2023). The great resignation: Managing people in a post COVID 19 pandemic world. *Personnel Review, 52*(2), 401–407.

Northwood, K., Siskind, D., Suetani, S., & McArdle, P. A. (2021). An assessment of psychological distress and professional burnout in mental health professionals in Australia during the COVID-19 pandemic. *Australasian Psychiatry: Bulletin of Royal Australian and New Zealand College of Psychiatrists, 29*(6), 628–634.

Nowakowski, A. X. C. H. (2023). Same old new normal: The ableist fallacy of "post-pandemic" work. *Social Inclusion, 11*(1), 16–25.

Nowell, L. (2022). Helping nurses shift from the great resignation to the great reimagination. *Journal of Advanced Nursing, 78*(10), e115–e117.

Pannoni, A. (2023). *Microsoft Announces Four New Employee Workforce Initiatives.* Microsoft. Available at: Microsoft.com Accessed on: 16 November 2023

Podrekar, N., Kozinc, Ž., & Šarabon, N. (2020). The effects of cycle and treadmill desks on work performance and cognitive function in sedentary workers: A review and meta-analysis. *Work, 65*(3), 537–545.

Prakash, N., Alagarsamy, S., & Hawaldar, A. (2022). Demographic characteristics influencing financial wellbeing: A multigroup analysis. *Managerial Finance, 48*(9/10), 1334–1351.

Prawitz, A., & Cohart, J. (2014). Workplace financial education facilitates improvement in personal financial behavior. *Journal of Financial Counseling and Planning, 25*(1), 5–26.

Puolakanaho, A., Tolvanen, A., Kinnunen, S. M., & Lappalainen, R. (2020). A psychological flexibility-based intervention for Burnout: A randomized controlled trial. *Journal of Contextual Behavioral Science, 15*, 52–67.

Ramakrishnan, S., & Arokiasamy, L. (2019). Flexible working arrangements in Malaysia; A study of employee's performance on white collar employees. *Global Business and Management Research, 11*(1), 551–559.

Rashid, T., & Zarowsky, Z. (2023). Resilience and wellbeing strategies for pandemic fatigue in times of Covid 19. *International Journal of Applied Positive Psychology, 8*(1), 1–36.

Richter, A. (2020). Locked-down digital work. *International Journal of Information Management, 55*, 102157.

Robertson, L. J., Maposa, I., Somaroo, H., & Johnson, O. (2020). Mental health of healthcare workers during the COVID-19 outbreak: A rapid scoping review to inform provincial guidelines in South Africa. *South African Medical Journal, 110*(10), 1010–1019.

Ryan, R. M., & Deci, E. L. (2001). On happiness and human potentials: A review of research on hedonic and eudaimonic well-being. *Annual Review of Psychology, 52*(1), 141–166.

De Ruiters, M. & Peters, P. (2021). Flexible work initiatives, employee workplace well-being, and organizational performance. In P. Brough, E. Gardiner & K. Daniels (Eds.), *Handbook on management and employment practices* (pp. 1–889). Switzerland: Springer Nature.

Sabri, M., Wijekoon, R., & Rahim, H. (2020). The influence of money attitude, financial practices, self-efficacy and emotion coping on employees' financial wellbeing. *Management Science Letters, 10*(4), 889–900.

Sadick, A. M., & Kamardeen, I. (2020). Enhancing employees' performance and wellbeing with nature exposure embedded office workplace design. *Journal of Building Engineering, 32*, 101789.

Scerri, M., & Grech, V. (2021). Practicing medicine in the COVID-19 pandemic. *RHiME, 28*, 29–37.

Ścieszko, E., Budny, E., Rotsztejn, H., & Erkiert-Polguj, A. (2021). How has the pandemic lockdown changed our daily facial skincare habits? *Journal of Cosmetic Dermatology, 20*(12), 3722–3726.

Selinger, E., & Whyte, K. (2011). Is there a right way to nudge? The practice and ethics of choice architecture. *Sociology Compass, 5*(10), 923–935.

Shahane, A. D., & Denny, B. T. (2019). Predicting emotional health indicators from linguistic evidence of psychological distancing. *Stress and Health, 35*(2), 200–210.

Shahriar, S. H. B., Arafat, S., Islam, I., Nur, J. E. H., Rahman, S., Khan, S. I., & Alam, M. S. (2023). The emergence of e-learning and online-based training during the COVID-19 crisis: An exploratory investigation from Bangladesh. *Management Matters, 20*(1), 1–15.

Shrikrishna, D., Karan, A., & Dhillon, R. S. (2023). Making the air in the office clean. *Harvard Business Review*. Available at: https://hbr.org/2023/07/making-the-air-in-the-office-cleaner Accessed on: 15 November 2023.

Siemsen, E., Roth, A. V., Balasubramanian, S., & Anand, G. (2009). The influence of psychological safety and confidence in knowledge on employee knowledge sharing. *Manufacturing & service operations management, 11*(3), 429–447.

Sinha, S., & Jain, N. K. (2022). The jury is out–Can the HR managers be the choice architects in a post-pandemic work setting? *Journal of Organizational Change Management, 35*(1), 165–168.

Sliter, M., & Yuan, Z. (2015). Workout at work: Laboratory test of psychological and performance outcomes of active workstations. *Journal of Occupational Health Psychology, 20*(2), 259.

Smet, A., Tegelberg, Thiunissen, R., & Vogel, T. (2020). Overcoming pandemic fatigue: How to reenergize organizations for the long run. *McKinsey and Company*. Available at: https://www.mckinsey.com/capabilities/people-and-organizational-performance/our-insights/overcoming-pandemic-fatigue-how-to-reenergize-organizations-for-the-long-run#/ Accessed on: 16 November 2023

Song, X., English, M. T. M., & Whitman, M. V. (2017). Exploring organizational smoking policies and employee vaping behavior. *Journal of Occupational and Environmental Medicine, 59*(4), 365–368.

Sousa, M. J., & Rocha, Á. (2019). Skills for disruptive digital business. *Journal of Business Research, 94*, 257–263.

Sufi, T. (2021). Management research post-covid-19 pandemic. *Journal of Business Strategy Finance and Management, 3*(1–2), 1.

Swartz, S., Barbosa, B., Crawford, I., & Luck, S. (Eds.). (2021). *Developments in Virtual Learning Environments and the Global Workplace*. Manchester: IGI Global.

Tabuchi, T., Hoshino, T., & Nakayama, T. (2016). Are partial workplace smoking bans as effective as complete smoking bans? A national population-based study of smoke-free policy among Japanese employees. *Nicotine and Tobacco Research, 18*(5), 1265–1273.

Tangka, F. K., Subramanian, S., Jones, M., Edwards, P., Flanigan, T., Kaganova, Y., ... Guy, G. P. (2020). Insurance coverage, employment status, and financial well-being of young women diagnosed with breast cancer. *Cancer Epidemiology, Biomarkers and Prevention, 29*(3), 616–624.

Tannenbaum, S. I., Traylor, A. M., Thomas, E. J., & Salas, E. (2021). Managing teamwork in the face of pandemic: Evidence-based tips. *BMJ Quality and Safety, 30*(1), 59–63.

Taormina, R. J., & Gao, J. H. (2013). Maslow and the motivation hierarchy: Measuring satisfaction of the needs. *The American Journal of Psychology, 126*(2), 155–177.

Tariq, M. U., Khan, S., & Araci, Z. C. (2020). Self-directed learning through YouTube: Challenges, opportunities, and trends in the United Arab Emirates. *International Journal of Mechanical and Production Engineering Research and Development (IJMPERD), 10*(3), 1949–1965.

Taylor, G. M., Sawyer, K., Kessler, D., Munafò, M. R., Aveyard, P., & Shaw, A. (2021). Views about integrating smoking cessation treatment within psychological services for patients with common mental illness: A multi-perspective qualitative study. *Health Expectations, 24*(2), 411–420.

Taylor, S. (2022). The psychology of pandemics: Lessons learned for the future. *Canadian Psychology/Psychologie canadienne, 63*(2), 233.

Teasdale, N. (2020). Flexible Working in the UK: interrogating policy through a gendered Bacchi lens. *Feminismo/s, 35*, 155–177.

TheGuardian (2024). 'Are you loud budgeting or doom spending?' Finance according to Gen Z. Available at: https://www.theguardian.com/lifeandstyle/2024/jan/31/are-you-loud-budgeting-or-doom-spending-finance-according-to-gen-z Accessed on: 17 July 2024.

Thorndike, A. N., Riis, J., Sonnenberg, L. M., & Levy, D. E. (2014). Traffic-light labels and choice architecture: Promoting healthy food choices. *American Journal of Preventive Medicine, 46*(2), 143–149.

Vieira, K. M., Potrich, A. C. G., Bressan, A. A., & Klein, L. L. (2021). Loss of financial well-being in the COVID-19 pandemic: Does job stability make a difference? *Journal of Behavioral and Experimental Finance, 31*, 100554.

Vogt, F., Hall, S., & Marteau, T. M. (2010). Examining why smokers do not want behavioral support with stopping smoking. *Patient Education and Counseling, 79*(2), 160–166.

Whitehead, L. C. (2006). Quest, chaos and restitution: Living with chronic fatigue syndrome/myalgic encephalomyelitis. *Social Science and Medicine, 62*(9), 2236–2245.

Williams, M., & Penman, D. (2011). *Mindfulness: An Eight-Week Plan for Finding Peace in a Frantic World*. USA: Rodale.

Zhou, Y., Zhou, Y., Song, Y., Ren, L., Ng, C. H., Xiang, Y. T., & Tang, Y. (2021). Tackling the mental health burden of frontline healthcare staff in the COVID-19 pandemic: China's experiences. *Psychological Medicine, 51*(11), 1955–1956.

Zhu, X. (2023). Mapping linguistic shifts during psychological coping with the COVID-19 pandemic. *Journal of Language and Social Psychology, 42*(2), 203–216.

Chapter 3

The Use and Misuse of Employee Voice

3.1 Understanding Employee Voice

The coining and the emergence of the 'employee voice' theme trace back to the 'exit-voice-loyalty' theory proposed by Hirschman (1970), which whilst focusing on customers (not employees) stated that 'dissatisfied customers could either decide to exit or "voice" when faced with an objectionable state of affairs'. Farrel (1983) later applied this to employees as organisational stakeholders. With varying definitions across diverse contexts, 'employee voice' has been broadly understood as 'the ability of employees to express their views, opinions, concerns and suggestions and for these to influence decisions at work' (CIPD, 2023; Nechanska, Hughes, & Dundon, 2020). Most employees experience 'voice' prospects manifesting in the form of one to one meetings with their line managers/colleagues, team meetings, employee surveys, intra and inter departmental meetings. Still other organisations employed employee voice boxes within the organisation, investing in employee focus groups, online forums or chat room. Relatively fewer number of employers were found to urge encourage employees to engage in non-union staff associations or consultation committees (Lewin & Mitchell, 1992). Employee voice has been distinguished from 'employee silence'. Individuals choose not to speak on matters of importance to them, despite having something to say, if they believe the costs of doing so outweigh the benefits (for instance, if their position in the organisation is threatened) (Hirschman, 1972; Nechanska et al., 2020).

Approachable and transformational leadership, managers with high self-efficacy, the existence of clear, bottom-up communication channels, an employee perceiving their organisational environment as safe and trusted, and an employer's evidenced track record of responding respectfully and meaningfully to employee concerns have been recognised and affirmed as 'facilitators' of employee voice. Transactional and overly formal managers, poorly designed channels for employee voice, an employee's lack of trust in their manager/organisation and an employer's track record of poorly addressing their employees' concerns were appraised as 'voice inhibitors' (Abdulgalimov, Kirkham, Lindsay, Nicholson, Vlachokyriakos, Dao, & Olivier, 2023).

DOI: 10.4324/9781032705125-3

Effective management of employee voice begins with understanding its significance and purpose, including its contribution to management decision-making, demonstration of partnership, articulation of individual dissatisfaction and expression of collective bargaining (Miles & Mangold, 2014). Pre-pandemic evidences highlight how a significant number of employees (more than 50%) from within the UK report being highly satisfied with their work when they feel they have a 'voice' at work and are involved in decision-making. Studies demonstrate a significant, positive correlation between employee voice opportunities and employee pro-social meeting behaviours (and pro-social behaviours, in general) (Allen, Yoerger, Lehmann-Willenbrock and Jones, 2015; CIPD, 2019). Individuals who often raised concerns and had this addressed proactively by the management, seldom engaged in irrelevant discussions or complaining behaviours about other attendees and peers, arrived late, contributed poorly to meetings or engaged in other disruptive behaviours (Allen et al., 2015).

Alfes, Gatenby and Rees (2013) confirm a strong positive correlation between employee voice opportunities and employee engagement. The relationship, however, was significantly moderated the employee levels of trust in the senior management and the line manager-employee relationship quality. High-quality, positive and reciprocal social exchanges with line managers result in trust and stronger relationships, fostering voice, high levels of engagement, workplace outcomes and EW (Alfes et al., 2013).

Failing to foster employee voice meant crippling employee and organisational motivation to engage in problem-solving and decision-making behaviours, and affecting willingness to engage in activities that foster creativity and innovation.

Critics argue that the over-estimation of employee voice may lead to negative consequences. This is particularly prevalent amongst employees who underestimate or disregard their failures (/perceived failures). When voice opportunities are availed of more than necessary/deemed appropriate, line managers may perceive this as the employee not being pro-social or having an 'improvement-oriented' voice (Burris, Detert, & Romney, 2013). Employees may be seen as 'bossy'; 'voice' may be misconstrued as 'unsolicited interference' or an 'attempt to underestimate the credibility of supervisors and/or co-workers' (Burris et al., 2013).

The *Google Walkout* – 2018

The Google Walkout in 2018 appraised how employee voices cannot be snubbed or shunned (Karkoulian, Kertechian, Balozian and Nahed (2023). The incident witnessed thousands of Google employees, in different parts of the world, raising their voices in organised rallies and demonstrating their disagreement with various organisational procedures. The knowledge workforce and other highly proficient and well-paid employees chose to take to the streets to get noticed and be heard. They posted their list of demands on Instagram – many of which revolved around demanding more transparency, equality and participation in organisational problem-solving and decision-making. This was a wake-up call for human resource leaders and stakeholders from within the management of organisations, globally, to pay heed to the 'employee voice' (Karkoulian et al., 2023; Vanka & Singh, 2019).

Suggested Activity

Reflect on the organisations you have worked for, in the past. What factors, do you believe, fostered or curbed 'employee voice'?

The Employee Voice – Employee Wellbeing Correlation

A study by Li, Xi, Xu and Yang (2021) surveyed 400 Chinese employees for their research and established a significant, positive correlation between employee voice and EW. The findings whilst being analysed through the lens of Maslow's hierarchy of needs, confirm how offering employees an opportunity to express their opinions addresses their needs of relatedness, competency and autonomy, which consequentially influences social health and overall levels of wellbeing. The researchers, however, illustrate how this correlation is fully mediated by 'authentic self-expression'. When employees were able to voice their opinions and concerns, in resonance with their true selves and not having to hide their authentic selves, they were more likely to experience positive affect (Li et al., 2021).

More recent evidences from the pandemic such as De Clercq and Pereira (2022), surveyed 158 employees from a large-scale, Portugal-based organisation during the pandemic and appraised how employee voice behaviours significantly moderated employee perceptions of pandemic threats and heightened levels of anxiety. The study was found to distinguish between employee prohibitive (expressions about organisational shortcomings) versus promotive (expressions that focus on the solutions for those shortcomings) voices. Findings established how promotive voices fostered individual-organisational goal alignment. Goal/value congruence further enhanced the likelihood of employees engaging in organisational citizenship behaviours; individuals were less likely to report work-related strain/anxieties.

This is of significance during unprecedented times, such as the pandemic, when prohibitive voices and consequential, persistent rumination are likely to be upsetting, deplete energy resources, increase the likelihood of negative work experiences, the avoidance of positive work behaviours and diminish performance-enhancing efforts. Catastrophising or appraising the harmful effects of the pandemic was evidenced as psychologically distressing to internal and external organisational stakeholders (De Clercq and Pereira 2022).

'Continuous Listening' Strategy, 'Listen First' Approaches and 'Rapid Listening' Sessions

Technological advancements and the employing of people analytics enabled organisations such as McKinsey & Company (2023) build and implement a 'continuous, employee listening' strategy. This offered employers opportunities to quickly identify factors that were affecting colleagues, subordinates and other stakeholders within the organisation and determine ways to address this. In resonance with the strategy, the organisation conducted a 'weekly pulse check', exploring how employees were feeling (items on the survey were multiple choice questions). The survey explored whether employees were challenged with financial, childcare or caregiving concerns, employee perceptions about their professional development, work-life balance and concerns with inclusion (Ferrar & Green, 2021).

In attempts to obtain a 'team level' perspective on employee experience, team leaders received alerts that included an overview of potential concerns that their teams were concerned or being challenged with. The 'alert' notification enabled employers/leaders recognise potentially, emerging challenges before they turned into grave issues. They were consequentially able to initiate objective and constructive team conversations whilst guiding their teams towards more sustainable practices. By enhancing team and organisational performance and reputation, this people analytic 'continuous listening' strategy significantly enhanced the quality of relationships shared by team members, levels of employee satisfaction and experience – their zest and commitment towards their work. It gave the company a competitive edge in the industry during a global health emergency (the pandemic) and a local crisis when leaders had to swiftly understand which employees were affected and the best ways to intervene and assist (Ferrar & Green, 2021; Ruck, 2021).

On an additional note, Pannoni (2022) particularly appraised how Microsoft benefitted from employing a 'listen first approach'. The methodology enabled the organisation to appraise what worked, what did not and how best to adjust. Microsoft enhanced their 'employee listening systems' with an anonymous daily pulse and biannual employee signal surveys (Pannoni, 2022). Researchers suggest that 'technology-based crowdsourcing tools' (which enabled virtual connection with employees and the subsequent compilation of large volumes of rich data concerning the causal factors of employee burnout, anxiety and overall deteriorating levels of EW) as beneficial during the pandemic (Vermicelli, Cricelli, & Grimaldi, 2021). In addition to hour-long crowdsourcing 'rapid listening sessions', natural language processing, employee experience surveys, mental health and wellbeing survey data and aggregating benefits and disability claims have been evidenced as being effective in the understanding of employee mental health and wellbeing needs. The tools and practices enabled organisations to appropriately identify which employee needs require faster management attention and investment (Vermicelli et al., 2021).

'Leader Listening' Tours

Contemporary researchers have strongly reaffirmed investing in 'leader listening' tours. During the course of the tour, leaders are trained in active and deep listening skills and encouraged to share their vulnerabilities, communicating powerfully that possessing weaknesses, experiencing failures and 'not being okay' is okay (Janusik, 2023). During one of the experiments conducted by a financial institution, top directors were sent on a 'listening tour' to better understand 'work from home' employee experiences. Participating employees reported bleak workplace boundaries, and deteriorating levels of psychological safety and a sense of belongingness. Regular check-ins by line managers felt transactional. Informal meetings which embraced no schedule were spontaneous and casual were deemed necessary to combat and subsequently enhance employee experience and productivity (Emmet et al., 2020).

Suggested Activity

Think of your own experiences (or interview employees from other organisations) during the pandemic.

1. What strategies did your organisation adopt to foster employee voice? Were these strategies effective? How did this impact your wellbeing?
2. What mechanisms could your employer have possibly employed to address employee anxiety during the time?

HR 'Breakathon' Intervention

CISCO, an IT giant employing more than 70,000 employees globally, implemented a non-tech employee voice intervention. A twenty four hour long intervention, the 'HR breakathon' activity was a systematic approach to revamping the human resource team at CISCO (Vanka & Singh, 2019). Employing 600 human resource professionals and 200 employees, the employees were grouped into cross-functional teams of five to eight individuals. Employing a systematic approach and a design thinking methodology, teams were required to reflect and note domains (including employee onboarding, employee job design, training and development initiatives, and employee wellbeing) within which the HR department had a substantial influence. Participants further identified challenges and appraised potential propositions for resolving these concerns. At the end of the 24-hour initiative, participants collaboratively offered more than 100 innovative ideas pertaining to talent acquisition, onboarding, team building and leadership. These recommendations were implemented by employees at different levels, initiating changes at different levels. The organisation on the basis of employee advice, initiated a mobile application – Youbelong@CISCO for its employees. The voice intervention successfully revamped the human resource department (Vanka & Singh, 2019).

Della Torre (2019) elucidated the significance of employers formulating an 'effective and holistic strategy' in fostering individual and collective forms of employee voice. Whilst drafting policies, practices and specific strategies to enhance employee voice provisions, it may be beneficial for leaders to inform themselves about employee statutory rights and consult with employees to discuss health and safety concerns. Implementing and ensuring a wide range of two-way communication and consultation methods and ensuring that voice methods (such as weekly/monthly team meetings, surveys for employee voice for individual voice, and staff and joint consultation forums for collective voice) are employed regularly enabled employers foster voice behaviours.

Implicit-Inclusive Leader Language Recommendations

Team meetings which include i) one-to-one meetings (to enhance the quality of work relationships and build trust); ii) onboarding – to affirm employer expectations, values and understanding; iii) brainstorming – to collaborate and creatively generate ideas; iv) department meetings – to build a sense of connectedness and cohesiveness amongst team members; v) kick-off project meetings – to establish goals, offer clarity and establish a system of regular feedback; vi) post project meetings – to discuss successes, challenges and failures; and vii) organisation meetings have been evidenced to increase engagement from senior leaders with all employees (Marchington, 2007).

However, Weiss, Kolbe, Grote, Spahn and Grande (2018) place significance on the leader's language employed during team meetings for promoting employee voice behaviours. Whilst distinguishing between leader language such as implicit-inclusive (using collective pronouns such as 'we', 'us', 'our', etc. in highlighting superordinate or organisational identity) or explicit-inclusive (using 'I', 'you', etc., which employs direct invitations to voice and appreciation of follower input), the authors established that implicit-inclusive leader language was relatively more effective at encouraging employees to 'speak up'. Implicit-inclusive leader language draws on social identity, mobilises employees by de-emphasising hierarchical barriers and places significance on the group as a whole (for instance, 'we need to re-check the patient's blood pressure', 'the oxygen saturation is decreasing, we need to do something now!').

Consequentially, extra-role behaviours such as 'voice' are promoted within teams and organisations, and individuals are more willing and likely to challenge the status quo with alternative ideas and solutions (Weiss et al., 2018). This is in contrast to employing explicit-inclusive language (for instance, 'what do you think about this?' and 'stop, you can't do that!'), which made employees feel they were part of a 'lower status, out-group', consequentially less likely to contribute and voice their opinions within teams.

Additionally, informationally and financially investing in training and development workshops and educating line managers on the significance and specific ways in which voice mechanisms can be implemented is suggested (Jones, Blake, Adams, Kelly, Mannion, & Maben, 2021). Gupta, Sexton, Milne and Frush (2015) have made attempts to address employee voice challenges within the healthcare sector and chose to administer a training intervention; this included content on the significance of fostering employee voice within teams and organisations. By conducting pre- and post-implementation surveys, the analysts found a statistically significant difference in employee perceptions of their team working climate. A smaller number of employees were found to report challenges with speaking up when experiencing problems with patient care or any mistakes/errors within the healthcare setting.

Transnational policy interventions such as the European Commission Whistleblowing Legislation and the European Convention on Human Rights have led to national policy interventions. This includes the NHS England's raising concerns policy, the introduction of the 'Freedom to Speak Up Guardians' and UK-wide professional standards and regulatory guidance on raising concerns in the form of codes of conduct for nursing, dentistry, allied health professionals and medicine (Jones, et al., 2021). The transnational and national policy interventions subsequently initiated local/workplace policy initiatives for employee voice within the NHS in England. These included the implementation of employee 'speak up' hotlines, standard operating procedures to address employee concerns, executive walk rounds, 'speak up' training and staff induction courses (Jones, et al., 2021).

3.2 Technology, Digitalisation and Social Media for Employee Voice

Implementing 'Enterprise Social Networking Systems' for Employee Voice

The Enterprise Social Networking Systems (ESNs) offer effective internal channels for organisational communication, and employee knowledge-sharing and management (Ellison, Gibbs & Weber, 2015). Intended to foster engagement between colleagues and access to knowledge bottom-up, ESNS initiatives offer those employed with opportunities to form groups on the basis of shared goals and interests. It fostered collective resilience and cohesiveness amongst team members, enhances employee innovativeness, creativity, problem-solving and decision-making abilities (Ellison et al., 2015).

Critics argue that employers may use the platform to monitor and moderate employees' perceptions of the organisation. The organisation may be faced with a backlash, with employees experiencing intrusion and a deteriorating sense of power. A lack of anonymity on the ESNS platform could discourage employees from engaging with the system, networking, collaboratively learning and working with each other, and demonstrating creative and innovative work behaviours (Olfat, Shokouhyar, Ahmadi, Tabarsa, & Sedaghat, 2020).

Irrespective of the limitations of the ESNS, Abdulgalimov et al. (2023) operationalised the characteristics of civility, validity, safety and egalitarianism as 'a set of design goals' (including 'assured anonymity, constructive moderation, adequate slowness and controlled access') as being imperative to the building of a secure, confidential, employee voice system. Deploying this to 600 employees, the investigators urged participants to discuss the positive and negative aspects of a new university building. Participants were found to raise concerns pertaining to gender pay, equal opportunities and workplace discrimination on the ESNS platform. There were a few potential uncivil/impolite entries or those that contributed little to the discussion. The implementation of the system had significant implications for organisational policies and practices after an appraisal of concrete complaints of discrimination and the expression of genuine grievances to senior management. The system, however, did not ensure effective and timely action by the leadership team (Abdulgalimov et al., 2023).

'Gather–Analyse–Respond' Model

Exploring the use of technology to facilitate continuous employee listening, analysts propose the use of the 'gather–analyse–respond' model. In this light, evidence from the literature highlights how online and pulse surveys such as those employed by McKinsey & Company (2020) allow employers quick, inexpensive, targeted and regular opportunities to listen to employees and gather relevant data. Designed and administered on tools such as Microsoft Forms or other built-in survey tools, the survey allows for data to be collected or presented anonymously (Denison, Dickson, Mullins, & Sanchez, 2020).

In addition to using spreadsheets, organisations could consider employing statistical software, qualitative analysis software or data visualisation software to systematically analyse employee voice. Some platforms possess built-in analytics that automatically produce tables and charts, and the ability to produce a sentiment analysis of employee feedback. Responding to employee 'voice' has become relatively easy with the emergence of platforms such as Microsoft Teams and Workplace from Meta, which offer a forum for multi-way conversations (CIPD, 2023; Dension et al., 2020).

On another note, Stage Coach, UK, and Metroline subscribe to Blink – a mobile application that fosters employee voice. The application enhances levels of internal organisational communication, assists with the designing and dissemination of employee surveys, offers secure e-chat rooms, options to publish and share employee shift schedules, HR information, company calendars and allows for access to shared files (Blink, 2024). Other organisations such as Travellodge, UK, avail of services from Hive HR. Hive HR offer organisations HR benchmarking services, appraising them with an 'employee voice certified' recognition. In addition to enabling surveys and messenger chat services, their products build a culture of recognition and appreciation. These propositions enhanced employee levels of positive affect and brand reputation (HiveHR, 2024).

Suggested Activity

Observe and reflect on the employee voice listening strategies your organisation employs or initiate research on the employee listening strategies of an organisation you have access to -

  i) Appraise the extent to which the employer/human resource team/ line manager employs the 'gather-analyse-respond' model.
 ii) Which specific methodology (for instance, pulse checks, focus group interviews) do they employ in order to implement this model effectively?
iii) Critically analyse the use of these methods for the effective implementation of the model.

The Use of Social Media for Employee Voice

Employing social media for the attainment of organisational goals and objectives was initiated and further gained momentum in the early 2000s. The use of multiple media channels such as social networking sites such as Facebook, video-based platforms such as YouTube, video messaging platforms such as Skype, micro-blogs such as Twitter, direct messaging platforms such as WhatsApp has been analysed in the literature. Blog communities and sub-channels for internal organisational communication make it possible for individuals to engage in lengthy and insightful discussions (Ghani & Malik, 2022). Social media enabled employees to build high quality relationships and extend their social network within and outside their workplace.

Conway, Rosati, Monks and Lynn (2019) investigated the use of Twitter (an online form of blogging, designed in 2006) for 'employee voice' whilst analysing 817,235 tweets posted by 650,958 users in 2014. Appraised as 'the microphone of the masses', employees have an opportunity to post about both significant and insignificant events in their workplaces. Tweets are disseminated to a wider audience through 'retweeting', 'replying' and 'adding hashtags'. The findings established how postings on this social media platform were predominantly positive. Any negative voice, thought or experience included justice-seeking posts or the desire for employees to distance themselves from corporate culture, concerns relating to working hours, the work itself and the employee's relationship with his/her manager. Employing Twitter for 'employee voice' needs was primarily found to be individualistic; there was little evidence that suggested 'collectivism' (Conway, et al., 2019).

Supporting research from Holland, Cooper and Hecker (2016) highlighted how the use of social media platforms to voice satisfaction/dissatisfaction with their employer was particularly prevalent amongst younger (Generation Z) employees; older employees seldom tweeted. In essence, as channels employed to disseminate information, enable horizontal communication with internal and external organisation stakeholders, and bring an opportunity to build and draw support, the use of social media platforms for voicing significantly influences employee wellbeing (Van Zoonen, Verhoeven, & Vliegenthart, 2016).

Employee Voice as a Social Media 'Time Bomb' – The Case of a 'Golden Corral' Buffet Chef

Critics argue that social media channels hold the potential to breed racism and foster oppression and discrimination, further fuelling any stigmatisation, overt and covert violence or abuse within the workplace (El Ouirdi, El Ouirdi, Segers, & Henderickx, 2015). Studies conducted by Miles and Mangold (2014) elucidated an example of a Golden Corral buffet chef who made attempts to notify management and the Volusia County Health Department in Florida, USA, of flies infesting raw burgers. When they paid no heed to his complaints, the chef posted a YouTube video, later re-posted on the social news site Reddit, 'depicting raw burgers, ready to grill, stored next to an outside dumpster, surrounded by flies' (Miles & Mangold, 2014). Having a devastating impact on the organisation's reputation and unknown damage to its market share and profitability, the study appraised 'employee voice' as a potential 'social media time bomb' (Miles & Mangold, 2014).

Suggested Activity

Research and appraise some of the other cons to employing social media for employee voice.

Nampak, UK, and the 'Yammer' Social Media Tool

Other organisations include *Nampak*, a successful manufacturer of milk bottles in the UK, which recognised the need to implement a social media tool after a number of employee voice initiatives such as annual conferences, excellence awards evening, and conducting regular team meetings and surveys. 'Yammer', the social media tool, was easily accessible, engaging and easy to use (Parry, Martin, & Dromey, 2019). The organisation urged employees to contribute ideas for improvement; if these were implemented, employees received 5% of the savings, resulting from the administration of the intervention. Few employees, however, were not comfortable and lacked trust in using social media for employee voice. To combat these challenges, the organisation proactively marketed 'Yammer' during business conferences and within their company magazine. Also, 'Yammer' champions were recruited to assist employees with using the tool (Parry et al., 2019).

'We Create' Social Media Tool

Similarly, the *London Borough of Lewisham* introduced the 'We Create' social media tool with the objective of 'crowdsourcing ideas from employees' for the re-design of their services, sustaining the quality of service, business outcomes and reducing organisational costs. Findings established how employees often contributed their ideas, and leaders were able to recognise which ideas were appraised by their teams. Employees whose ideas were chosen for implementation were chosen for the delivery of that proposition (Parry et al., 2019). This strategy fostered employee engagement and was found to enhance employee positive affect.

Analysts conclude that 'employee voice' must be guided with evidence-based policy and practices to ensure its effective use to build and preserve the organisation's reputation and competitive advantage (Ghani & Malik, 2022; Miles & Mangold, 2014). Continually investing in training employees to employ social media to augment jobs, marketing products and services, enhancing public relations efforts and capturing the organisation's expertise whilst serving society and in resonance with the organisation's culture, companies such as *Dell* and *IBM* have successfully manoeuvred around the opportunities and challenges of technological advancements and employed social media platforms to their advantage (Miles & Mangold, 2014).

Alang, Stanton and Rose (2022) and Bennett (2010) reinstate the significance of governments drafting and implementing evidence-based policies and strategies that reinstate the significance of 'voice' within workplaces. Policy-makers, whilst emphasising the monitoring and attraction of high-quality individuals, may additionally choose to offer financial aid for the training and reskilling/upskilling of those employed in the people profession (Bennett, 2010). Working in resonance with professional bodies meant reciprocally investing in high-quality research and collectively engaging in knowledge-sharing and public dissemination of findings. This ensured the formulation and implementation of the best 'voice' practices within contemporary workplaces. Governmental bodies may choose to roll out workshops/training sessions for human resource professionals, leaders and employees on appropriately availing of 'voice' opportunities and effectively employing 'social media' for employee voice (Alang et al., 2022; Bennett, 2010).

'WorkTango' and 'Hyphen' Applications to Capture Real-Time Employee Voice

Using applications such as WorkTango and Hyphen can capture and attend to real-time employee voice. The applications permit organisations to include/exclude features, as per their requirements. Offering customised user interfaces, WorkTango equips leaders with resources to foster employee voice effectively, conduct employee engagement and lifecycle surveys, assist with action planning and hold anonymous conversations. The application also enables the posting of incentivisation, nominations and service awards. With similar services, Hyphen makes possible an instant screenshot of trending topics within the company, red flag concerns and suggestions that could potentially be implemented (BetterWorks, WorkTango, 2024).

Although lacking a formal structure, 'power and knowledge asymmetry' and often resulting in information overload, the implementation of these applications reaffirms employee belief in the significance an employer places on diverse voices and the voice of the 'collective'. The proposition has found to foster a culture of inclusion, build bonds of trust, enhancing levels of confidence to communicate in the digital sphere, with stakeholders, particularly crucial during public health emergencies (Bernauer & Kornau, 2024).

TeamSTEPPS Interventions

On a similar note, various other team working propositions such as Crew Resource Management and TeamSTEPPS (Team Strategies and Tools to Enhance Performance and Patient Safety) have been drawn from highly reliable industries such as the aviation industry and implemented within other contexts such as the healthcare context. An evidence-based curriculum drafted, compiled and implemented collaboratively between the Department of Defence and the Agency for Healthcare Research and Quality, TeamSTEPPS offers specific strategies and instructional resources to improve team working relationships and patient safety within the healthcare context, consequentially enhancing product/service quality (Gupta, et al., 2015). Gupta et al. (2015), when implementing TeamSTEPPS in an academic interventional ultrasound service and using sonographers, physicians and other healthcare professionals as participants, found that 'teamwork climate' components such as 'inputs being well received' and 'speaking up' improved the most. This meant a psychologically safe organisational climate, where employees were confident to speak up.

Weiss et al. (2017) argue how team-based interventions, solely did not foster effective voice behaviours. Using anaesthesia nurses for their study and conducting pre- and post-intervention analysis, the participants were more likely to speak up following an assertiveness-based team training course (Weiss et al., 2017). Sayre, McNeese-Smith, Leach and Phillips (2012) conducted a quasi-experimental study to firmly establish the effectiveness of multi-faceted, educational interventions using scenarios, personal reflection and peer support with small groups of registered nurses. The findings reported a significantly positive difference in mean employee 'speaking up' scores.

Employee Voice Interventions for the LGBTQ Community

Maji, Yadav & Gupta (2024) in his writings highlights how heterosexual norms and routines, identified as 'normal' in most workplaces, silence the voices of the LGBTQ and other minority communities. Discrimination and stigmatisation often curb their 'voice'. Employees from these communities are often found to report micro-aggression at work. This can include the pressure to 'play along' during sexual discussions, humour or actions compared to their straight employees. A significant number of LGBTQ employees have experienced being 'targets of sexist comments/jokes' or have been targets of 'sexual harassment' (Maji, Yadav & Gupta, 2024).

McNulty, McPhail, Inversi,Dundon and Nechanska (2018), by analysing data from 15 LGBTQ employees, describe how formal and informal, social and business-oriented employee resource groups offer mechanisms for unheard or missing voices to be heard. The findings indicate many positive outcomes such as positive role model building, opportunities to offer and avail of mentoring and coaching services, personal development and greater access to new networking opportunities. Employee resource groups reduced employer recruiting costs, reduced turnover rates of employees from LGBTQ and minority communities, and consequentially led to better-performing teams and organisations (McNulty et al., 2018).

On another note, researchers advise employers and human resource professionals to scrutinise all organisational policies and practices for a sexual orientation bias. These inclusive policies and practices must make provisions for i) confidential, complaint mechanisms; ii) offering constructive feedback without being harassed or discriminated against; and iii) safe spaces for employees belonging to the LGBTQ community to network.

The establishing diversity and inclusion councils, virtual or face-to-face intra-organisational LGBTQ networks that ensure a fair representation of the minority employee community within union groups count as key initiatives for 'expression as a collective' (Bell, Özbilgin, Beauregard, & Sürgevil, 2011; Yvonne McNulty et al., 2018). Allocating adequate funds for sexual orientation equality efforts, integrating the voices of the LGBTQ employee community in organisational training and development programmes, and recognising and appraising champions of sexual orientation equality are some of the initiatives proposed by Bell et al. (2011) in their research.

Supporting evidence from the literature highlights successful interventions initiated by organisations such as Accenture and Ernst and Young in attempts to foster employee voice in employees from the LGBTQ and minority communities. Accenture, by building a global LGBTQ network, has successfully driven its LGBTQ community to collaborate with its LGBTQ allies, subsequently enhancing networking and mentoring opportunities (Syed, 2014). Appraising the significance of inclusion, the organisation has made individuals more aware of sexual orientation/gender identity and discrimination within the workplace; consequentially, they were successful at preventing discriminatory behaviours against LGBTQ and minority communities at work. In 2012, reports claimed how thousands of *Accenture* employees joined the global LGBTQ network, taking equal responsibility to ensure workplace inclusion. Lastly, organisational policies and practices should reflect an open and proactive acceptance of employees from the LGBTQ community and place significance on the training and career development of individuals from the group (Syed, 2014).

On an additional note, Ernst and Young initiated the EYGLES network for LGBTQ employees; this was recognised as a 'Star Performer Network Group'. Embracing inclusive leadership, the organisation continually invests in their client network to effectively tackle workplace challenges (including that of voice and wellbeing) when including the LGBTQ and minority communities (Bell et al., 2011; Yvonne McNulty et al., 2018; Syed, 2014).

Robotics, Artificial Intelligence and the Future of 'Employee Voice'

Contemporary workplace literature appraise the role of rapidly evolving technologies in the collation, analysis and dissemination of employee voice (Belloc, Burdin & Landini, 2023). Smarter, smaller, lighter and inexpensive voice tools including sensors, cameras, speech and image processing, biometrics, mobile and cloud technologies, geo tagging and more increasingly powered advancements in AI are likely to evolve the ways in which employee voice is addressed (Paluch & Wirtz, 2020). Analysts demonstrate robotics and artificial intelligence methodologies as positively correlated with employee voice representation, particularly in relatively 'centralised wage setting, employee relations and grievance managing work environments' (Belloc et al., 2022). This necessitated employee upkilling, job redesigning and re-evaluating work time management. Subsequently, Lopes, Ferreira & Prada, (2023) discuss how social robots may hold greater potential in delivering personalised employee feedback and counselling, in contrast to traditional, telemedicine applications. The authors contemplate the probabilities of robots building therapeutic and high-quality relationships with employees within contemporary workplaces. Affirming the significance of AI and robotic science methodologies in the employee voice – employee wellbeing narrative, Palauch & Wirtz (2020), however, demonstrate the 'service robot development' model, suggesting these techniques to be of greater importance for simple, cognitive and analytical tasks. They foresee the services of human beings (and not robots) as continuing to contribute to complex, socio-emotional tasks.

Suggested Activity

Research and recommend other initiatives or interventions that organisations could potentially employ to foster employee voice, inclusion and wellbeing of employees belonging to the LGBTQ community.

3.3 Employee Whistleblowing: Evidence from the Pandemic

Deemed as 'the voice of the conscience', whistleblowing is recognised as a former or current employee's avenue of disclosure of unethical, illegitimate or immoral practices that are under the control of the employer. Disclosures can be both internal and external to the organisation, although employers benefit when whistleblowing is internal. Cavazos and Heese (2021), in offering greater clarity on the theme, discuss how within most organisations, top-down monitoring is prevalent. However, 'whistleblowing' counts as a 'bottom-up' employer monitoring mechanism, which permits employees to report actions taken by their superiors that are or could be harmful to the organisation.

Healthcare Workers 'Blowing the Whistle'

The onset of the pandemic, whilst significantly impacting healthcare sectors across the globe, saw many healthcare workers 'blowing' the whistle. Studies conducted by Gagnon et al. (2022) drew from 15 semi-structured interviews with nurses and systematically analysed 83 news stories and 597 reports from a whistleblowing platform to establish how employees within the healthcare sector were experiencing wavering loyalty and significantly, changing workplace relationships (Gagnon, Perron, Dufour, Marcogliese, Pariseau-Legault, Wright, & Carnevale, 2022). A significant number of nurses felt 'discredited, ignored, instrumentalised, devalued and abandoned' by their organisation and governmental authorities. They witnessed a soaring number of wrongdoings, the consequences of which intensified due to poor management and other long-standing issues. Necessitated to work overtime within unsafe working environments and with a lack of personal protective equipment (PPE), healthcare sector employees were challenged with poor sleep hygiene. A lack of trust and transparency, whilst tackling illnesses and being challenged with inadequate informational, financial and social resources, necessitated external whistleblowing (such as the use of social media) during the crisis. External whistleblowing was employed to expose the wrongdoings of employers, advocate for better responses to COVID-19 and more importantly reclaim the rights of healthcare workers who were silenced by their management (Gagnon et al., 2022). Not having adequate resources/facilities to get tested for COVID-19 was particularly challenging for pregnant and immune-compromised employees.

Critics draw attention to how choosing to engage in whistleblowing behaviours was a difficult decision to make. This was deemed as 'ethically justifiable' only under exceptional, extenuating circumstances and was perceived as extremely risky, given the consequences (for instance, termination of the employment contract) that the employee may consequentially face. Nevertheless, most studies in the literature frame whistleblowing behaviours undertaken by employees within the healthcare sector as a positive action rather than negative, a decision that healthcare sector employees undertook as professionals committed to the best interests of the public, as members of a collective and as employees endowed with basic, inalienable rights (Gagnon et al., 2022).

The Use of Social Media for Whistleblowing Behaviours

Lazar (2022) describes the case of a major conflict between an Israeli telecommunication company and union employees, during the course of which a senior leader was covertly video-recorded whilst he instructed his employees to withdraw their union membership. An edited version of the video was later published on YouTube by the employees/union activists, who acted as whistleblowers. When organisational scandals unfold as a 'drama' on social media, viewers, including a number of stakeholders from within the organisation, engage in public conversations, speculating, critically assessing and appraising morality, law and order. Unethical conduct, deceitful practices and corruption are brought to the attention of the public. This, however, is severely detrimental to the whistleblower and the organisation's reputation and wellbeing (Lazar, 2022).

One of the potential benefits of whistleblowing or reporting organisational misconduct to an external regulator includes the monetary incentive. Research from Dey, Heese and Pérez-Cavazos (2021) described how the 'approximate monetary benefit for whistleblowers accounts to $200,000 ($406,000 for public firms), representing four (eight) times the annual compensation of the median employee working for a publicly traded firm'. 'Cash for information' programmes, particularly prevalent in the United States, heavily compensate whistleblowers for having reported corporate fraud, whilst compensating them for the risks they carry for having reported wrongdoings. Perceived whistleblower benefits may have 'altruistic origins' – the individual may believe their actions to be aimed at correcting the wrongdoings of the organisation that may harm the interests of society (Dey et al., 2021). In most cases, whistleblowers are faced with weak incentives, gaining little from revealing wrongdoing (Vandekerckhove & Commers, 2004).

'Employer retaliation', accounting for a major challenge/cost associated with whistleblowing, usually takes the form of a loss of income by demoting the employee, limiting career training, development and advancement opportunities, terminating the work contract or challenging the whistleblower with legal cases/expenses (Vandekerckhove & Commers, 2004). Other analysts claim that 50% of whistleblowers were fired and others were faced with on-the-job harassment and disciplinary actions.

Stigmatisation, as a consequence of whistleblowing is severely detrimental to employee self-esteem and self-confidence. There likely will be a tarnishing of one's public esteem – the employee's accomplishments and failures are judged on the basis of some code that society is perceived to value. In the professional context, this often translates as employee underperformance, trouble-making behaviours or even 'theft of company information'. Whistleblowers are perceived as upsetting the 'moral order' by highlighting the organisation's deficiencies and immorality or lack of integrity (Foxley, 2019). Alford (2001) describes stigmatisation as a 'means of social control'. By initiating processes and practices to prevent or diminish levels of deviance, organisations employ stigmatisation as a political weapon to punish the instigator whilst proactively disciplining others.

Gao and Brink (2017) analysed the determinants of the act. Characteristics of the whistleblower – such as the personality characteristics, moral judgements and demographic characteristics of the whistleblower – were a crucial moderator. Findings affirmed how employees possessing an internal locus of control (i.e. attributing events to internal factors such as an individual's hard work or perseverance) and exhibiting a judging, ethical style were more likely to engage in whistleblowing behaviours (Curtis & Taylor, 2009). Individuals scoring high on alpha traits (such as agreeableness, conscientiousness and emotional stability), beta traits (such as self-development and preservation) and those possessing higher levels of idealism or a defined set of behaviours (in contrast to relativistic individuals who do not possess a defined set of behaviours) demonstrated greater tendencies to participate in the act of whistleblowing (Brink, Cereola, & Menk, 2015).

Supporting evidence was drawn from studies such as Dalton and Radtke (2013), who, in conducting a between-subjects experiment with more than 100 MBA learners, reported a negative correlation between employee 'Machiavellian' characteristics (or a tendency to deceive others to achieve personal goals) and the likelihood to engage in whistleblowing behaviours. In addition to illustrating the significance of the characteristics (including personality characteristics, moral judgements and demographic characteristics) and levels of idealism of the report recipient, the reporting channel and the wrongdoer, the model places significance on the characteristics of the organisation. Organisational climate (closed versus open climate, for instance) and organisational structure (simple versus complex) moderated tendencies of engaging in whistleblowing and the ways in which this was perceived within and outside the organisation.

Elucidating future implications of these occurrences, other researchers have proposed the drafting and implementation of strong, whistleblowing protection policies that protect the rights of employees. Here, 'protection' implies protection from the management team/employers and governments who choose to silence employees and retaliate against those who choose to blow the whistle (Gagnon et al., 2022). Measures that can be included in the whistleblowing policy could include guaranteeing anonymity, punishing officials who breach confidentiality and reveal employee identity, and framing mechanisms to systematically report, investigate and sanction retaliation. Lastly, access to free counselling services, helplines offering advice and financial aid for whistleblowers could be offered (Agnew, McInnes, & Vian, 2022).

Suggested Activity

From your reading and research, reflect and appraise, under what circumstances, do you believe, should employee whistleblowing be justified? Analyse this with reference to public health emergencies, specifically.

3.4 Coping with Stigmatisation and the Psycho-Social Impact

Whistleblower Retaliation Checklist

Buck and Garrick (2020) describe 'whistleblowing' retaliation as 'an employer, taking or failing to take, threatening to take or not to take a personnel action, because of a whistleblower's disclosure'. The Whistleblower Retaliation Checklist was designed and propagated with the intent of helping employees identify toxic tactics of retaliation and subsequently effectively manage psycho-social consequences. The constructs of the checklist include gaslighting, mobbing, marginalisation, shunning, devaluation, double binding ('associated with mixed messages and contradictions usually from someone from greater power – a line manager/senior colleague, to manipulate the mental status of the victim'), blacklisting, (counter) accusations and violence. Other retaliatory tactics highlighted in the workplace literature, although not included on the checklist however, include employer intimidation/threats, blackballing ('where the whistleblower tries to move to another organisation or field of practice, but their professional reputation is so tarnished, that it hindered their ability to obtain substantial gainful employment'), treating family members unfairly and the spreading of false rumours (Brink et al. 2017).

These constructs/tactics employed to silence, discredit and/or forcibly remove the individual from the organisation result in 'moral injury'. Organisational retaliations often undermine the employee's sense of morality and self, isolating the employee from the society that he/she deeply values. Consequentially, there is an increasing likelihood of experiencing post-traumatic stress disorder (PTSD), heightened levels of anxiety and depression, substance abuse and suicidal thoughts (Brink & Gao, 2017).

Buck and Garrick (2020) conducted a study through a link on the WoA website, running this openly for a year. Individuals who googled 'whistleblowing' or 'retaliation' could find the website survey. The research instrument was a 72-item scale comprising two sections. The first section entailed open-ended questions that captured the nature of workplace stressors, and the second section measured the nine toxic tactic domains. The instrument took into consideration details from the PTSD checklist and the clinician-administered PTSD scale, both scales having acquired gold stand-ards for assessing traumatic stress and having evidenced a correlation (Buck & Garrick, 2020). Additionally, Beck's Depression Inventory and the Columbia Suicide Severity Rating Scale were consulted. After using 72 participants for their study, the researchers found that more than 50% of whistleblowers had experienced 'gaslighting' or others questioning their recollections of facts. Consequentially, a significant number of participants reported experiencing intrusive thoughts and nightmares and a diminished sense of confidence and clarity in their own judgement.

More than 60% of participants described how they sensed a hostile mob organised against them at work and sensed some level of persecution for their ethical beliefs or morals. They were being held against different work standards than other employees, with 100% of employees being highly con-cerned about their own health and safety within their workplace. In addi-tion, all participants reported experiencing marginalisation and 'shunning'; they felt humiliated and embarrassed to talk about the situation with family and friends. As a consequence, their levels of self-efficacy, self and social esteem, and sense of belongingness, purpose and meaning were threatened, increasing the likelihood of depression and suicidal tendencies. Lastly, more than 80% of employees experienced bullying, intimidation or harassment that made them feel extremely fearful, were accused of misconduct or insub-ordination, and were unemployed for a prolonged period of time. This had a detrimental impact on the individual's earning capacity and their perceived future financial security (Buck & Garrick, 2020).

Other Methods

Examining employee coping behaviours amongst South Africans, Uys and Smit (2016) contacted and used participants in multiple ways – some were contacted upon the publishing of their experiences in newspaper articles, oth-ers approached the author following requests for participation in the media, and a few were recruited after they sought assistance to cope with organisa-tional toxic retaliation tactics. Employing the episodic, narrative interviewing technique, the researchers found participants using appropriate intrapersonal resources (such as having an optimistic outlook on life, being determined to succeed and continuing to embrace a strong system of internalised values) (Uys & Smit, 2016).

Further, by making use of external resources such as seeking professional legal advice and trade union support, whistleblowers experienced a decrease in their financial resources. The invaluable financial, moral and emotional support from kin, family members and close friends, in this light, was reported to be instrumental in coping with organisational retaliation behaviours. The employee's attempts and the extent to which they were able to meaning-fully construct or make sense of their past and present circumstances, and continue to perceive the world as benevolent and the self as 'worthy' fostered coping and consequential emotional healing (Fotaki, Kenny, Scriver & Galway, 2015).

Lastly, whistleblowers remaining firm in their convictions by perceiving their behaviour as a 'choiceless choice' further enabled sense-making and fostered effective coping. Given these findings, the analysts, in essence, particularly appraise the whistleblower's sense of coherence or comprehensibility or their ability to discern between stimuli, situations and his/her world. Moreover, the whistleblower's ability to identify, avail and mobilise necessary legal, financial, interpersonal and intrapersonal resources to cope with the emotional turmoil was recognised as crucial (Fotaki et al., 2015).

3.5 Summary

Discussing 'employee voice' as 'the ability of employees to express their opinions and suggestions and for these to influence decisions at work', the author drew the reader's attention to the 'Google Walkout' 2018 – an incident that urged employers to reflect and design effective employee voice mechanisms. The correlation between employee voice and wellbeing; findings from the literature established a firm positive correlation – however, authentic self-expression significantly moderated this relationship. Studies from the pandemic period distinguished between promotive and prohibitive employee voices – analysing their role in appraising or catastrophising harmful consequences of the pandemic. Later, 'voice' interventions employed by organisations such as Microsoft were explored. Here, implementing a people analytic driven 'continuous listening strategy', leader listening tours, 'listen first' approaches and 'rapid listening' sessions with employees were evidenced as beneficial.

Stakeholders could consider and adopt models such as the 'gather–analyse–respond' model, the HR 'breakathon' intervention, and the TeamSTEPPS intervention to implement employee voice mechanisms. Implicit leader language was additionally appraised as beneficial. The ESNS proposition was concluded to be beneficial; however, the characteristics of civility, validity, safety and egalitarianism – 'a set of design goals' – were reported as crucial to the design and implementation of an effective employee voice system.

Lastly, the chapter explored the role of social media – interventions employed by organisations to effectively foster 'voice'. The author critically analysed the potential perceived misuse of employee voice in employee whistleblowing behaviours, as well as its contextualisation during the pandemic and the specific ways in which employees cope with employer retaliating behaviours. Exploring the case of a 'Golden Corral' buffet chef, the chapter cautioned stakeholders against employee voice being a potential social media 'time bomb'. It additionally offered readers an opportunity to reflect, critically analyse and potentially employ the 'Yammer' and 'We

Create' social media tools for employee voice. Future analysts could consider further building on and strengthening these interventions. Employing applications for employee voice fostered a culture of inclusion, reaffirmed an employee's belief in the employer placing significance on diverse voices, consequentially enhancing engagement and wellbeing. In the next chapter, the author discusses employee incivility, bullying and evidence-based interventions that organisations could potentially employ to diminish the possibilities of conflicts within contemporary workplaces.

3.6 Further Readings

Budd, J. W., Gollan, P. J., & Wilkinson, A. (2010). New approaches to employee voice and participation in organisations. *Human Relations*, *63*(3), 303–310.

Dent (2023). What the whistleblowing review means for employers. Available at: https://www.peoplemanagement.co.uk/article/1826818/whistleblowing-review -means-employers Accessed on: 6 November 2023

Dundon, T., Wilkinson*, A., Marchington, M., & Ackers, P. (2004). The meanings and purpose of employee voice. *The International Journal of Human Resource Management*, *15*(6), 1149–1170.

Gorden, W. I., Infante, D. A., & Graham, E. E. (1988). Corporate conditions conducive to employee voice: A subordinate perspective. *Employee Responsibilities and Rights Journal*, *1*, 101–111.

Kaufman, B. E. (2015). Theorising determinants of employee voice: An integrative model across disciplines and levels of analysis. *Human Resource Management Journal*, *25*(1), 19–40.

Kougiannou, N., & Holland, P. (2022). Employee voice and silence in the digital era. T. Garavan & K. Grant, In *The Emerald Handbook of Work, Workplaces and Disruptive Issues in HRM*. Bingley: Emerald Publishing Limited (pp. 513–531).

Morrison, E. W. (2011). Employee voice behavior: Integration and directions for future research. *Academy of Management Annals*, *5*(1), 373–412.

Whiting, S. W., Maynes, T. D., Podsakoff, N. P., & Podsakoff, P. M. (2012). Effects of message, source, and context on evaluations of employee voice behavior. *Journal of Applied Psychology*, *97*(1), 159.

Wilkinson, A., Gollan, P. J., Kalfa, S., & Xu, Y. (2018). Voices unheard: Employee voice in the new century. *The International Journal of Human Resource Management*, *29*(5), 711–724.

3.7 Suggested Websites

American Psychological Association (2023). Listen to what employees need and act on it. Available at: https://www.apa.org/topics/healthy-workplaces/mental-health/ listen-employee-needs Accessed on: 6 November 2023

Guinan, G. (2022). Whistleblowing: A guide for employers. Available at: https://www .peoplemanagement.co.uk/article/1804087/whistleblowing-guide-employers Accessed on: 6 November 2023

The British Psychological Society (2015). Whistleblowers – Heroes not headaches. Available at: https://www.bps.org.uk/psychologist/whistleblowers-heroes-not -headaches Accessed on: 6 November 2023

The British Psychological Society (2023). Whistleblowing policy. Available at: https://www.bps.org.uk/whistleblowing-policy Accessed on: 6 November 2023

3.8 Reflective Questions – For Learners

From your reading and research

1. Can the act of 'whistleblowing' have any benefits within the workplace? Why or why not?
2. How did the role of social media, when considering employee voice, evolve during and post-pandemic?
3. Are there any disadvantages to the fostering of 'employee voice'?

3.9 Reflective Questions – For Researchers/Practitioners

From your reading and research:

1. What employee voice mechanisms does your organisation employ?
2. Post-pandemic, what employee voice mechanisms do you believe could have proven to be beneficial to the organisations, or employees more specifically?
3. To what extent do you believe social media is useful in fostering employee voice?
4. In what specific ways does your organisation regulate the use of social media and its use for 'employee voice'?

References

Abdulgalimov, D., Kirkham, R., Lindsay, S., Nicholson, J., Vlachokyriakos, V., Dao, E., & Olivier, P. (2023). Designing for the embedding of employee voice. *Proceedings of the ACM on Human-Computer Interaction, 7*(CSCW1), 1–31.

Agnew, B., McInnes, K., & Vian, T. (2022). Whistleblowing as an anti-corruption strategy in health and pharmaceutical organizations in low- and middle-income countries: A scoping review. *Global Health Action, 51*(1), 214–494.

Alang, T., Stanton, P., & Rose, M. (2022). Enhancing employee voice and inclusion through inclusive leadership in public sector organizations. *Public Personnel Management, 51*(3), 309–329.

Alfes, K., Gatenby, M., & Rees, C. (2013). Employee voice and engagement: Connections and consequences. *The International Journal of Human Resource Management, 24*(14), 2780–2798.

Alford, C. F. (2001). Whistleblowers and the narrative of ethics. *Journal of Social Philosophy, 32*(3), 402.

Allen, J. A., Yoerger, M. A., Lehmann-Willenbrock, N., & Jones, J. (2015). Would you please stop that!? The relationship between counterproductive meeting behaviors, employee voice, and trust. *Journal of Management Development*, *34*(10), 1272–1287.

Bell, M. P., Özbilgin, M. F., Beauregard, T. A., & Sürgevil, O. (2011). Voice, silence, and diversity in 21st century organizations: Strategies for inclusion of gay, lesbian, bisexual, and transgender employees. *Human Resource Management, 50*(1), 131–146.

Belloc, F., Burdin, G., & Landini, F. (2023). Advanced technologies and worker voice. *Economica, 90*(1), 1–38.

Bernauer, V. S., & Kornau, A. (2024). E-voice in the digitalised workplace. Insights from an alternative organisation. *Human Resource Management Journal, 34*(2), 369–385.

Bennett, T. (2010). Employee voice initiatives in the public sector: Views from the workplace. *International Journal of Public Sector Management, 23*(5), 444–455.

BetterWorks (2024). Employee engagement: Build a better culture with real-time employee feedback. Available at: https://www.betterworks.com/product/employee -survey-tools/ Accessed on: 5 August 2024.

Blink. (2024). Blink and everyone's productive. Available at: https://www.joinblink .com/. Accessed on: 2 June 2024.

Brink, A. G., Cereola, S., & Menk, K. B. (2015). The effects of fraudulent reporting, materiality level, personality traits, and ethical position on entry-level employee whistleblowing decisions. *Journal of Forensic and Investigative Accounting, 7*(1), 180–211.

Brink, A. G., & Gao, L. (2017). Whistleblowing studies in accounting research: A review of experimental studies on the determinants of whistleblowing. *Journal of Accounting Literature, 38*, 1–13.

Buck, M., & Garrick, J. (2020). Whistleblower retaliation checklist: A new instrument for identifying retaliatory tactics and their psycho-social impact after an employee discloses workplace wrongdoing. *Crisis, Stress and Human Resilience: An International Journal, 2*(2), 76–93.

Burris, E. R., Detert, J. R., & Romney, A. C. (2013). Speaking up vs. being heard: The disagreement around and outcomes of employee voice. *Organization Science, 24*(1), 22–38.

Cavazos, G. & Heese, J. (2021). The effect of retaliation costs on employee whistleblowing. *Journal of Accounting and Economics, 71*(2–3), 101385.

CIPD. (2019). Talking about voice: Employee experiences. Available at: www.cipd .org/uk. Accessed on: 26 May 2024.

CIPD. (2023). People analytics. Available at: https://www.cipd.org/uk/knowledge/ factsheets/analytics-factsheet/. Accessed on: 26 May 2024.

Conway, E., Rosati, P., Monks, K., & Lynn, T. (2019). Voicing job satisfaction and dissatisfaction through Twitter: Employees' use of cyberspace. *New Technology, Work and Employment, 34*(2), 139–156.

Curtis, M. B. & Taylor, E. Z. (2009). Whistleblowing in public accounting: Influence of identity disclosure, situational context, and personal characteristics. *Accounting and the Public Interest, 9*(1), 191–220.

Dalton, D. & Radtke, R. R. (2013). The joint effects of Machiavellianism and ethical environment on whistle-blowing. *Journal of Business Ethics, 117*, 153–172.

De Clercq, D., & Pereira, R. (2022). Let's work together, especially in the pandemic: Finding ways to encourage problem-focused voice behavior among passionate employees. *Journal of Organizational Effectiveness: People and Performance, 9*(2), 169–192.

Della Torre, E. (2019). Collective voice mechanisms, HRM practices and organizational performance in Italian manufacturing firms. *European Management Journal, 37*(3), 398–410.

Denison, D., Dickson, M. W., Mullins, M. W., & Sanchez, J. (2020). The unique role of corporate culture in employee listening systems. *Employee Surveys and Sensing: Challenges and Opportunities, 1*, 135–152.

Dey, A., Heese, J., & Pérez-Cavazos, G. (2021). Cash-for-information whistleblower programs: Effects on whistleblowing and consequences for whistleblowers. *Journal of Accounting Research, 59*(5), 1689–1740.

Ellison, N. B., Gibbs, J. L., & Weber, M. S. (2015). The use of enterprise social network sites for knowledge sharing in distributed organizations: The role of organizational affordances. *American Behavioral Scientist, 59*(1), 103–123.

El Ouirdi, A., El Ouirdi, M., Segers, J., & Henderickx, E. (2015). Employees' use of social media technologies: A methodological and thematic review. *Behaviour & Information Technology, 34*(5), 454–464.

Farrel, D. (1983). Exit, voice, loyalty, and neglect as responses to job dissatisfaction: A multidimensional scaling study. *Academy of Management Journal, 26*(4), 596–607. https://doi.org/10.2307/255909.

Ferrar, J., & Green, D. (2021). *Excellence in People Analytics: How to Use Workforce Data to Create Business Value.* London: Kogan Page Publishers.

Foxley, I. (2019). Overcoming stigma: Whistleblowers as' supranormal' members of society? *Ephemera, 19*(4), 847–864.

Gagnon, M., Perron, A., Dufour, C., Marcogliese, E., Pariseau-Legault, P., Wright, D. K., & Carnevale, F. A. (2022). Blowing the whistle during the first wave of COVID-19: A case study of Quebec nurses. *Journal of Advanced Nursing, 78*(12), 4135–4149.

Gao, L. & Brink, A. G. (2017). Whistleblowing studies in accounting research: A review of experimental studies on the determinants of whistleblowing. *Journal of Accounting Literature, 38*(1), 1–13.

Ghani, B. & Malik, A. R. (2022). Social media and employee voice: A comprehensive literature review. *Behaviour and Information Technology, 42*(1), 1–21.

Gupta, R. T., Sexton, B., Milne, J., & Frush, D. P. (2015). Practice and quality improvement: Successful implementation of TeamSTEPPS tools into an academic interventional ultrasound practice. *AJR. American Journal of Roentgenology, 204*(1), 105–110.

Hirschman, A. O. (1970). *Exit, voice, and loyalty: Responses to decline in firms, organizations, and states.* London: Harvard University Press.

Hirschman, A. O. (1972). *Exit, Voice, and Loyalty: Responses to Decline in Firms, Organizations, and States* (Vol. 25). London: Harvard University Press.

HiveHR. (2024). The employee voice platform for leaders who want to make change, not spreadsheets. Available at: www.hive.hr.com. Accessed on: 2 June 2024.

Holland, P., Cooper, B., & Hecker, R. (2016). Use of social media at work: A new form of employee voice? *The International Journal of Human Resource Management, 27*(21), 2621–2634.

Janusik, L. (2023). Listening training in organizations. *Current Opinion in Psychology, 52*, 101631.

Jones, A., Blake, J., Adams, M., Kelly, D., Mannion, R., & Maben, J. (2021). Interventions promoting employee "speaking-up" within healthcare workplaces: A systematic narrative review of the international literature. *Health Policy, 125*(3), 375–384.

Karkoulian, S., Kertechian, K. S., Balozian, P., & Nahed, M. B. (2023). Employee voice as a mediator between leader-member exchange and creative performance: Empirical evidence from the Middle East. *International Journal of Process Management and Benchmarking, 14*(3), 311–328.

Lazar, A. (2022). Organisational scandal on social media: Workers whistleblowing on YouTube and Facebook. *Information and Organisation, 32*, 100–390.

Lewin, D., & Mitchell, D. J. (1992). Systems of employee voice: Theoretical and empirical perspectives. *California Management Review, 34*(3), 95–111.

Li, L., Xi, B., Xu, J., & Yang, Y. (2021). Voice more and be happier: How Employee Voice Influences Psychological wellbeing in the Workplace. *International Journal of Mental Health Promotion, 23*(1), 43–55.

Lopes, S. L., Ferreira, A. I., & Prada, R. (2023). The use of robots in the workplace: Conclusions from a health promoting intervention using social robots. *International Journal of Social Robotics, 15*(6), 893–905.

Maji, S., Yadav, N., & Gupta, P. (2024). LGBTQ+ in workplace: A systematic review and reconsideration. *Equality, Diversity and Inclusion: An International Journal, 43*(2), 313–360.

Marchington, M. (2007). Employee voice systems. The Oxford Handbook of Human Resource Management, Available at: www.oxfordhandbook.com. Accessed on: 27 May 2024.

Mckinsey & Company (2020). The next competitive advantage in talent: Continuous employee listening. Available at: https://www.mckinsey.com/capabilities/people -and-organizational-performance/our-insights/the-next-competitive-advantage-in -talent-continuous-employee-listening Accessed on: 31 October 2023.

McKinsey and Company (2023) The next competitive advantage in talent: Continuous employee listening. Available at: https://www.mckinsey.com/capabilities/people -and-organizational-performance/our-insights/the-next-competitive-advantage-in -talent-continuous-employee-listening, Accessed on: 17 July 2024.

McNulty, Y., McPhail, R., Inversi, C., Dundon, T., & Nechanska, E. (2018). Employee voice mechanisms for lesbian, gay, bisexual and transgender expatriation: The role of Employee-Resource Groups (ERGs) and allies. *The International Journal of Human Resource Management, 29*(5), 829–856.

Miles, S. J. & Mangold, W. G. (2014). Employee voice: Untapped resource or social media time bomb? *Business Horizons, 57*(3), 401–411

Nechanska, E., Hughes, E., & Dundon, T. (2020). Towards an integration of employee voice and silence. *Human Resource Management Review, 30*(1), 100674.

Olfat, M., Shokouhyar, S., Ahmadi, S., Tabarsa, G. A., & Sedaghat, A. (2020). Organizational commitment and work-related implementation of enterprise social networks (ESNs): The mediating roles of employees' organizational concern and prosocial values. *Online Information Review, 44*(6), 1223–1243.

Ouyang, C., Ma, Z., Ma, Z., & Su, J. (2023). Research on employee voice intention: Conceptualization, scale development, and validation among enterprises in China. *Psychology Research and Behavior Management, 16*, 2137–2156.

Paluch, S., & Wirtz, J. (2020). Artificial intelligence and robots in the service encounter. *Journal of service management research, 4*(1), 3–8.

Pannoni, A. (2022). Microsoft announces four new employee workforce initiatives. Available at: www.microsoft.com. Accessed on: 26 May 2024.

Parry, E., Martin, G., & Dromey, J. (2019). Scenarios and strategies for social media in engaging an giving voice to employees. In P. Holland, J. Teicher, & J. Donaghey (Eds.), *Employee Voice at Work* (1st ed., pp. 201–215) (Work, Organization, and Employment). Springer. https://doi.org/10.1007/978-981-13-2820-6.

Ruck, K. (2021). Employee voice and internal listening: Towards dialogue in the workplace. *Current Trends and Issues in Internal Communication. Theory and Into Practice, 1*, 93–111.

Sayre, M. M., McNeese-Smith, D., Leach, L. S., & Phillips, L. R. (2012). An educational intervention to increase "speaking-up" behaviors in nurses and improve patient safety. *Journal of Nursing Care Quality, 27*(2), 154–160.

Syed, J. (2014). Diversity management and missing voices. In A. Wilkinson, J. Donaghey, T. Dundon, & R. Freeman (Eds.), *Handbook of Research on Employee Voice* (pp. 421–438). Cheltenham: Edward Elgar.

Uys, T., & Smit, R. (2016). Resilience and whistleblowers: Coping with the consequences. *South African Review of Sociology, 47*(4), 60–79.

Van Dyne, L., & LePine, J. A. (1998). Helping and voice extra-role behaviors: Evidence of construct and predictive validity. *Academy of Management Journal, 41*(1), 108–119.

Van Zoonen, W., Verhoeven, J. W., & Vliegenthart, R. (2016). How employees use Twitter to talk about work: A typology of work-related tweets. *Computers in Human Behavior, 55*, 329–339.

Vandekerckhove, W. & Commers, M. R. (2004). Whistle blowing and rational loyalty. *Journal of Business Ethics, 53*(1), 225–233.

Vanka, S. & Singh, S. (2019). Voice matters: why HR should listen to employee voice? *Strategic HR Review, 18*(6), 268–271.

Weiss, M., Kolbe, M., Grote, G., Spahn, D. R., & Grande, B. (2017). Why didn't you say something? Effects of after-event reviews on voice behaviour and hierarchy beliefs in multi-professional action teams. *European Journal of Work and Organizational Psychology, 26*(1), 66–80.

Weiss, M., Kolbe, M., Grote, G., Spahn, D. R., & Grande, B. (2018). We can do it! Inclusive leader language promotes voice behavior in multi-professional teams. *The Leadership Quarterly, 29*(3), 389–402.

WorkTango (2024) Guide to employee voice. Available at: https://www.worktango.com/resources/guides/how-to-actively-listen-to-employee-voice-guide   Accessed on: 5 August 2024.

Chapter 4

Addressing Workplace Conflicts
Employee Incivility and Bullying

4.1 Employee Incivility and Bullying Behaviours

Workplace conflicts cover a wide spectrum of employee behaviours, from a difference of opinion to incidences of incivility. Employee individual differences, differences in individual employee competence or performance, level of employee support or resources and agreeing on employee deliverables or setting targets accounted for some of the many sources of workplace conflict. A relatively smaller number of employees report contracts of employment/ terms and conditions, employee absence or absence management, and/or consideration for promotion as causal factors (CIPD, 2020). During the course of a conflict, more than 30% of employees demonstrated a lack of respect, engaged in bullying, intimidation and harassment behaviours, or refused to work together/cooperate. Comparatively fewer employees engaged in shouting or heated arguments, verbal abuse or insult, or physical threats or assaults (Egerová & Rotenbornová, 2021).

A significant number of employees were challenged with workplace conflict-related stressors, with women reporting this relatively more often than men. More than 20% of the CIPD-surveyed participants reported unworkable relationships, a steep drop in motivation or commitment towards work and/ or the organisation, a loss of self-confidence, and anxiety and/or depression. Women were more likely to report this set of consequences, suggesting they are more likely to feel a lack of psychological safety ('referring to levels of trust, support and/or presence or not of a blame culture at work') within their workplace in comparison to men. Changing job roles, increasingly availing of sickness absence leave, employees resigning from their jobs, formal disciplinary actions and/or legal disputes account for other consequences of workplace conflicts. Workplace disciplinary actions and legal disputes were relatively more common for men (CIPD, 2020; De Dreu & Breesma, 2005; Kuriakose, Jose, Anusree & Jose, 2019). Irrespective of the circumstance, age, gender or context, workplace conflicts indisputably decreased the desire of employees to engage in workplace fun, heightened employee negative affect

DOI: 10.4324/9781032705125-4

and consequentially reduced levels of job satisfaction, engagement, work meaningfulness and wellbeing (Kuriakose, et al., 2019).

'Me Too' Movement – 2017

Pre-pandemic evidence particularly draws attention to the 'Me Too' movement, from 2017. A large-scale, anti-sexual harassment movement, marked by 'high profile scandals', the naming and shaming of celebrity figures, and awareness campaigns, the movement received much attention within various strata of society and the media and the effects of the movement trickled to workplaces globally. 'Me Too' was concerned with the prevalence of misconduct or 'harassment' ('unwanted conduct related to a relevant protected characteristic, which has the purpose or effect of violating an individual's dignity or creating an intimidating, hostile, degrading environment, for that individual'), incivility, bullying and abusive behaviours, and the impact of these factors on employee health and wellbeing (Pelfrey, 2019). More than 30% of employers reported a general workplace culture shift around sexual harassment. A greater number of organisations were engaged in re-writing human resource policies and focused on running training and development programmes. Also, internal pressures from within the organisations, with employees demanding stronger HR policies, were noted post-2017 (Fortado, 2018).

Suggested Activity

Reflect on the conflicts you have witnessed at your workplace or conduct interviews with employees working at an organisation.

1. What factors do you believe fuelled these conflicts?
2. What knowledge and skills do you believe the individuals needed to possess to effectively tackle and cope with the challenge/conflict?

Employee Incivility

Employee incivility is a specific form of social mistreatment (insensitive, disrespectful and rude behaviour), causing distress and indicating a lack of regard for the other person, even if only occurring occasionally (Porath, MacInnis, & Folkes, 2010). Instances of workplace incivility include making 'demeaning, derogatory or condescending remarks and raising one's voice'. Employee incivility has proven to be expensive (Leiter, Day, Oore, & Laschinger, 2012; Porath et al., 2010). Incivility has a strong, positive correlation with

increasing costs of employee presenteeism, absenteeism and turnover intentions. Supporting evidence from Erez and Porath (2011), in a study that encom-
passed 74 participants from the United States, confirms that rude behaviours
negatively influenced not only the work outcomes of victims but also those
of witnesses. Many people are concerned with the wellbeing of others. Most
employees possess an innate concern for the individuals they work with. As
a consequence, witnessing any harm to others may arouse strong negative
affect such as irritation, anger and 'even hostility related to perceptions of
injustice', as human beings tend to believe that all employees are deserving of
respect from others. Other research further established how these experiences
of negative affect significantly deteriorated workplace task performance and
tendencies to engage in creative/innovative work behaviours (Erez & Porath,
2011). This was additionally detrimental to team, organisational culture and
employee wellbeing (Leiter, Laschinger, Day, & Oore, 2011).

Pandemic studies particularly highlight the prevalence of incivility within
the healthcare sector globally (Gaan & Shin, 2023). Evidences from the literature elucidate how pandemic-related stressors (increasing physiological and
psychological depleters) contributed to poor quality working relationships
(marked by intervening in an employee's personal affairs, abandonment,
unfriendly communication and inconsiderate behaviours); inappropriate,
disruptive and abusive physician behaviours; power challenges and gender
discrimination within the workplace; and communication and team-working
challenges. Interpersonal mistreatment from or between senior leaders on the
organisational hierarchy and horizontal aggression (aggression coming from
one's own colleagues) increased absenteeism tendencies and the likelihood
of employees wanting to quit work (Gaan & Shin, 2023). Supporting findings from Alsaif, Almutairi, Elmelegy, Abdelrahman, & Algahtani, (2023) and
El Ghaziri, Johnson, Purpora, Simons & Taylor (2022) particularly appraise
increasing occurrences of incivility, amongst health care professionals, during the pandemic. Shortages of Personal Protective Equipment (PPE), lack of
informational and financial resources during the time, role conflict, ambiguity and overload fractured working relationships.

Leiter et al. (2011), during the course of their investigation, designed and
propagated a research instrument comprising three sub-scales: i) supervisor
incivility, ii) colleague incivility and iii) instigated incivility (the employee's
own behaviour towards other employees). Items on the scale included 'how
frequently have you ignored or excluded another individual from the professional camaraderie?' and 'people treat each other with respect in my work
group'. Participating employees were required to respond to the statements
on a five-point scale ranging from 'never' to 'most of the time'. Systematically
measuring uncivil behaviours such as disrespect and rudeness, in terms of
employee perceptions and experiences, the instrument was deemed as psychometrically robust (Smidt, De Beer, Brink, & Leiter, 2016).

Burnfield, Clark, Devendorf and Jex (2004) proposed an option of administering a validated, multi-dimensional incivility scale, including both verbal and non-verbal behaviours, direct and indirect behaviours, and active and passive forms of employee incivility. This measure of incivility addresses uncivil work behaviours from both internal (supervisors/colleagues) and external (customers) stakeholders (Burnfield et al., 2004). Critics argue that the social desirability bias distorts incivility research and findings; this is given the socially sensitive nature (for instance, workplace deviance) of the items on the scale. The subjective perceptions of individuals of items on the scale can further interfere with the researcher's investigation. In this light, authors from within the organisational psychology literature advise adopting a mixed methodological approach to workplace incivility investigations (Smidt et al., 2016).

Suggested Activity

Appraise and critically analyse the specific methodologies your employer adopts to gauge the prevalence of employee incivility at work.

Employee Bullying

A moderately severe form of workplace incivility, 'bullying' according to ACAS (2023) has been recognised as 'offensive, intimidating, malicious or insulting behaviour, an abuse or misuse of power, through means that undermine, humiliate, denigrate or injure the recipient'. Including a wide spectrum of behaviours, reports from the CIPD (2020) elucidated how more than 40% of surveyed employees within the UK experienced being undermined or humiliated at their workplace, receiving persistent, unwarranted criticism, and having unwanted personal remarks made to them (for instance, making jokes at the employee's expense). Further, more than 10% of the participating employees reported public humiliation within the workplace, shouting or very heated arguments. Other employees experienced isolation or exclusion from social activities, personal intrusion from pestering, spying and/or stalking behaviours, written or verbal comments of a sexual nature, unwanted physical contact of a sexual nature, physical assault or intimidation, sexual assault, coercion for sexual favours, and other offensive and threatening behaviours (Hasan, Shafin & Akter, 2023; Lindert, Sisenop, Agay-Shay, Etzel, Mollica, & Baccarelli, 2023).

When investigating further, more than 20% of employees experienced one or more of these bullying behaviours from their line manager/supervisor, a colleague in their team or a colleague within their organisation. More than

4% reported someone whom their line manager reports to, a customer or client, an indirect reportee (someone working in a function, department or organisation that the employee leads but does not manage) or a member of the public (whilst at work). Others claimed that employees in other organisations, direct reportees (someone the employee line manages or supervises), partner organisations or suppliers engaged in bullying behaviours (Gao, Feng & Zhao, 2021; Lutgen-Sandvik, Namie, & Namie, 2010).

In this light, the findings discovered that most employees did not often report bullying behaviours, as they believed that this would not be taken seriously by the management or that the leaders would take no action against the perpetrator. More than 30% of the surveyed employees stated that any claims made could harm their relationships at work or their future career prospects. Others did not want to go through a formal process, were concerned about confidentiality or did not believe that the issue was serious enough. A small number of employees reported how they had had concerns that had not been addressed in the past and therefore did not believe in raising any more claims. Expressing fear that the employer/leader would not believe them, feeling embarrassed or not knowing how to report workplace bullying behaviours, they chose to stay silent about their experiences (Khan, Nazir & Shafi, 2021; Lutgen-Sandvik et al., 2010).

Studies from Asaoka, Sasaki, Kuroda, Tsuno and Kawakami (2021); Ikeda, Hori, Sasaki, Komase, Doki, Takahashi and Sasahara (2022); and Tsuno and Tabuchi (2022) confirmed the increasing prevalence of employee bullying and cyberbullying behaviours during the pandemic in Japan. This was particularly found to be more prevalent with low-skilled or poorly skilled employees and with 'middle-managers', commonly identified as 'player managers'. The latter group of employees were relatively more challenged with heavy workloads and limited autonomy. Given labour market fluctuations, unemployment, social comparisons and consequential poor physical, social and financial wellbeing during COVID-19, employee levels of stress and subsequent engagement in bullying and other counterproductive behaviours were relatively high globally. Poor working conditions heightened levels of employee vulnerability (Asaoka et al., 2021; Ikeda et al., 2022; Tsuno & Tabuchi, 2022).

Suggested Activity

Reflect on your experiences at work. Have you ever witnessed or been a victim of bullying behaviours? What factors do you believe contribute to or aggravate these tendencies?

The Challenges

Most employees report a lack of trust in senior management, a lack of leadership and role modelling by senior management, and line managers lacking the confidence to challenge inappropriate workplace behaviours as some of the many organisational barriers to managing workplace conflicts (De Dreu & Breesma, 2005). Other organisations claimed to lack adequate appropriate guidance from HR, a scarcity of resources (in terms of time, money and budget) and a lack of employee understanding of what constituted workplace bullying/harassment, which amounted to additional challenges. Still fewer employers explicated how an organisational culture that does not foster dignity and respect and has inadequate training and guidance for line managers, poor working relationships with the organisation, and inadequate policies and procedures to tackle employee complaints and conflicts amount to other barriers to workplace conflict management (Kuriakose, 2022; Rayner & Lewis, 2020).

Evidence Based Recommendations and Interventions

By formulating and implementing stronger inclusion policies, modern-day workplaces are effectively able to prevent employee conflicts, biases/stereotypes and unfair treatment, fostering acceptance and respect. In addition to being built on the grounds of acceptance, inclusive workplaces wish to celebrate every individual, despite their background, identity and circumstances (Scarborough, Lambouths & Holbrook, 2019). In this light, research places importance on assessing workplace inclusion. Creating a bespoke survey to collect inclusion data and systematically measuring individual-level perceptions of inclusion at multiple levels can facilitate this assessment (Pal, Galinsky, & Kim, 2022).

On an additional note, Nishii (2013) recommends the implementation of an instrument that assesses 'workplace inclusion climate', which is an analysis of an employee's perception of i) whether work practices are fair and are designed in a non-biased way, ii) whether the organisation permits employees to be themselves at work, without recrimination; the employer/leaders recognise and value individual differences, and iii) whether all employees are included in decision-making processes, even if their opinions differ from that of the status quo (CIPD, 2020; Pal et al., 2022). Further, adding/updating inclusion questions to existing surveys (for instance, considering nuances of 'employee voice', employee sense of belongingness and organisational values relating to diversity), and employing and critically analysing existing survey data (that inform researchers of employee engagement, equality of opportunity or fairness of policies and practices) can help inform the implementation of employee inclusion policies and practices, thus reducing the occurrences of workplace conflicts (Nishii, 2013).

Supporting evidences also encourage the initiation of employee focus groups or employee feedback sessions to comprehensively gather employee perspectives and/or make amendments to organisational policies, practices and norms. Critics argue that despite employing the most detailed and well-designed initiatives, employers fail to combat conflicts, including work-place incivility, bullying and abusive employee behaviours. In this light, they recommend that employees must be well informed as to why employee inclusion data is being collected and what outcomes the employer/human resource team hope to find from the findings. It is crucial for employees to be offered multiple methods to offer feedback ('online or through any other mechanism, if employees don't have access to their work devices') (Nishii, 2013; Pal et al., 2022).

Suggested Activity

Think about what specific policies/practices your organisation particularly implements in order to accommodate individual differences, diversity in employee needs and the fostering of an inclusive climate.

Activity Reduces Conflict-Associated Strain (ARCAS) Model

Kuriakose, et al. (2019), in their studies investigated employee conflict and wellbeing amongst 554 software engineers and affirmed the significance of the ARCAS model. The proposition appraised how employee lack of proactivity or 'passiveness' in managing conflicts, strengthened the detrimental consequences of stressors on EW. Passive approaches aggravated physiological and psychological strain (Kuriakose, et al., 2019). Organisational psychologists recommend that employers invest in employee training and development, appraising the significance of proactive, conflict management styles.

Educational Interventions

Studies conducting pre and post intervention experiments and analysis highlight the significance of educational activities, employee training and development workshops to raise awareness, reduce the overall frequency and impact of employee incivility and bullying behaviours (Howard & Embree, 2020). Post intervention findings established a significant decrease in disruptive work behaviours. The researchers demonstrated evidence to support the efficacy of asynchronous provider-directed and learner-paced e-learning educational activity interventions in decreasing incivility and increasing perceived psychological comfort level during critical conversations, between employees (Howard & Embree, 2020). More recent evidence from A Saleh, Sarhan, Jabri, Amin, Awadi, Eshah & Rayan (2023), in addition to affirming the significance of facilitated discussions, team building interventions and experiential learning activities, appraise the dissemination of written instruction material and didactic instruction to address disruptive work behaviours, enhance workplace outcomes and the foster EW.

Suggested Activity

Research, reflect and discuss the specific ways in which employers can assess and address the effectiveness of these educational interventions (aimed reduce workplace conflicts)?

Civility, Respect and Engagement in the Workplace (CREW) Intervention

Hodgins, MacCurtain and Mannix-McNamara (2014) propose the 'Civility, Respect and Engagement in the Workplace' (CREW) intervention, initially formulated and employed by the Veteran's Hospital Administration, USA. During the six-month intervention, employees worked with facilitators to identify specific facets of their relationships at work that needed to be addressed, with the objective of increasing the frequency and enhancing the quality of civil interactions between employees in their own departments. Subsequently, a plan of action was drafted, implemented and assessed for how effective this could be in addressing challenges with relationships at work (Hodgins et al., 2014).

The implementation of an 'employee incivility' toolkit, which comprised specific activities focused on enhancing the quality of relationships amongst colleagues. Consisting of 40 exercises and discussion topics, the toolkit offered specific advice for 'group facilitation, forms for making reports' and background information on the fundamental concepts of group dynamics (Hodgins et al., 2014). Initiating conversations with questions such as 'how do we show respect to one another here?' or 'how do we show disrespect to one another here?', the facilitator, in addition to addressing the theme of 'mutual respect', also included topics such as employee assertiveness, accountability, cooperation, conflict resolution, professionalism, disputes and rationales for justifying one's own rude behaviour and leadership.

Activities in the toolkit included the practising of employee active and empathetic listening, resolving conflicts between two other individuals, employing metaphors in conflict resolution and a 'force field analysis of likes and dislikes within a group and brainstorming' (Hodgins et al., 2014).

Findings from the study evidenced a significant decrease in employee incivility after the CREW intervention/tool kit intervention; civility exchanges subsequently enhance employee self-esteem and energy levels at work. Pleasant, quality interactions at work enhanced employee's sense of belongingness, levels of psychological safety, their experiences at work and subsequent levels of wellbeing (Hodgins et al., 2014). These findings were in resonance with Fredrickson and Branigan's (2005) proposition of the Broaden and Build model, which postulated how positive social interactions and fostering psychological safety subsequently enabled employees to build and hone their repertoire of skill sets and potentialities. Hodgins et al. (2014) reinstated that the CREW intervention does not promise a positive spiral leading to ever-increasing levels of civility and attitudes; rather the proposition only improve employee attitudes and civility. Other supporting evidences from the literature clarify two goals of the CREW intervention, related processes and strategies (Laschinger, Leiter, Day, Gilin-Oore, & Mackinnon, 2012). The first goal entails the fostering of respectful interactions between employees within the department. In resonance with this, potential organisational practices/processes include holding team meetings every week for the selection of a specific 'incivility' strategy from either the tool kit or their own ideas.

Researchers further recommend the use of 'colour analysis' to recognise and analyse personality characteristics and individual differences in communication styles (Laschinger et al., 2012). Employees could design a square for a quilt depicting what CREW meant to them; all squares when stitched together indicated the team's perspective on CREW. This quilt could then be hung in the lunch room or the common area of the department. Initiating 'huddles' at the beginning of the 'work-day', another potential process, could act a reminder to members of the group to pay heed to the quality of their interactions on the shift.

To address the second goal of building and honing skills for conflict management, researchers advise participating in the practice/process of engaging in regular team meetings. During the course of this, employees design and participate in role-playing scenarios to practice managing challenging social interactions (Laschinger et al., 2012). Additionally, team building within departments can be encouraged by socially, financially and informationally investing in team building exercises (process).

'Icebreaker' and 'Secret Angel' Strategies

Employing 'icebreakers' to 'start each meeting, to transition group from work activities to crew activities and get to know each other' may account as one of the many strategies. Creating teams for Nintendo Wii tournaments, for instance, to have fun together at work, fostered cohesiveness and collaboration (strategy). Whilst designing and implementing systems to enable to appreciation of peers, employers could organise social/gift funds to celebrate special events such as a long-serving employee's retirement, employee birthday celebrations or new staff joining events. 'Secret angel' initiatives, during which employees acted as 'angels' to appraise proactive behaviours or special occasions, have been evidenced as an effective intervention to fostering a sense of belongingness and team cohesiveness, subsequently countering employee incivility tendencies and bullying behaviours (Laschinger et al., 2012).

'Brag Board'

Leaders and employees can consider sharing successes within teams by creating a 'brag board' for employees to share their accomplishments and to show gratitude to fellow colleagues/senior leaders for any assistance or advice they may have received. Summarising what is 'working' in monthly meetings and through regular emails to employees can prove to be effective. Lastly, in order to eliminate cynical, pessimistic or disrespectful communication resulting from poor resource systems (for instance, blaming others for not replacing supplies) (goal), simple strategies such as formulating a system within which a team leader is assigned to check inventories and ensure access to resources needed for employee care can prove to be beneficial (Laschinger et al., 2012).

Suggested Activity

Elucidate the factors, you believe, that contribute to these interventions positively contributing to employee conflict management.

Gratitude Interventions

In addition to CREW interventions, Ambrose, Locklear and Taylor (2020), whilst analysing workplace incivility, gossip ('negative evaluative talk about someone who is not present') and ostracism, employed a 10-day gratitude list intervention, in attempts to further strengthen inter-personal behaviours and subsequently foster desirable workplace employee behaviours and performance outcomes. Two field experiments, amongst more than a 140 employees in both studies. In addition to listing things for which the employee was grateful, employers urged employees to engage in 'expressive writing' including 'musings about the reasons behind a kindness received'. Findings established a significant increase in self-control resources and subsequent decrease in mistreatment incidences (as reported by co-workers). The gratitude intervention was particularly found to be even more effective amongst employees who perceived higher norms for gratitude in their workplace. Fewer reports of employees criticising others behind their back, ignoring or excluding others (i.e. ostracism) were reported (Ambrose et al., 2020).

In addition to this, 'gratitude letter writing' has been affirmed as useful in managing uncivil behaviours. During the course of this intervention, employers/leaders instruct employees to write a letter to a benefactor, expressing gratitude for something and reading the letter aloud for him/her. The implementation of this proposition has demonstrated greater positive affect. The literature further draws attention to how organisations could design and employ psycho-educational group interventions to foster gratitude, amongst their employees. The facilitator, whilst using structured lesson plans, encouraging team discussions, administering writing assignments and conducting role play activities, educate employees about the various workplace circumstances that elicit gratitude. This could potentially include an employee's/leader's intention to help, the costs associated with helping a benefactor and understanding the benefits received from benefactors. Critics argue that gratitude lists and gratitude letters have proven to be relatively more effective than the implantation of psycho-educational groups. Although, the latter intervention, prompted positive thoughts about events, individuals and material objects, gratitude interventions within workplace have proven to increase positive affectivity, more effectively (Ambrose et al., 2020).

Ford, Wang, Jin and Eisenberger (2018) explicate how employees who experienced a 'sense of gratitude' towards their employer, engaged in fewer uncivil, deviant work behaviours (such as criticising organisational policies and practices, taking unnecessary breaks). There were marked improvements in inter-personal interactions, quality of relationships; consequentially in experiences of joy, positive affect and over all levels of wellbeing.

Find-Remind-Bind Theory of Gratitude for High Quality Workplace Relationships

These findings were in resonance with the 'find-remind-and-bind' theory of gratitude, sourcing from the relationships literature. When employees notice that another employee/senior leader has been responsive to them, i.e. 'given them a benefit for which they felt grateful for', the consequential gratitude signalled that the employee understands, approves or cares about them. Employing the 'finding, reminding and binding' approach brought employees closer to their workplace relationship partners (Algoe, 2012). Findings from Williams and Bartlett (2015) conclude perceptions of interpersonal warmth (e.g., friendliness, thoughtfulness) serve as the mechanism via which gratitude expressions facilitate affiliation; gratitude expressions signalled interpersonal

warmth of the expresser, enhanced positive affect and tendencies of reciprocal, altruistic behaviours.

Challenges with the Implementation of the Intervention

Critics argue that with interventions targeted at employee incivility and bullying behaviours, the challenge is with sustaining the improvements in attitudes
and behaviours.

'The Loss Momentum Model', in this light, assumes that changes (post the
implementation of interventions) in employee attitudes/behaviours, have no
internal momentum. As soon as the intervention ceases to guide and per-
suade employees to engage in new behaviours, the employees return to their
previous state. When the organisation ceases to invest energy into maintaining their new behaviour, the previous social dynamics reassert themselves,
returning the system to its previous state (Leiter et al., 2012). This implied
that organisations had to continually invest in drafting and implementing
evidence based, employee incivility policies, practices and interventions, in
order to foster respectful and pro-social behaviours amongst employees.

The formulators of the 'The Steady State Model' argue that improvements
attained post intervention, are maintained. At an individual level, employees
create self – sustaining behaviours. At the level of the team, the new dynamics amongst team members become 'self-sustaining'. Employees, whilst
sustaining their levels of improvement in social behaviours and attitudes,
continue to behave in resonance with the propositions of the intervention,
without any further instruction (Leiter, et al., 2012). Supporting evidences
from the literature suggest that 'reciprocity' or balanced, reciprocal social
exchanges possess the potential to maintain the quality of social relationships or 'even to support spirals that increase the intensity of exchanges'.
In this light, the 'tit-for-tat' reciprocity is in resonance with the Steady State
Model; i.e. when employees experience respectful, empathetic and cooperative behaviours from others, reciprocal efforts can build and foster pleasant
working environments (Kim & Qu, 2020).

On another note, the 'Augmentation Model' proposes that new insights
from the intervention promote a civility spiral, in which respectful, empathetic
and cooperative behaviours, promote more of the same; consequentially this
may increase the intervention's 'range of influence' (Kelly & Barsade, 2001).
This means, employees who did not engage or invest in the intervention, continually, may align their behaviours with increased civility (whilst decreasing
the proportion of behaviours that reflects incivility), occurring within their
departments (Kelly & Barsade, 2001). Evidences suggest that 'social climate
improvements' from a civility intervention that take on the pattern of the
'Augmentation Model' may occur through a process of emotional contagion'
(Leiter, et al., 2012). The spread of positive affect amongst individuals could
initiate attitudinal and behavioural improvements over time (Kelly & Barsade,

2001). A significant improvement could also imply a honed, genuine empathy for other individuals and an increasing capacity for emotional perception and perspective taking (Coplan, 2011).

Workplace investigators, in the future, must place significance on the analysis of inter-personal dynamics that consequentially lead to enduring changes in employee attitudes and behaviours. Studies that comprehensively consider employee perspectives on reciprocity within their relationships and the role of social/emotional contagions; although intrusive and urging participants to closely evaluate their relationships, would offer value and move research within this domain, forward (Kelly & Barsade, 2001).

4.2 Mindful Self-Compassion

'Conceptualized as a state in which one is highly aware of the present moment, acknowledging and accepting it, without getting caught up in thoughts about the present experience or in emotional reactions to it', mindfulness interventions have been comprehensively explored within the workplace literature (Slutsky, Chin, Raye, & Creswell, 2019). Of similar significance within the domains of positive and organisational psychology, 'self-compassion' pertains to an 'individual's capacity to soothe themselves, to motivate ourselves with encouragement, when we suffer, fail or feel inadequate' (Dodson & Heng, 2022). 'Mindful self-compassion', more specifically, whilst combining both these themes, 'is the process of combining the skills developed through mindfulness, with the emotional practice of self-compassion' (Dodson & Heng, 2022).

Shapiro, Bishop and Cordova (2005) demonstrated how mindfulness-based stress reduction (MBSR) programme interventions were effective in reducing levels of employee distress, anxiety and depression, thereby enhancing self-compassion and quality of life. Consisting of eight two-hour sessions, participants in the experimental group received training in sitting meditations, body scans, hatha yoga and a 'mini-meditation' or 'three-minute breathing space activity'. In addition to this, a 'loving kindness meditation' intervention (discussed later in the chapter) was implemented. On a similar note, Beddoe and Murphy (2004) describe how the implementation of these interventions enabled healthcare employees to develop more compassion and empathy for their patients. They were found not psychologically 'absorbing' the negative emotions of their patients, thereby (deteriorating tendencies of incivility and experiences of angst) enhancing their own levels of self-compassion (Beddoe & Murphy, 2004).

The 'Mindfulness-Based Cognitive Therapy Program' has further been recommended by contemporary researchers within workplaces (Grégoire & Lachance, 2015). Implementing the intervention for a span of two weeks, Grégoire & Lachance (2015) showed that employees reported higher levels of mindfulness and decreased levels of emotional exhaustion. In this light, analysts suggest that in order to develop mindful self-compassion, employees must reflect, explore and understand the challenges that may prevent them from emotionally soothing/comforting themselves (Grégoire & Lachance, 2015). Subject to individual experiences and beliefs, the most recommended method is for employees to reflect on their core (predominantly negative) beliefs that they hold about themselves and write this down. By encouraging employees to think about how writing this down made them feel, the practice also encouraged employees to think about how they first developed this belief and what experiences were connected to it. Other questions included i) what external situations or experiences trigger this belief about yourself? ii) who encourages this belief about yourself? and iii) how would your life look if you didn't believe this about yourself? These questions account for a first step towards cultivating mindful self-compassion.

The employing of the 'how would you treat a friend?' exercise within workplaces has proven to be beneficial. This enabled the employee reflect on how they would treat others in challenging/emotionally difficult circumstances, and then compare and contrast this with how they were treating themselves. Implementing the 'identify what you want' exercise has additionally been evidenced as useful. The intervention focuses on the ways in which employees often use criticism as a motivator (which has been scientifically proven to be ineffective) and rectify this faulty way of thinking to use mindful self-compassion to motivate the individual to achieve his/her goals.

Another intervention that has been designed and propagated by positive psychologists in the literature is 'The Criticizer, the Criticized and the Compassionate Observer' exercise. By encouraging the employee to become more connected with the three different versions (the Criticizer, Criticized and the Compassionate Observer) of themselves, the intervention encourages the employee to label three different chairs as i) the Criticizer (the inner critic), ii) the Criticized (the internal self that feels judged) and iii) the Compassionate Observer (the part of you that is able to offer wisdom and compassion). In taking the seat of the 'criticiser', the employee is encouraged to voice any opinions they have about themselves whilst reflecting on the volume, tone and language and phrases used (Neff, 2003). Employees are later, encouraged to think about how they felt about this. On the second chair, after reflecting on how the criticiser made the employee feel, he/she has to express the degree to which anger/sadness or any other emotion was experienced. Lastly, whilst assuming the role of a compassionate observer, employees are urged to tap into their most compassionate selves, reflecting on the phrases, tone and the ways in which they built compassion into the words they spoke to themselves (Chu, 2016; Neff, 2023).

4.3 Compassion-Cultivating Training/Compassion-Focused Therapy

Jazaieri, Jinpa, McGonigal, Rosenberg, Finkelstein, Simon-Thomas and Goldin (2013), whilst investigating methods to alleviate individuals from negative emotional states, initiated the compassion cultivation intervention programme with 100 individuals. Comprising of a structured protocol, the intervention comprised of a two hour introductory orientation, programme, once a week, for eight weeks, and a regular compassion-focused meditation practice. The intervention engaged participants in active group discussions, guided group meditations,, interactive, practical exercises that prime feelings of open heartedness or connection to others, either through reading poetry or through reflecting on inspiring stories.

During implementation, it addressed four key components: 'i) an awareness of suffering (cognitive/empathic awareness), ii) sympathetic concern related to being emotionally moved by suffering' (affective component), iii) a wish to see a relief to that suffering (intention) and iv) a responsiveness or readiness to help relieve that suffering (motivational) (Jazzaieri et al., 2013). Wellbeing findings before and after the nine-week intervention were analysed with findings demonstrating a significantly positive difference in all three domains of compassion – compassion for others, receiving compassion from others and self-compassion (Gilbert, 2009).

4.4 Loving- Kindness Meditations

Recently investigated and propagated by contemporary researchers and psychologists, 'loving kindness' meditations (LKM) draw from Buddhism. The practice places significance on possessing a mental state of unselfish and unconditional kindness to all beings. When practising LKM, employees pass through a number of distinct stages differing in focus, whilst proceeding from 'easier to more challenging types of contemplation'. This included i) focusing on one self, ii) focusing a good friend (an individual who is alive and does not invoke sexual desires), iii) focusing on a neutral person (an individual who does not elicit positive or negative feelings but is commonly encountered during a normal day), iv) focus on a 'difficult' person (an individual who is typically associated with negative feelings), v) focusing on the self, good friend, neutral and difficult individual (with attention being equally divided between them), and vi) focusing on the entire universe (Hofmann, Grossman, & Hinton, 2011). As in the case of this sequence, employees experience warm feelings, typically initiated and directed towards oneself; this later 'extends to an ever-widening circle of others, ultimately radiating in all directions' (Hoffmann et al., 2011).

In this light, Hutcherson, Seppala and Gross (2008) recruited and randomised participants to receive either a loving kindness meditation intervention or an imagery experimental condition, investigating whether LKM had any influence on affect towards neutral strangers (perceived isolation, social connectedness). Findings demonstrated a significant positive influence on affect and employee sense of 'social connectedness' (Hutcherson et al., 2008). This evidence was supported by studies such as that by Fredrickson, Cohn, Coffey, Pek and Finkel (2008), who drew links between the intervention and frequent experience of positive affect, and a subsequent increase in personal, social and informational resources. Evidencing a shift in a whole range of positive emotions, including love, joy, contentment, gratitude, hope, pride, interest, amusement and awe, the implementation of LKM activities strengthened relationships and held positive consequences for an employee's mental health.

Elucidating the benefits of the practice, contemporary researchers appraise how the intervention is useful in tackling interpersonal challenges such as anger, social anxiety and marital issues or challenges with partnerships (Gillbert & Proctor, 2006). Addressing challenges of caregiving professionals or non-professionals who are required to provide long-term care and support to an ailing relative, friend or colleague, the technique enhances an employee's threshold to experience and offer unconditional positive regard and kindness (Fredrickson et al., 2008).

4.5 Summary

In summary, this chapter elucidated how employee personality and individual differences, and lack of social support and informational, financial and social resources within the workplace fundamentally contribute to conflicts. This inevitably heightens employee frustration and angst. The prevalence and the intensity of conflicts in contemporary workplaces, including harassment, incivility and bullying behaviours, were significantly appraised in the context of the 'Me Too' movement of 2017. The movement marked a cultural shift within workplaces, empowering employees to report incidents that violated their dignity. Human resource departments globally were found to invest considerably more in employee training and development. Evidence from the literature particularly recommended the implementation of 'CREW' and gratitude interventions. Scientific experiments confirmed a significant decrease in the prevalence of employee incivility, bullying behaviours and consequentially poor physiological and psychological health.

Additionally, employing mindful self-compassion, compassion-focused therapies and engaging in loving kindness meditations have proven to be beneficial in addressing the 'compassion deficit', psychologically replenishing employees and fostering greater levels of wellness. This was particularly evidenced as beneficial for health care workers. Having summarised the essence of this chapter, the author will now move on to addressing challenges and interventions pertaining to employee engagement.

4.6 Further Readings

Bassman, E. S. (1992). Abuse in the Workplace: Management Remedies and Bottom Line Impact. Westport, CT: Quorum Books.

Einarsen, S., Hoel, H., & Cooper, C. (2002). Bullying and Emotional Abuse in the Workplace: International Perspectives in Research and Practice. *1*, 439-446

Hoel, H., Rayner, C., & Cooper, C. L. (1999). Workplace bullying. Manchester: John Wiley & Sons Ltd.

Leiter, M. (2013). Analyzing and Theorizing the Dynamics of the Workplace Incivility Crisis. New York, NY: Springer.

Rayner, C., Hoel, H., & Cooper, C. (2001). Workplace Bullying: What We Know, Who is to Blame and What Can We Do? London: CRC Press.

4.7 Suggested Websites

Cartwright and Cooper (2007). Hazards to health: The problem of workplace bullying. Available at: https://www.bps.org.uk/psychologist/hazards-health-problem-workplace-bullying Accessed on: 6 November 2023

Erez & Porath (2011). How Rudeness Takes Its Toll. British Psychological Society. Available at: https://www.bps.org.uk/psychologist/how-rudeness-takes-its-toll Accessed on: 6 November 2023

West (2021). Collective and Compassionate Leadership. British Psychological Society. Available at: https://www.bps.org.uk/psychologist/collective-and-compassionate-leadership Accessed on: 6 November 2023

4.8 Reflective Questions – For Learners

1. Elucidate the significance of leaders engaging in the drafting and implementation of compassion-driven policies and practices.
2. What specific nuances account as 'ethical' in the implementation of employee counselling interventions?
3. What are the challenges that employers/HR departments can potentially be faced with when assessing and addressing employee incivility, bullying and abuse within the workplace?

4.9 Reflective Questions – For Researchers/Practitioners

1. Have you witnessed any occurrences of incivility/bullying/abuse at your workplace? If yes,

   i) What factors do you believe contributed to this?
   ii) How did your human resource department respond to this?
   iii) Critically analyse the effectiveness of the interventions they employed to address the challenge.

2. How do you believe organisations can effectively address employee incivility/bullying/abuse?
3. Conduct a Psychinfo/EBSCOhost search covering literature published in the past using the terms 'employee incivility', 'employee bullying', 'employee abuse' and 'employee wellbeing', individually or in combination. Identify a study that resonates with your interests and that is feasible to replicate and extend. Conduct the replication.
4. Design and conduct a study to analyse whether and the extent to which compassion-focused therapy, mindful self-compassion, compassion-cultivating training, emotional balance interventions and compassion and loving kindness meditations foster employee wellbeing.

References

A Saleh, A., Sarhan, W., Jabri, A., Amin, M., Awadi, T., Eshah, N., & Rayan, A. (2023). Strategies combating workplace incivility: An integrative review of literature. In Second International Nursing Conference *"Nursing Profession in the Current Era" (INC 2023)* (pp. 95–113). Atlantis Press.

ACAS. (2023). Workplace conflict: Research and commentary. Available at: https://www.acas.org.uk/research-and-commentary/workplace-conflict. Accessed on: 27 May 2024.

Algoe, S. B. (2012). Find, remind, and bind: The functions of gratitude in everyday relationships. *Social and Personality Psychology Compass, 6*(6), 455–469.

Alsaif, B., Almutairi, Y. M. N., Elmelegy, R. I., Abdelrahman, M., & Algahtani, F. D. (2023). Exposure to workplace incivility during the COVID-19 pandemic and turnover intentions among nursing professionals. *International Journal of Pharmaceutical Research and Allied Sciences, 12*(4), 104–111.

Ambrose, M. L., Locklear, L. R. & Taylor, S. G. (2020). How a gratitude intervention influences workplace mistreatment: A multiple mediation model. *Journal of Applied Psychology, 106*(9), 1314–1331. https://doi.org/10.1037/apl0000825.

Asaoka, H., Sasaki, N., Kuroda, R., Tsuno, K., & Kawakami, N. (2021). Workplace bullying and patient aggression related to COVID-19 and its association with psychological distress among health care professionals during the COVID-19 pandemic in Japan. *The Tohoku Journal of Experimental Medicine, 255*(4), 283–289.

Beddoe, A. E., & Murphy, S. O. (2004). Does mindfulness decrease stress and foster empathy among nursing students? *Journal of Nursing Education, 43*(7), 305–312.

Burnfield, J. L., Clark, O. L., Devendorf, S. A., & Jex, S. M. (2004, April). Understanding workplace incivility: Scale development and validation. Poster presented at the 19th Annual Conference of the Society for Industrial and Organizational Psychology, Chicago, IL.

Chu, L. C. (2016). Mediating positive moods: The impact of experiencing compassion at work. *Journal of Nursing Management, 24*(1), 59–69.

CIPD. (2020). Managing conflict in the modern workplace. Available at: www.cipd.org. Accessed on: 27 May 2025.

Coplan, A. (2011). Will the real empathy please stand up? A case for a narrow conceptualization. *The Southern Journal of Philosophy, 49,* 40–65. https://doi.org /10.1111/j.2041-6962.2011.00056.x.

De Dreu, C. K. W., & Beersma, B. (2005). Conflict in organizations: beyond effectiveness and performance. *European Journal of Work and Organizational Psychology, 14*(2), 105–117.

Dodson, S. J., & Heng, Y. T. (2022). Self-compassion in organizations: A review and future research agenda. *Journal of Organizational Behavior, 43*(2), 168–196.

Egerová, D. & Rotenbornová, L. (2021). Towards understanding of workplace conflict: An examination into causes and conflict management strategies. *Problems of Management in the 21st Century, 16*(1), 7–18.

El Ghaziri, M., Johnson, S., Purpora, C., Simons, S., & Taylor, R. (2022). Registered nurses' experiences with incivility during the early phase of COVID-19 pandemic: Results of a multi-state survey. *Workplace Health & Safety, 70*(3), 148–160.

Erez, A. & Porath, C. L. (2011). How rudeness takes its toll. British Psychological Society. Available at: https://www.bps.org.uk/psychologist/how-rudeness-takes-its -toll. Accessed on: 6 November 2023.

Ford, M. T., Wang, Y., Jin, J., & Eisenberger, R. (2018). Chronic and episodic anger and gratitude toward the organization: Relationships with organizational and supervisor supportiveness and extrarole behavior. *Journal of Occupational Health Psychology, 23*(2), 175–187.

Fortado, S. (2018). Workplace sexual abuse, labor and the# MeToo movement. *Labor Studies Journal, 43*(4), 241–244.

Fredrickson, B. L. & Branigan, C. (2005). Positive emotions broaden the scope of attention and thought-action repertoires. *Cognition & Emotion, 19*(3), 313–332.

Fredrickson, B. L., Cohn, M. A., Coffey, K. A., Pek, J., & Finkel, S. M. (2008). Open hearts build lives: Positive emotions, induced through loving-kindness meditation, build consequential personal resources. *Journal of Personality and Social Psychology, 95*(5), 1045.

Gaan, N., & Shin, Y. (2023). Supervisor incivility and frontline employees' performance amid the COVID-19 pandemic: A multilevel moderated mediation analysis. *Journal of Retailing and Consumer Services, 73,* 103347.

Gao, H., Feng, Z., & Zhao, Z. (2021). The impact of customer bullying on employees' job performance: The locus of control as a moderating effect. *Emerging Markets Finance and Trade, 57*(5), 1333–1348.

Gilbert, P. (2009). Introducing compassion-focused therapy. *Advances in Psychiatric Treatment, 15*(3), 199–208.

Gillbert, P., & Proctor, S. (2006). Compassionate mind training for people with high shame and self-criticism: overview and pilot study of a group therapy approach. *Clinical Psychology and Psychotherapy, 13*(6), 353–379.

Grégoire, S., & Lachance, L. (2015). Evaluation of a brief mindfulness-based intervention to reduce psychological distress in the workplace. *Mindfulness, 6*(4), 836–847.

Hasan, M. M., Shafin, F., & Akter, N. (2023). The role of employee stress in workplace bullying and its effect on organizational performance-a study on bangladeshi workplace. *Cultural Communication and Socialization Journal, 4*(1), 18–22.

Hodgins, M., MacCurtain, S., & Mannix-McNamara, P. (2014). Workplace bullying and incivility: A systematic review of interventions. *International Journal of Workplace Health Management, 7*(1), 54–72.

Hofmann, S. G., Grossman, P., & Hinton, D. E. (2011). Loving-kindness and compassion meditation: Potential for psychological interventions. *Clinical Psychology Review, 31*(7), 1126–1132.

Howard, M. S., & Embree, J. L. (2020). Educational intervention improves communication abilities of nurses encountering workplace incivility. *The Journal of Continuing Education in Nursing, 51*(3), 138–144.

Hutcherson, C. A., Seppala, E. M., & Gross, J. J. (2008). Loving-kindness meditation increases social connectedness. *Emotion, 8*(5), 720.

Ikeda, T., Hori, D., Sasaki, H., Komase, Y., Doki, S., Takahashi, T., ... Sasahara, S. (2022). Prevalence, characteristics, and psychological outcomes of workplace cyberbullying during the COVID-19 pandemic in Japan: A cross-sectional online survey. *BMC Public Health, 22*(1), 1087.

Jazaieri, H., Jinpa, G. T., McGonigal, K., Rosenberg, E. L., Finkelstein, J., Simon-Thomas, E., ... Goldin, P. R. (2013). Enhancing compassion: A randomized controlled trial of a compassion cultivation training program. *Journal of Happiness Studies, 14*(4), 1113–1126.

Kelly, J. R. & Barsade, S. G. (2001). Mood and emotions in small groups and work teams. *Organizational Behavior and Human Decision Processes, 86*(1), 99–130.

Khan, K., Nazir, T., & Shafi, K. (2021). Could workplace bullying and emotional exhaustion be reasons of employee silence?. *Journal of Workplace Behavior, 2*(2), 35–51.

Kim, H., & Qu, H. (2020). The mediating roles of gratitude and obligation to link employees' social exchange relationships and prosocial behavior. *International Journal of Contemporary Hospitality Management, 32*(2), 644–664.

Kuriakose, V. (2022). Behavioural conflict on employee wellbeing: Role of negative affect state and workplace fun. *Benchmarking: An International Journal, 30*(8), 2634–2654.

Kuriakose, V., Jose, H., Anusree, M. R., & Jose, S. (2019). Process conflict and employee well-being: An application of activity reduces conflict associated strain (ARCAS) model. *International Journal of Conflict Management, 30*(4), 462–489.

Laschinger, H. K. S., Leiter, M. P., Day, A., Gilin-Oore, D., & Mackinnon, S. P. (2012). Building empowering work environments that foster civility and organizational trust: Testing an intervention. *Nursing Research, 61*(5), 316–325.

Leiter, M. P., Laschinger, H. K. S., Day, A., & Oore, D. G. (2011). The impact of civility interventions on employee social behaviour, distress, and attitudes. *Journal of Applied Psychology, 96*(6), 1258–1274.

Leiter, M. P., Day, A., Oore, D. G., & Spence Laschinger, H. K. (2012). Getting better and staying better: Assessing civility, incivility, distress, and job attitudes one year after a civility intervention. *Journal of Occupational Health Psychology, 17*(4), 425–434.

Lindert, J., Sisenop, F., Agay-Shay, K., Etzel, R., Mollica, R., & Baccarelli, A. A. (2023). Threats and humiliation in the workplace. *European Journal of Public Health, 33*(Supplement_2), ckad160–424.

Lutgen-Sandvik, P., Namie, G., & Namie, R. (2010). Workplace bullying: Causes, consequences, and corrections. In P. Lutgen-Sandvik & B. Sypher (Eds.), *Destructive Organizational Communication* (pp. 43–68). New York: Routledge.

Neff, K. (2003). Self-compassion: An alternative conceptualization of a healthy attitude toward oneself. *Self and Identity, 2*(2), 85–101.

Neff, K. D. (2023). Self-compassion: Theory, method, research, and intervention. *Annual Review of Psychology, 74*, 193–218.

Nishii, L. H. (2013). The benefits of climate for inclusion for gender-diverse groups. *Academy of Management Journal, 56*(6), 1754–1774.

Pal, I., Galinsky, E., & Kim, S. (2022). Employee health and well-being after a crisis–re-imagining the role of workplace inclusion. *Community, Work and Family, 25*(1), 30–62.

Pelfrey, S. W. (2019). Employment law-how the# metoo movement has rocked the workplace. *American Journal of Trial Advocacy, 43*, 259.

Porath, C., MacInnis, D., & Folkes, V. (2010). Witnessing incivility among employees: Effects on consumer anger and negative inferences about companies. *Journal of Consumer Research, 37*(2), 292–303.

Rayner, C., & Lewis, D. (2020). Managing workplace bullying: The role of policies. In *Bullying and Harassment in the Workplace* (pp. 497–519). CRC Press.

Scarborough, W. J., Lambouths III, D. L., & Holbrook, A. L. (2019). Support of workplace diversity policies: The role of race, gender, and beliefs about inequality. *Social Science Research, 79*, 194–210.

Shapiro, S. L., Astin, J. A., Bishop, S. R., & Cordova, M. (2005). Mindfulness-based stress reduction for health care professionals: Results from a randomized trial. *International Journal of Stress Management, 12*(2), 164.

Shin, Y., Hur, W. M., & Hwang, H. (2022). Impacts of customer incivility and abusive supervision on employee performance: A comparative study of the pre-and post-COVID-19 periods. *Service Business, 16*(2), 309–330.

Slutsky, J., Chin, B., Raye, J., & Creswell, J. D. (2019). Mindfulness training improves employee well-being: A randomized controlled trial. *Journal of Occupational Health Psychology, 24*(1), 139.

Smidt, O., De Beer, L. T., Brink, L., & Leiter, M. P. (2016). The validation of a workplace incivility scale within the South African banking industry. *SA Journal of Industrial Psychology, 42*(1), 1–12.

Tsuno, K., & Tabuchi, T. (2022). Risk factors for workplace bullying, severe psychological distress and suicidal ideation during the COVID-19 pandemic among the general working population in Japan: A large-scale cross-sectional study. *BMJ Open, 12*(11), e059–860.

Williams, L. A. & Bartlett, M. Y. (2015). Warm thanks: Gratitude expression facilitates social affiliation in new relationships via perceived warmth. *Emotion, 15*(1), 1.

Chapter 5

Employee Engagement
Challenges and Interventions

5.1 Employee Presenteeism

'Presenteeism' is 'a combination of an employee's physical presence but functional absence in the workplace, i.e. an employee being present at work when they should be at home, either because they are ill or working such long hours that they are no longer effective' (Cooper & Dewe, 2008). Driven by stress, poor physical, mental or financial wellbeing or lack of sleep, pre-pandemic evidence appraises how more than 50% of presenteeism cases were explained by these factors.

Survey findings from CIPD (2020) further detailed how 30 productive days were lost per employee, per year, due to presenteeism. Other evidence from the United States reports how employee presenteeism costs the country more than $150 billion, annually, accounting for 71% of the total cost of lost productivity (Prochaska, Evers, Johnson, Castle, Prochaska, Sears, & Pope, 2011). Significant links have been established between employee presenteeism and employee physical and emotional health, risk factors and life evaluation (Prochaska et al., 2011).

Suggested Activity

'Employee presenteeism costs the United States more than $150 billion'. In this light,

Why do you believe employees report to work when they are ill or are not at that time effective?

Ho, Ng, Teo and Hee (2022) whilst examining the prevalence of presenteeism during the pandemic, in Malaysia, elucidated how unprecedented challenges and the organisation's downsizing trend heightened levels of employee anxiety. The consequential physical and mental exhaustion resulted in increasing presenteeism. Findings further demonstrated how coworker COVID-19

DOI: 10.4324/9781032705125-5

health-related ailments significantly contributed to time pressures at work. This physiological and psychological urgency to complete tasks was found to be positively correlated to employee presenteeism (Ho et al., 2022).

Additionally, the need to constantly stay connected across all organisational communication channels resulted in information overload and insufficient rest and increased the likelihood of presenteeism. Having demonstrated that time pressures and the need for constant connectivity were positively correlated to presenteeism, the author further established a negative correlation between employee presenteeism (resulting from factors such as organisational changes, job insecurity and a lack of psychological safety) and psychological wellbeing (Ho et al., 2022).

Research studies recommend employing the 'Wellbeing Assessment for Productivity' scale for assessing employee presenteeism. Deemed as a psychometrically robust research instrument, the scale comprises 12 questions measuring employee reduced functioning within the domains of personal and work wellbeing. The scale comprises items such as 'During the past four weeks (28 days), how often have you had trouble at work concentrating or doing your best because of each of the 12 different reasons?'. Possible responses were 'not at all', 'some' or 'a lot'. Scoring of this measure ranged from 0 (not at all) to 100 (Prochaska et al., 2011).

Employer Interventions

During and post pandemic, a significant number of employers proactively urged employees who were unwell to take time off sick in attempts to address 'presenteeism'. With employers encouraging leaders to be role models by not working when ill, organisations took proactive efforts to tackle the challenge by offering better training and guidance for all employees to spot warning signs. Other companies chose to review their health and wellbeing policies, investigate potential causes (such as employee workload) of presenteeism, update the organisation's attendance policies, introduce new ways to monitor presenteeism and/or urge the organisation's company board to recognise the issue as a priority (CIPD, 2020; Kinman, 2019).

Takano, Iwano, Aoki, Nakano and Sakano (2021) systematically analysed whether and which sleep interventions (including cognitive behavioural therapy for insomnia, sleep hygiene education, yoga, mindfulness interventions, weight loss programmes and changing the colour temperature of fluorescent lights in the workplace) deteriorated employee tendencies of presenteeism. Findings established sleep restriction, stimulus control, relaxation and cognitive reconstruction, cognitive behavioural therapy for insomnia as being the most effective in tackling challenges pertaining to employee presenteeism. Sleep hygiene education fostered better management of employee time, mental and interpersonal demands, and output demands, reflecting an alleviation of employee presenteeism symptoms (Takano et al., 2021).

Other evidences from Ammendolia, Côté, Cancelliere, Cassidy, Hartvigsen, Boyle & Amick (2016) recommend implementing the 'intervention mapping methodology' ('a systematic and comprehensive approach employing all stakeholder involvement to tailor interventions/programs to address employee presenteeism in a specific context'). During their study with an international financial organisation, for instance, employee mental health was appraised as the key cause for presenteeism behaviours. Employing the intervention mapping methodology, analysts initiated regular sharing focus groups, social networking, monthly personal stories from leadership using webinars and multi-media communications, expert-led workshops, lunch and learn sessions and manager and employee training were part of a comprehensive program. Specific strategies were developed, encouraging healthy behaviours such as regular exercise, proper nutrition, adequate sleep, smoking cessation, socialization and work-life balance. Intervention mapping was evidenced as a useful methodology for the designing of a 'health promotion and wellness' intervention, aiming to deteriorate tendencies of employee presenteeism. The methodology offered a systematic process to address a complex problem (Ammendolia, et al., 2016).

5.2 Employee Quiet Quitting Behaviours

Presenteeism is distinct from 'quiet quitting'. The latter refers to a phenomenon where employees disengage from work and carry out the bare minimum of their responsibilities. Pendell and Wigert (2022) in this light highlights how disengaged employees and their subsequent loss of productivity costed the global economy approximately $7.8 trillion annually. A serious sign of dissatisfaction, feeling 'undervalued' and a 'lack of appreciation', 'quiet quitters' are unwilling to establish themselves as an 'extra mile' performer. Investing minimally at work is often marked by a lack of employee efficiency, deteriorating productivity, non-attendance at meetings, a lack of motivation or failure to contribute to team endeavours (Caldwell & Mahand, 2023).

Research evidence from Formica and Sfodera (2022), whilst particularly analysing the 'quiet quitting' phenomenon during and after the pandemic, clarifies how the onset of COVID-19 did not count as a 'source' of employee 'quiet quitting'; rather, it simply fuelled and intensified its prevalence. The virtual/hybrid nature of work, changing work dynamics and the quality of workplace relationships significantly deteriorated the extent to which employees felt cared about. 'Quiet quitting' occurrences typically accelerate when employees do not perceive their work as being adequately recognised; they feel disrespected, do not feel valued. Workplace process and role ambiguities and the ineffective designing and implementation of training and development sessions, negatively influenced employee perceptions of opportunities to learn and grow. Lack of face-to-face social interactions resulted in employees feeling disconnected from their organisation's purpose.

Galanis, Katsiroumpa, Vraka, Siskou, Konstantakopoulou, Moisoglou and Kaitelidou (2023) whilst discussing the formulation and the validation of the 'quiet quitting scale', inform stakeholders of the 11 items that the research instrument consists of. The items included statements such as 'I feel detached from my job', 'I feel inspired when I work' and 'I feel isolated at work'. Seven items were reverse scored – this included statements such as 'I give my best at work' and 'I feel inspired when I work'. Deemed as possessing psychometrically robust properties, the scale is easy to administer and can be employed across diverse cultures and societies.

Suggested Activity

Conduct interviews with employers/line managers of an organisation you have access to. Appraise and analyse the extent to which employee quiet quitting behaviours are prevalent within their organisation.

Critically analyse the methodologies they adopt for assessing prevalence and the factors they believe, as contributing to quiet quitting behaviours.

Employer Interventions

Drawing from evidences reported by Formica and Sfodera (2022), it is crucial for employers to demonstrate 'knowledge, interest and involvement' about an employee's needs satisfaction at work; this consequentially strengthens the employer-employee partnership. In this light, during recruitment, selection and onboarding process, human resource teams can consider exploring the following: i) 'a list of top needs prospective employees would want to have strongly met, who should meet them and how', ii) after having completed three months of the role, employees must report the extent to which their needs were met as a percentage; subsequently, an action plan to reach the highest level of employee need satisfaction must be drafted and implemented (Pevec, 2023).

The authors elucidate an example of an employee whose top need is 'growth'; the measure of employee need satisfaction at work was reported as being 35%. Researchers advise that this is discussed with the line manager, appraising specific ways in which this percentage could increase to 50% or higher in three months. These actions entail engaging in potentially challenging tasks of modifying employee tasks, and processes in order to achieve a fine balance between employee needs and organisational performance (Aydin & Azizoğlu, 2022).

Factors such as an employee's perception of their organisation's culture as toxic and a perceived lack of opportunities to train and grow contribute to 'quiet quitting' behaviours. Supporting evidence from the literature states that 'employer-employee value alignment' is crucial. In order to gauge and build on employee value alignment, identifying an employee's values, determining the 'person-organisation' value fit, checking for an alignment between employee values and behaviour, and understanding and showing interest in the values of others was claimed to be useful. These include, asking employees to reflect on a long-lasting legacy, they would like to leave once they decease (Akinloye, 2022). Urging them to reflect on 'multiple scenarios in which they have limited time to live from: six months to one week and a final scenario, where they have only one day of life' can account as a 'second step'. Lastly, sharing these details with their peers within the team/workplace is expected to foster clarity and strengthen 'the depth and breadth' of their relationships. Whilst systematically building on 'purpose', employers can check for a resonance between employee and organisational purpose alignment and consider implementing further appropriate interventions to address the gap (Pevec, 2023).

On another note, Serenko (2023), having employed secondary data, advises how 'investing in knowledge sharing, capturing the knowledge of potential quiet quitters, conducting a comprehensive knowledge audit, particularly focusing on high performers and initiating employee burnout management programmes can assist with addressing employee "quiet quitting"'. Moreover, fostering interactional justice between employers/line managers and subordinates and fairly compensating for employees 'going above and beyond' count as additional initiatives when making attempts to cope with the challenge. Propagating work-life balance as a 'national core value', and financially and informationally investing in employee physical and mental health resources, interventions, and employee efficiency innovations can potentially enhance employee engagement and productivity (Shah & Parekh 2023).

5.3 Employee Proactivity

'Proactivity' or 'taking initiative' accounts for a 'form of motivated behaviour at work' (Ashford & Grant, 2008). Proactive employees, whilst actively pursuing personal and organisational goals, adapt to new environments or to any changes quickly and with ease, 'express voice', take charge and 'act in advance to influence individuals and groups' (Ashford & Grant, 2008). Evidence from extensive studies in the literature has established how employee proactivity has strong, positive links with employee goal-setting behaviours, the building, expanding and maintaining of social networks, timely responses to client/colleague/employer requests (engaging in pro-social behaviours) and, subsequently, effective problem solving, decision-making and work outcomes (Rioux & Penner, 2001).

Cangiano and Parker' (2015) analysed the correlation between employee proactivity, appraising motivational antecedents (such as self-efficacy/'can do' attitudes), the need for self-determination or a 'reason to', and an activated positive affect or 'an energised to' nuance. Employee proactivity is positively correlated to employee wellbeing. The extent to which these variables are correlated, however, depends on the feedback that employees receive. Consequentially, this can result in positive health and wellbeing outcomes (work-related self-efficacy, employee basic needs satisfaction, activated positive affect, such as employee vitality) or negative mental health outcomes (including job strain, role overload and regulatory depletion).

Grant (2023), further to his investigations, formulated and propagated using a 'proactivity' scale. The scale consisted of statements such as 'I am always looking for better ways of doing things', 'I love to challenge the status quo', 'I enjoy being a champion for ideas, even against opposition' and 'I like to be the one taking initiative'.

The 'MCE' Approach to Proactivity

Grant (2023) recommends that leaders model 'proactivity' in order to encourage 'proactivity', for instance, initiating a clean-up campaign or a 'tree/flower planting' campaign if the street requires sprucing up. Further, 'celebrating', 'applauding' or rewarding proactivity enabled others to recognise the behaviour and associate it with a positive response or consequence. Lastly, employers/leaders can 'enable' proactivity by inviting employees to raise problem questions/concerns, even if they are unaware of the solutions. Ask a question and give everyone a chance to answer, so they all have a voice. Criticise yourself out loud, showing people you are open to being challenged – this has proven to be beneficial.

5.4 Employee Grit

In 1907, William James, an American psychologist and philosopher, sought to investigate the various diverse means by which individuals unleash their innate abilities and the reasons why some people accomplish more than others with equivalent cognitive acumen. There was an underlying psychological quality that was crucial for success, irrespective of the realm of study, work or performance. This scientific inquiry became a starting point for the discovery of the 'grit' construct in psychological sciences (Duckworth, Kelly, Matthews, & Peterson, 2007). High achievers at work possessed a ferocious determination. Unusually resilient and hardworking, they had an enduring, unparalleled interest and direction.

The research team propagated 'grit' as 'passion and perseverance for long-term goals'. Metaphorically, it was described as 'sweat not swagger, character not charisma' (Singh & Chopra, 2016). The psychological, 'non-cognitive' asset embraced 'working strenuously' towards demanding goals, sustaining effort and undivided attention for years, despite adversity and failure. The trait can be developed and gradually refined over time. The 'grit' terminology, in essence, found to encapsulate three definitional aspects which remain constant throughout the literature: passion, goals and perseverance (Ferris, Jordan, Hochwarter, & Wright, 2019).

Although synonymously used with 'employee conscientiousness', 'employee grit' is unique. Duckworth and Quinn (2009) clarify how 'grit' places greater emphasis on 'long-term stamina', entailing the capacity to sustain both effort and interest in projects that take months or even longer to complete rather than short-term stamina (relatively more relevant to the 'conscientiousness' construct). The employee with grit not only completes the assignment in hand but pursues a given objective over years. Another theme that 'grit' has been connected with is the 'need for achievement'. Employees who score high on the 'need for achievement' dimension put effort into tasks that are neither too easy nor too difficult, and that are dependent on immediate feedback for performance. This is in contrast to those who score high on the 'grit' dimension, who intentionally set and maintain for themselves, purposefully and consciously, extremely long-term objectives and do not swerve from them – even in the absence of positive feedback (Duckworth et al., 2007). Lastly, an employee demonstrating 'resilience' is often misunderstood as having 'grit'. However, resilience only considers 'bouncing back from failure or adversity' or the 'perseverance' component of 'grit' – disregarding the 'passion' element of the variable.

'Grit' in Collectivistic Contexts

There have been multiple studies that have analysed 'grit' and its psychological constructs; however, most investigations were conducted in the Western context or within individualistic societies. Given that collectivistic societies demand greater degrees of selflessness, altruism and interdependence, the role that 'grit' plays in collectivistic societies such as the Asian context has been debatable. Drawing from the educational domains of study and research, Datu (2017) suggests that, in addition to perseverance of effort and consistency of effort, a 'sense of relatedness' or the degree to which an employee feels accepted by different social partners (such as the employer, colleagues, customers) accounts as a crucial construct to the constitution, implementation and development of the 'grit' theme in a collectivistic context. Social and contextual factors strongly relate to a wide range of cognitive, emotional and motivational outcomes. Grit is deemed as a psychological resource that can potentially crystallise as a result of meaningful, interpersonal relationships.

Chen, Datu and Yuen (2016) claim that the characteristic of 'adapting to situations' was a relatively more significant, third dimension to the 'grit' theme. Employees who appreciated changes or 'gave up' on their plans for other equally appealing pathways in order to achieve distant goals in life had elevated levels of employee passion, perseverance and subsequent workplace performance and employee wellbeing within collectivistic societies. In essence, possessing a 'sense of relatedness' and the ability to 'adapt to situations' are crucial for workplace and career-related goal-setting behaviours, workplace, career decision-making self-efficacy and employee career maturity (Ting & Datu, 2020).

Assessing 'Employee Grit'

'Grit' Scales

The 'grit' literature primarily informs organisational stakeholders of three research instruments: the Grit – O scale, Grit – S scale and the Triarchic Model of Grit scale. Possessing strong psychometric properties, the 12-item, Grit – O scale or the Original Grit scale was developed by Duckworth et al. (2007) to assess grit. The study comprised of reversed and non-reversed statements such as 'I have overcome setbacks to conquer an important challenge', 'my interests change from year to year' and 'setbacks don't discourage me'. Having been criticised for being lengthy and lacking predictive validity for the interest and perseverance factors on crucial achievement outcomes, researchers compiled a relatively shorter version of the scale: the Grit – S scale.

Kuruveettissery, Gupta and Rajan (2023) argued that a different scale had to be formulated in order to assess grit in collectivistic contexts. The research instrument did not only have to assess the consistency of interest/passion and the perseverance of effort components but also 'adaptability to situations' as a characteristic. The third component was crucial to thriving in a collectivistic context, 'enabling the individual to accept new challenges, facilitate flexibility and possessing an inner drive to overcome, as they arise'.

It was in this light that the Triarchic Model of Grit scale was developed – borrowing some items from the Grit – O scale. More specifically, three items measured passion (e.g. 'new ideas and projects sometimes distract me from previous ones'), three items assessed perseverance of effort (e.g. 'I am a hard worker), and four items evaluated adaptability to situations (e.g. 'I am able to cope with changing circumstances in life') on the scale. These instruments are however prone to biases as employees are able to easily fake their responses on the scale. In this, analysts from multi-national cooperations recommend hiring for 'grit' by using the following questions on the interview schedule (Ting, et al., 2020).

The 'Grit' Interview Schedule

First, check for the candidate's biggest professional failure and what they learned from their experience. Whilst assessing the employee's determination despite past mistakes (rather than being discouraged) and their ability to embrace humility and adaptation, in the face of failure, human resource teams should wait to listen for whether and how the employee owns up to their failures, rather than passing on the blame. Further, empathetically listening for self-reflection on what went wrong with a clear sense of what to do differently next time proves to be beneficial (Browne, Fleming, Gorksi, & Tham, 2023).

Second, it would be useful to ask for a goal that the employee is working towards, personally or professionally, and check on their progress so far. By analysing their enthusiasm and diligence in achieving long-term goals, and their motivation and perseverance when something goes unexpectedly, employers will be able to better evaluate the individual's ability to engage in thoughtful, advanced planning behaviours and the concrete steps they undertook to sustain focus whilst achieving their goals (Browne et al., 2023).

Lastly, checking if and when the employee decided to stop pursuing a goal can prove to be useful information. When assessing the employee's ability to recognise a lost cause, demonstrate poise in backing out and the ability to minimise unwanted consequences, human resource professionals must listen and be wary of employees centring around negative, futile consequences of continuing down the same path and the employee's lack of ability to evaluate the pros and cons of giving up and considering alternative solutions (Browne et al., 2023).

Interventions to Build a 'Gritty' Organisational Culture

One of the ways by which organisations can build a culture of 'grit' is by acknowledging that interest is not developed and sustained through introspection. Rather, it is by engaging in the process of discovering and sustaining interest through interactions and experiences in the outside world. Employing creative, inductive methods such as polling, group discussions, reflective methods during training and development sessions, employing gamification and organising events with experts in the domain of work/study can accelerate an employee's process of discovery, passion building and subsequent development and deepening of one's knowledge base and skill sets (Duckworth, 2019).

Second, Lyons and Bandura (2023) and Duckworth, Southwick, and Tsay (2019) whilst investigating the antecedents to workplace grit, was that leadership was crucial. An organisation was an extended shadow of its leader, and perhaps the most obvious way to build grit was to 'model' it. If successful and high-status leaders had a deep-rooted passion and love for what they were pursuing, they should make this widely known – wearing passion on the sleeve. Sharing failures and learnings from their experiences was key. Human learning is from observation, and in this light, employees continually observe and emulate the behaviours and attitudes of their role models within the organisational space. Leaders, therefore, must embrace this responsibility and engage in intentional rather than accidental role modelling.

Further, drawing attention to or 'celebrating' when an employee demonstrates their passion and perseveres is crucial. Fostering a culture of appreciation for when grit is exhibited increases the likelihood of the individual to continue to stay committed to their interest and engage in goal-directed behaviours (Caza & Posner, 2019). The 'paradox of grit' in the workplace or in other contexts lies in how the steely determination of individuals is still dependent on the goodwill, support and warmth of loved ones.

Lastly, leaders must foster and engage in effective communication and feedback mechanisms. When followers are given relevant, timely instructions and offered evaluative and corrective information, they are more likely to persevere, learn and progress with tasks of interest (Kuruveettissery et al., 2023). Building a culture of 'grit', in essence, meant investing in the nuances of employee eudaimonic wellbeing.

Cultivating Interest

Attributes associated with employee 'interest' are curiosity, self-awareness, courage and patience. Employees who were 'curious' or continually sought to explore and seek answers were more likely to build on their knowledge, intellectual and creative capacities (Kashdan, Disabato, Goodman, & McKnight, 2018). Residing in a psychologically 'pleasurable state', this characteristic fuelled intrinsic motivation and the urge to deeply engage with an assigned work task. A substantial amount of evidence has reported a positive correlation between job performance, job crafting, quality work relationships and innovation outcomes within the workplace.

In this light, researchers urge employers to administer a curiosity scale to gauge the extent to which individuals within the organisation engage in internal and external explorations. The scale consists of reflective statements such as 'I got so absorbed in learning that I lost track of time', 'I talked to someone who gave me a new idea or changed my mind' and 'I took the initiative to learn more about one of my interests'.

Supporting evidence has established that employee curiosity and subsequently employee interest and grit can, first, be fostered by stakeholders within the organisation by 'modelling' curiosity. For instance, a leader confessing what he/she does not know and taking the initiative to collaborate and learn or explore each other's interests cooperatively can count as a step to modelling and subsequently fostering curiosity, interest and grit (Grazer & Fishman, 2016). Further, 'celebrating' or praising curiosity or 'question asking' ('What a great question! I love the ideas it's sparking!'), showing admiration for incorrect answers ('No, that's not right. Explain to me how you're thinking about this!') and building on curiosity expressed as statements ('I bet that if we use all our pencils we can build a skyscraper!', 'That's cool, let's see how we can do that!').

However, the 'curiosity' construct only fuels 'interest' and subsequent grit when integrated with 'self-awareness'. New tasks, events and experiences are more likely to encourage the employee to persevere when he/she possesses a comprehensive understanding of themselves. The self-reflection process enables the employee to identify discrepancies between current and desired behaviours, according to salient standards (Kashdan et al., 2018).

The Growth Mindset

Carol Susan Dweck, an American psychologist and a professor at Stanford University, in the early 1970s began studying how human beings coped with failure. She found that some individuals were not merely 'coping' but 'relishing' the challenge, striving to learn and building on new skills. This firm belief that one's personal characteristics, such as intelligence, can be developed, was categorised as the 'growth mindset'. A 'fixed mindset', on the contrary, is a 'belief that intelligence is not likely to be changed' (Dweck, 2017). Heslin and Keating (2017) elucidate how the mindset is unidimensional – i.e., that 'an employee's mindset changes along a continuum and is often about responsiveness to challenges'. In this light, another antecedent to 'grit' is the extent to which leadership practices fostered a 'growth mindset', urging employees to continually strive and build on their skill sets (Dweck, 2009).

Employer Interventions

Employing Behavioural Interviewing Questions in the Hiring Process

Drawing from Dweck's mindset propositions, the CME Group, a large-scale financial services company, recommends employing behavioural interviewing, using mindset-focused questions such as 'describe a time when you were confronted with a challenge – how did you work through it to confront your doubts ?'. Although solely employing growth mindset questions on an interview schedule is not recommended, evidence of employees possessing a growth mindset is a quality for employers to seek (Butz, Stratton, Trzebiatowski, & Hillery, 2019).

The 'MCE' (Model–Celebrate–Enable) Model

Leaders can model this mindset by sharing stories of when they failed or were rejected and what they learned from this experience. In addition to modelling the mindset, it was also crucial to celebrate it. Praising the 'process of learning' instead of appreciating the individual for being 'talented', 'gifted' or being a 'natural' was found to positively impact performance, learning and wellbeing (Lyon & Bandura, 2023). Awarding 'innate talent' or 'giftedness' can result in a negative self-fulfilling prophecy amongst the less talented.

On another note, leaders were able to 'enable' this mindset by creating authentic opportunities for learning. Providing employees with meaningful challenges, consistent support and timely and constructive feedback fostered employee engagement and development (Lyon & Bandura, 2023). More specifically, in engaging in an 'experiential learning process', prompts should be included, such as i) what is the objective of the effort, ii) how will the learning and changes be outlined and identified, iii) what specific goals are being identified, iv) what resources will be applied by employee and manager, and v) what positive outcomes are anticipated. This specific process is often referred to as 'approach–action–reflection' intervention and/or experiential learning and is useful for stimulating interest, knowledge and skill acquisition. Moreover, urging employees to engage in reflection can be crucial for enabling a 'growth mindset' and subsequently 'grit'. This reflective process can include focusing on what has been learned and what could have been done differently, subsequently enabling learning and growth (Lyon & Bandura, 2023).

Employing the 'Growth Mindset' Language

An additional method to 'enable' the mindset within organisations is to craft and employ a 'growth mindset' language which fosters the idea that human abilities can be developed (Canning et al., 2020). Dweck (2010) elucidates how exposing employees to conversations and activities in which abilities and skills are perceived as 'malleable' and that which can be honed, is useful. For instance, in attempts to deliberately create a growth mindset culture, Microsoft employed 'Hackathons' (Dweck & Hogan, 2016). Here, when an employee has an idea of business or social merit – a hack – other employees within the organisation who share similar interests can assist in developing a business plan, initiating a prototype and propagating this company-wide. The organisation finances the most creative and viable proposition.

An alternative intervention administered by Microsoft was being supportive of high-risk projects. Organisational analysts within the company believed that appreciating and incentivising risky endeavours inspired and led to the stepping up of new kinds of leaders. Further, organisations must encourage appropriate risk-taking behaviours, acknowledging that engaging in some risks may not be beneficial in the future. Collaboration outside team and organisational boundaries exposes and urges individuals to work and thrive in diversity rather than within departmental units. This does not solely foster passion but also creativity, innovation and inclusion (Duckworth, 2019).

'Talent Talks'

Moreover, the organisation employed 'talent talks' to redefine its talent programme. During the course of this initiative, the CEO and senior leadership meet and review their talent pool, discuss promotions and employee departmental transfers and rotations, and analyse means by which employee skills can be honed and how quality experiences within the organisation can be fostered. By creating opportunities for employees to grow, this intervention allows for early talent identification, unleashes the potential of the employee, and enables the organisation build employee leadership skills and creativity (Dweck & Hogan, 2016).

Urging Employees to Ask Themselves 'Growth Mindset' Questions

Dweck (2007) and Kent Julian, a leadership and employee engagement speaker, discuss how employees, when challenged with a crisis, often focus on the wrong questions, such as 'why is this happening? why did I miss that? why didn't I do this?'. This increases anxiety and deteriorates wellbeing significantly. Instead, reflecting on better questions can make a positive difference. These include 'what does this situation, make possible?', 'what have we learned during this crisis?', 'what is something we are doing currently that we need to do more of?', 'what is still in my control?' and 'what can we do, to make this a new beginning for us ?'. This change in perspective enhances the individual's quality of life and their possibility to succeed.

Recognising a 'False Growth Mindset' and other Misconceptions

Researchers and practitioners caution, however, that before and during the implementation of these interventions, there could be challenges. Some individuals or leaders within organisations claim that they already possess a 'growth mindset' and confuse the theme with being flexible, open-minded and positive. This 'false growth mindset' hinders the initiation and implementation of growth mindset strategies and the progress and development of employees and their leaders (McLaughlin & Cox, 2022). Another misconception that stakeholders within organisations falsely embrace is that the mindset solely emphasises appreciation and rewarding of effort. This is however incorrect – scientists clarify that outcomes do matter. Whilst it is crucial to appreciate effort, it is deep engagement in the process of learning and progress to achieve the bottom line – the outcome – that is fundamental (Dweck & Hogan, 2016).

Lastly, a common error made by leadership teams is embracing a 'growth mindset' in the mission statement, and not drafting and implementing concrete policies that reflect the mindset. This makes the 'mindset' unachievable and unauthentic (Duckworth, 2019). In essence, superiors who embrace the growth mindset, at their core, possess a deep-rooted belief that people can change and that skills and intelligence can always be honed – this fuels both follower passion and perseverance and enables the organisation to evolve for the better.

Fostering 'Purpose' at Work

Analysts appraise the themes 'purposefulness' and 'meaningfulness' as over-lapping, but not synonymous to one another. Purpose, an employee's 'sense of directedness and intentionality', is often instrumental to meaningfulness or significance of work (Kerns, 2013). In this light, Duckworth et al. (2019) and Malin, Reilly, Moran and Quinn (2014) discuss how building a 'sense of purpose' enables employees, teams and the organisation to contribute posi-tively internally and to society, working in resonance with their own interests and strengths. This, Brooks and Winfrey (2023) as reported in Chapter 1, enhanced their own sense of wellbeing. Individuals who are able to work and live more meaningfully and energetically are more resilient to setbacks and able to feel good about what they have accomplished.

Developed by Hackman and Oldham in 1976, the Job Diagnostics Survey, whilst determining the extent to which an employee perceived their job to be 'meaningful, valuable and worthwhile', measured whether job tasks were perceived as 'useless or trivial' or whether work was appraised as meaningful (Steger, Dik, & Duffy, 2012). Deemed as possessing fairly acceptable psychometric properties, researchers claimed that it had strong reliability but that there were relatively poor validity properties of the research instrument (Mostafa & Abed, 2020). Spreitzer (1995) proposed a three-item scale comprising of statements such as 'the work I do is very important to me', 'my job activities are personally very meaningful to me' and the 'work I do is meaningful to me'. This proposition, although found to possess fairly strong psychometric properties for purposes of research, could be criticised for the limited number of items (Spreitzer, 1995; Steger et al., 2012).

A more contemporary tool propagated as being useful for gauging per-ceived 'purpose' is the 'Meaningful Work Inventory' (MWI). The scale is a comprehensive, 64-item questionnaire consisting of eight sub-scales com-prising 'meaningful work', 'intrinsic rewards', 'extrinsic rewards', 'leadership and organisational features', 'supervisory relationships', 'coworker relation-ships', 'organisational support' and 'work demands and balance' (Fairlie, 2011). Possessing high reliability and concurrent validity, the instrument is relatively free of the social desirability bias (Fairlie, 2011).

Other investigators such as Dr. Angela Duckworth, the chief scientist of Character Lab, propose employing a 'pulse check' (Duckworth, 2019). Employees could reflect, ask and assess themselves whether they seek to have a positive impact on the lives of others, they reflect on their life's goals and the kind of person they want to be, and if they pay heed to all activities, how this resonates with what they wish to accomplish in life. Duckworth further recommends checking for what the individual can particularly offer the world whilst taking into consideration their strengths and interests and what the world needs. Lastly, reflecting on what really matters to the individual and why this matters counts as one of the crucial first steps to the assessment of 'purpose' (Duckworth, 2019).

Employer Interventions

Researchers propose the implementation of the following purpose-building interventions that subsequently foster grit and consequential wellbeing within workplaces:

The 'MCE' Approach

Duckworth's (2023) advice is to employ the 'model–celebrate–enable' approach, Employers model purpose when engaging in activities connecting to their own purpose. For instance, participating as a volunteer, creating art, or 'talking about what their goals are' and why they are of significance has been evidenced to enhance a sense of purpose amongst young people. Further, recognising and appreciating efforts and actions that serve a 'larger purpose' and pointing out connections between activities and long-term goals count as some of the many activities to celebrate and further hone employee purpose.

Lastly, encouraging freshers/interns or junior colleagues to voice their values, the contribution they wish to make to society and the kind of person they wish to be can further initiate and enable a sense of 'meaningfulness' at work. Employers may further reaffirm this by noticing sparks of interest and curiosity, guiding employees towards opportunities that engage them in meaningful and productive ways. This consequentially enables individuals, organisations and societies to emerge as more resilient and flourish in their given capacities.

The SPIRE and CARMA Models to Employee Purpose-Building

Steger et al. (2012) organised the predictors in the literature to propose two models – the SPIRE and CARMA models – to foster purpose at work.

The former model offered specific pathways for employees to adhere to for enhancing their perceived 'sense of purpose' at work. The author elucidates the significance of employees recognising their own 'strengths' and drawing from these characteristics to execute their responsibilities at work – irrespective of whether this required the individual to 'go above and beyond' their basic work responsibilities (Steger et al., 2012). Moreover, 'personalisation'

or 'being more of oneself at work', the researcher claims, will prove beneficial. Working in resonance with one's values, and embracing and demonstrating accountability for the work and the organisation is crucial. Integrating
the motivation of and execution of work to other elements of life, working
in ways that bring meaning to one's life further fosters a perceived sense of
'purpose'. Further, the 'resonance' between the employee's daily activities
at work and their life's personal mission can be reaffirmed by learning more
about their organisation's vision, mission, values and goals. Finally, 'expanding' or 'seeking ways in which work can be grown to benefit some "greater
good" or expanding concerns to embrace broader interests, beyond yourself'
can enable and further strengthen the employee's sense of 'meaningfulness'
at work (Jacob & Steger, 2021; Steger et al., 2012).

The CARMA model for employee purpose offers pathways and advice for
employers and business leaders to foster a sense of 'purpose' amongst their
employees. Whilst affirming the significance of meaningful work, the authors
state how employers must possess 'clarity' (a clearly defined vision, mission and goal must be communicated across all levels of the organisation),
'authenticity' ('phoney purpose and exploitation kill meaning' – leaders must
coach with transparency), 'respect', 'mattering' (communicating how the
employee adds value to the organisation) and 'autonomy' (offering followers opportunities for self-expression, self-direction, trial and error, innovation
and idea exchanges). The SPIRE and CARMA models must be implemented
together for effective purpose-building and consequential employee wellbeing (Jacob & Steger, 2021).

Mindful Engagement in Pro-Social/Helpful Behaviours

Allan, Duffy and Collisson (2018) aimed to examine potential mechanisms
that enhance an individual's sense of meaningfulness with 284 participants
who used a daily diary based on an experimental methodology. Findings
from the control group (which received no intervention) and the experimental
group of individuals (who were instructed to help other individuals during
the course of their day and then attempt the meaningfulness at work survey)
firmly established the significance of engaging in pro-social/helpful behav-
iours/tasks for further fostering employee 'meaningfulness at work'.

Additionally, the employee simply reflecting or having casual conversations on how their pro-social/helpful behaviours and tasks contributed to their
life or to the 'greater good', in general, was also deemed as positively corre-
lating with employees sense of purpose (Allan et al., 2018). Critics argue that
access to resources (financial, social or informational) moderated the extent to
which pro-social behaviours influenced 'meaningfulness' at work. This finding has noteworthy implications for employers and other organisational stakeholders (Klein, 2017).

'Datification'

Coined as 'the process of taking an activity, event or characteristic, codifying it and turning it into data', datification allows employers to use the collected data to analyse employee productivity and performance (Stein et al., 2019). Based on what has been codified, 'datification work', or the process of employees 'manually entering data about their work', can significantly change job roles, knowledge practices and labour processes of professional practice (Fenwick & Edwards, 2016). A highly objective, standardised and reductionist employee accountability system, datification work is imperative to initiate the process of 'knowing thyself'. The examination of self makes positive transformations feasible (Edwards et al., 2016).

The 'Grit' Lab

In 2020, Dr. Angela Duckworth, initiated the 'grit lab' at the University of Pennsylvania in the United States, giving learners an opportunity to learn about cutting-edge research within the domain of study. If implemented within the workplace, the objectives of the 'grit lab' would be two-fold: i) equipping employees and leaders with generalisable knowledge, including cutting-edge scientific discoveries on the science of passion and perseverance, ii) enabling employees to reflect on their own experiences and apply scientific insights to their life – work life, more specifically. In addition to developing the intellect, the lab could potentially prove to significantly contribute to individual, organisational and societal wellness, productivity and performance, service and citizenship (Berger, 2020).

In order to foster employee passion and perseverance for long-term goals, similar to within the educational domains of study and research at the University of Pennsylvania, organisational psychologists could build on three 'pillars' within the 'passion' centre (or the first phase of the course) and the 'perseverance' centre (or the second phase of the course) of the grit lab – an interactive session, a lecture and a conversation with a person of 'grit' (Berger, 2020).

Making a genuine investment in employee self-exploration, self-discovery and skill building and development, the interactive sessions could consider

i) Explaining what 'passion' is and encouraging employees to try and experiment with different tasks/assignments at work, and reflect on what they are deeply interested in or passionate about. It is crucial to note that 'passion', once recognised, must not be followed at once – rather 'fostered' (Duckworth, 2019; Pollack, J. M., Ho, V. T., O'Boyle, E. H., & Kirkman, B. L., 2020). Interests must be triggered repeatedly and patiently – 'the development of interests take time'.

ii) Elucidating what constitutes 'purpose' and its significance to employee personal and professional wellbeing. Reflecting, recognising and further strengthening employee reasons for why their 'interest' or 'passion' is worth pursuing is crucial. Acknowledging its positive contribution to the wellbeing of the individual, the wellbeing of the organisation and the wider society, perceiving that 'purpose' will enable the employee to maintain 'grit' in the face of challenges – given that 'purpose' is a remendously powerful source of motivation (Duckworth, 2019).

iii) Urging employees to draft a professional goal hierarchy, with specific and intentional goals that reflect their passion, fosters perseverance by reflecting on how their hierarchy aligns/resonates with the employee's team and organisation's goals (Grant, 2020).

iv) Advocating for self-administration and assessment of employee levels of grit. Acknowledging the drawbacks of the self-report measure, 'grit' could be monitored, and specific measures could be taken to foster this.

v) Encouraging employees to maintain a journal for reflection and creating a presentation to document what they learned about grit and how this benefitted their workplace performance, relationships and wellbeing (Berger, 2020).

vi) When faced with uncertain and challenging times such as the pandemic, initiatives such as the 'grit lab', in addition to encouraging employees to explore their interests and values, could propagate the necessity to think about social problems, psychological flexibility, challenges and possible interventions to maintain levels of grit, in the face of uncertainty.

5.5 The IKEA Effect

The 'IKEA' effect is named in honour of Swedish furniture manufacturer and retailer IKEA, which sells furniture that requires assembly. The idea behind the phenomenon is that 'by building things themselves, people control and shape their environments, thereby demonstrating their competence to themselves and others' (Mochon, Norton, & Ariely, 2012). There was 'an increase in the valuation of self-made products' (Ashtiani, Rieger, & Stutz, 2021).

Customers at IKEA were found to fall in love with the products they helped create, i.e. they felt a sense of ownership and pride, loved the fruit of their labour and experienced a stronger emotional attachment to the item (Mochon et al., 2012). This phenomenon was similarly observed by other organisations such as Lego, which urged people to build their creations using Lego bricks. Whilst tapping into their consumer's desire to create something themselves, the company built a strong brand that is synonymous with 'creativity, fun and innovation' (Spinney, 2011).

The pandemic witnessed significant changes in the ways in which people work, the nature of work and workplace relationships. Hybrid and flexible working hours and work-from-home practices emerged as the 'new norm'. Drawing from studies such as Ashtiani et al. (2021), Mochon et al. (2012) and Yun, Zhao, Kim and Sadoi (2022), this section makes the following recommendations in order to foster employee sense of accomplishment, satisfaction, loyalty and wellbeing:

i)   Given the surge in e-trade during and after the pandemic, offering employees an opportunity to customise and build on the virtual presence of the brand, encouraging employee voice, insights and feedback to further develop and propagate e-resources for the same, accounts for one of the strategies to build on the IKEA effect.

ii) Encouraging people to informationally, socially and financially invest in the building, integration and utilisation of video conferencing platforms (given the restrictions/limitations with face-to-face meetings, events and conferences). Employees are more likely to stay invested in e-recruitment, e-training and development and virtual networking practices when they have initiated the building of the platform or the proposition of the event (Yun et al., 2022).

iii) An increase in the use of technology and the embracing of remote work witnessed an increasing prevalence of cyber security threats and challenges. In this light, collectively investing in the building and sharing of knowledge and resources to drive and navigate through investments with minimum risk and protect one another's personal and intellectual property counted as an additional crucial initiative (Mochon et al., 2012).

iv) Creating opportunities for employees to invest time and money, social and intellectual resources in 'do-it-yourself' e-projects, e-instructional videos and e-workshops to enable the organisation to cope effectively with uncertain and challenging times (Ashtiani et al., 2021; Spinney, 2011).

5.6 Employing Artificial Intelligence and Gamification

'Gamification' or 'the application of game design principles to change behaviour in non-gaming contexts', is a tool that, if crafted and implemented properly, can increase employee engagement (Robson, Plangger, Kietzmann, McCarthy, & Pitt, 2016).

Research evidence describes 'player orientation' or 'the understanding of whether the participating employee is predominantly oriented themselves or with others' to be crucial for the designing, assessment and implementation of gamification methodologies administered to enhance levels of engagement and subsequent levels of wellbeing. In this light, they distinguish between slayers, strivers, scholars and socialities. Whilst strivers are those who participate in the game to achieve personal development and a 'personal best score', 'slayers' are those who play in order to be better than others, where 'relative standing' or winning is of significance. The typology further details scholars, 'who play in order to learn about the game'; here, importance is placed on the learning and comprehending of the gamified experience in itself. 'Socialities', on the other hand, are those who play in order to network, collaborate or bond. Understanding, empathising with and learning about other individuals is deemed imperative (Robson et al., 2016).

'Freshdesk' – A Helpdesk Software

Studies in the literature draw attention to 'Freshdesk', 'a helpdesk software program for customer support centres' that has the objective of enhancing employee productivity and customer satisfaction. By gamifying the everyday tasks of customer service employees, 'Freshdesk' solutions involve transforming customer inquiries (for instance, telephone queries and comments posted to social media accounts) into virtual tickets. These are then randomly assigned to players (customer service employees). Fostering a real-time, competitive environment, employing gamification in stressful and notorious call centre contexts can significantly increase fun, enthusiasm and excitement at work.

Further, this gamification methodology has been evidenced to appeal to and enhance levels of engagement, amongst all player types (employees). 'The first call resolution' trophy (for resolving a customer query on the first try), the 'customer casanova' quest (aiming at employees resolving ten tickets in a week and receiving a customer rating of 'awesome') and the 'fast resolution' badge (for players with particularly speedy responses to customers) particularly aim to invest and engage strivers and slayers. Employee players who acquire a certain number of points are moved and are appraised – ranging from a low position of a 'support newbie' to that of a 'support guru' (Robson et al., 2016). The earning of points, badges and trophies offers employees opportunities to acquire social status visible to superiors and other employees, enhancing socialisation, competitiveness and cooperativeness. This positively transforms an employee's attitude towards their work, addressing the nuances of employee eudaimonic wellbeing whilst resonating with the objectives of the organisation (i.e. addressing customer service inquiries effectively and efficiently).

Critics argue that although 'gamification' methodologies seem trendy, this methodology is not always easy and does not always help achieve the desired outcomes. Highly reputed and successful organisations, for instance, employed gamification methodologies, allowing users to win badges for reading the news. This initiative failed; employees did not want to share the kind of news they searched for with others. Seen as an example of poor gamification setup mechanics, this method resulted in undesirable dynamics and unwelcome emotions (Hammedi, Leclercq, Poncin & Alkire, 2021).

5.7 Enhancing Employee Experience

Referring to a 'set of psycho-cognitive sentiments about the experiential benefits of employment', the employee experience theme has recently been propagated as of significance to numerous stakeholders within many industries. Embracing a variety of factors, the theme concerns how employees build purpose at work and how they perceive, interact and respond to the organisational culture during the course of their employment (Patil & Gopalakrishnan, 2020).

Employer Interventions

Employing Virtual HR Assistants/Chatbots

Research has elucidated how artificial intelligence (AI) tools and methods are employed to foster employee experience and subsequently levels of employee engagement, satisfaction and organisational reputation (Patil & Gopalakrishnan, 2020). Facilitating the automation of various repetitive tasks within human resources, researchers propagate the use of 'virtual HR assistants/chatbots' for employee relations and the communication of policies and practices, specifically.

Designed to further assist in the drafting of employment letters, this concept saves time and manpower costs, enabling the organisation to redirect its resources and time to other domains of work. Supporting evidence elucidates how users of virtual HR assistants/chatbots experience both positive (contentment and happiness) and negative (anxiety) emotions. However, predominantly, 'connection emotions' such as a sense of belongingness and social connection, 'empathy, compassion, forgiveness, fairness and kindness' were reported by employees (Gkinko & Elbanna, 2022). Despite occasional frustrations and annoyance with incorrect answers, 'contentment' emotions or a sense of convenience and cognitive ease and 'amusement emotions – excitement, anticipation and playfulness were relatively more frequently reported' (Gkinko & Elbanna, 2022).

Casillo, Colace, De Santo, Lombardi and Santaniello (2021), additionally, suggest employing virtual coach bots for leaders and managers to assist them in having difficult conversations with their employees. Criticised for being unable to replace human coaching sessions, these bots enable the stakeholders to prepare for discussions involving complex situations. Further, they have proven to be of significance in meeting employee training and development needs – fostering the building of individual employee learning pathways and subsequently monitoring learning and progression (Mantravadi, Jansson, & Møller, 2020).

Evidence from the literature further advises how the use of 'personalised AI-based career development tools' such as AI-based developmental portals can suggest vacancies to employees that are suitable to their profiles and can recommend training sessions on the basis of the employee's personal development needs (Westman, Kauttonen, Klemetti, Korhonen, Manninen, Mononen, & Paananen, 2021).

5.8 Summary

This chapter highlighted how pandemic-induced stressors and anxieties contributed to time pressures at work, significantly heightening employee presenteeism tendencies. Whilst recommending the 'Wellbeing Assessment for Productivity' scale for assessing employee presenteeism, researchers recommend that employers encourage their employees to take time off when ill. Researchers established cognitive behavioural therapeutic interventions for insomnia and sleep hygiene education, to address employee presenteeism. When tackling challenges with employee quiet quitting behaviours and leavism, the literature particularly appraised employer-employee value alignment.

Further, investing in employee proactivity, potentially employing the 'MCE' approach, was deemed as beneficial to enhancing levels of employee engagement and consequentially wellbeing. It was, however, crucial to place significance on the role of employer feedback, which moderated employee proactivity and wellbeing outcomes.

The chapter moved on to elucidate the difference between employee grit, 'conscientiousness' and 'need for achievement'. Whilst critically appraising the themes and the methodologies by which 'employee grit' can be measured, the author makes recommendations for employers to assess candidates for 'grit' when hiring. Employing the 'MCE' approach to fostering grit within workplaces could additionally prove to benefit EW and business outcomes. The chapter explored the 'growth mindset', 'employee purpose' and 'employee hope' themes within the workplace literature and closes by suggesting that researchers further investigate the significance and the possible application of grit within collectivistic contexts.

Additionally, the design and implementation of an evidence-based 'grit lab' within organisations is recommended; this is expected to further contribute to research, and employee training and development in order to sustain employee engagement and foster employee wellness within contemporary workplaces.

5.9 Further Readings

Galanis, P., Katsiroumpa, A., Vraka, I., Siskou, O., Konstantakopoulou, O., Katsoulas, T., & Kaitelidou, D. (2023). The influence of job burnout on quiet quitting among nurses: The mediating effect of job satisfaction. https://doi.org/10.21203/rs.3.rs -3128881/v1

McBain, R. (2007). The practice of engagement: Research into current employee engagement practice. *Strategic HR Review*, 6(6), 16–19.

Morrison-Beedy, D. (2022). Are we addressing "quiet quitting" in faculty, staff, and students in academic settings?. *Building Healthy Academic Communities Journal*, 6(2), 7–8.

Peterson, S. J., & Byron, K. (2008). Exploring the role of hope in job performance: Results from four studies. *Journal of Organizational Behavior: The International*

Journal of Industrial, Occupational and Organizational Psychology and Behavior, 29(6), 785–803.

Richards, J., Pustelnikovaite, T., Ellis, V., & Canduela, J. (2020). The normalisation of overwork: A scoping study of Leavism. Paper presented at International Labour Process Conference, Newcastle.

5.10 Suggested Websites

Dhingra, N., Samo, A., Schaninger, B., & Schrimper, M. (2020). Help your employees find purpose or watch them leave. *Harvard Business Review*. Available at: https://www.mckinsey.com/capabilities/people-and-organizational-performance/our-insights/help-your-employees-find-purpose-or-watch-them-leave#/ Accessed on: 7 November 2023

Duckworth, A. L., & Lee, T. H. (2018). Organisational grit. *Harvard Business Review*. Available at: https://hbr.org/2018/09/organizational-grit Accessed on: 7 November 2023

Dweck, C. S. (2007). *Mindset: The New Psychology of Success*. USA: Ballantine Books.

Dweck, C. S. (2016). What having a growth mindset actually means. *Harvard Business Review*. Available at: https://hbr.org/2016/01/what-having-a-growth-mindset-actually-means Accessed on: 7 November 2023

Harvard Business Review (2023). Does gamified training get results ? Available at: https://hbr.org/2023/03/does-gamified-training-get-results Accessed on: 7 November 2023

Robson, K., Plangger, K., Keitzmann, J. H., McCarthy, I., & Pitt, L. (2016). Game on: Engaging customers and employees through gamification. *Harvard Business Review*, Business Horizons. Available at: https://store.hbr.org/product/game-on-engaging-customers-and-employees-through-gamification/BH714 Accessed on: 7 November 2023

5.11 Reflective Questions – for Learners

From your reading and research,

1. What is the 'IKEA' effect? How can this theme prove to be beneficial to employers to foster employee engagement?
2. Elaborate on four key interventions that could be employed to build on an employee's growth mindset. What challenges might employers be faced with when choosing to implement this, and how can the challenge be possibly addressed?
3. What are the potential benefits and challenges of employing 'gamification' techniques to enhance employee experience, engagement and subsequent wellbeing within workplaces?

5.12 Reflective Questions – for Researchers/Practitioners

1. Think about a time when you found yourself 'quiet quitting' on your job. What factors, do you believe contributed to this?
2. Think about your organisation's policies, practices and systems. In your opinion, do any of these promote leavism? If you were a member of the leadership and management team, what specific steps would you take to make amends?
3. Design your professional goal hierarchy, ensuring your lower-level goals align/resonate with your mid- and higher-level goals.
4. Design and conduct a study to test the hypothesis that there is a significant positive correlation between employee burnout and employee quiet quitting/presenteeism.
5. Conduct an EBSCOhost/Psychinfo search covering the literature published in the past couple of years using the terms 'employee presenteeism', 'quiet quitting', 'employee burnout' and 'employee wellbeing', individually or in combination. Identify a study that resonates with your interests and that is feasible to replicate and extend. Conduct the replication.

References

Akinloye, A. (2022). *Talent Management Agenda in a Post Covid-19 World: Managing Careers and Career Transitions: Work, Workforce & Workplace*. Author House.

Allan, B. A., Duffy, R. D., & Collisson, B. (2018). Helping others increases meaningful work: Evidence from three experiments. *Journal of Counseling Psychology, 65*(2), 155.

Ammendolia, C., Côté, P., Cancelliere, C., Cassidy, J. D., Hartvigsen, J., Boyle, E., ... & Amick, B. (2016). Healthy and productive workers: using intervention mapping to design a workplace health promotion and wellness program to improve presenteeism. *BMC Public Health, 16*, 1–18.

Ashford, S. J., & Grant, A. M. (2008). The dynamics of proactivity at work. *Research in Organisational Behaviour, 28*(1), 3–34.

Ashtiani, A. Z., Rieger, M. O., & Stutz, D. (2021). Nudging against panic selling: Making use of the IKEA effect. *Journal of Behavioral and Experimental Finance, 30*, 100502.

Aydin, E., & Azizoğlu, O. (2022). A new term for an existing concept: Quiet quitting—a self-determination perspective. In *International Congress on Critical Debates in Social Sciences* (pp. 285–295).

Berger, M. W. (2020). A lesson in grit from Angela Duckworth. Available at: https://penntoday.upenn.edu/news/lesson-grit-angela-duckworth Accessed on: 23 September 2023.

Browne, B., Fleming, D., Gorksi, N., & Tham, L. (2023). How to assess for grit. Available at: https://business.linkedin.com/talent-solutions/resources/interviewing -talent/how-to-assess-skills/grit#speakers Accessed on: 19 November 2023.

Brooks, A. C. & Winfrey, O. (2023). *Build the Life You Want*. USA: Random House.

Butz, N. T., Stratton, R., Trzebiatowski, M. E., & Hillery, T. P. (2019). Inside the hiring process: How managers assess employability based on grit, the big five, and other factors. *International Journal of Business Environment*, 10(4), 306–328.

Caldwell, C., & Mahand, T. (2023). Quiet quitting: Causes and opportunities. *Business Management and Research*, 12(1), 9–19.

Cangiano, F., & Parker, S. K. (2015). Proactivity for mental health and well-being. *The Wiley Blackwell Handbook of the Psychology of Occupational Safety and Workplace Health*, 1, 228–250.

Canning, E. A., Murphy, M. C., Emerson, K. T., Chatman, J. A., Dweck, C. S., & Kray, L. J. (2020). Cultures of genius at work: Organizational mindsets predict cultural norms, trust, and commitment. *Personality and Social Psychology Bulletin*, 46(4), 626–642.

Casillo, M., Colace, F., De Santo, M., Lombardi, M., & Santaniello, D. (2021). A chatbot for training employees in industry 4.0. In A. Visvizi, M. D. Lytras and N. R. Aljohani (Eds.), *Research and Innovation Forum 2020: Disruptive Technologies in Times of Change* (pp. 397–409). Cham: Springer International Publishing.

Caza, A. & Posner, B. Z. (2019). How and when does grit influence leaders' behavior? *Leadership & Organization Development Journal*, 40(1), 124–134.

Chen, G., Datu, J. A. D., & Yuen, M. (2016). Exploring determination for long term goals in a collectivistic context: A qualitative study. *Current Psychology*, 37, 263–271.

CIPD (2020). Managing the challenge of workforce presenteeism in the COVID 19 crisis. Available at: www.cipd.org, Accessed on: 18 July 2024.

Cooper, C. L., & Dewe, P. (2008). Well-being—Absenteeism, presenteeism, costs and challenges. *Occupational Medicine*, 58(8), 522–524.

Cooper, C. L., & Lu, L. (2019). Excessive availability for work: Good or bad? Charting underlying motivations and searching for game-changers. *Human Resource Management Review*, 29(4), 100682.

Datu, J. A. D. (2017). Sense of relatedness is linked to higher grit in a collectivistic setting. *Personality and Individual Differences*, 105, 135–138.

Duckworth, A. L. (2019). *Grit: Why Passion and Persistence Are the Secrets to Success*. UK: Penguin Random House.

Duckworth, A. L., Southwick, D. A. & Tsay, C.J. (2019). Grit at work. *Research in Organizational Behavior*, 39, 100–126.

Duckworth, A. L., Peterson, C., Matthews, M. D., & Kelly, D. R. (2007). Grit: Perseverance and passion for long-term goals. *Journal of Personality and Social Psychology*, 92(6), 1087.

Duckworth, A. L., & Quinn, P. D. (2009). Development and validation of the short grit scale (GRIT–S). *Journal of Personality Assessment*, 91(2), 166–174.

Duckworth, A. (2019). *Grit: Why passion and persistence are the secrets to success*. United Kingdom: Penguin Random House.

Duckworth, A. (2023). Purpose: Commitment to making a meaningful contribution to the world. Available at: www.character lab.org. Accessed on: 28 May 2024.

Dweck, C. S. (2010). Even geniuses work hard. *Educational Leadership*, 68(1), 16–20.

Dweck, C. S., & Hogan, K. (2016). How Microsoft uses a growth mindset to develop leaders. *Harvard Business Review*, Available at: www.hbr.org. Last Accessed on: 28 May 2024.

Dweck, C. (2017). *Mindset: Changing the Way You Think to Fulfil Your Potential.* London: Robinson.

Edwards, R. & Fenwick, T. (2016). Exploring the impact of digital technologies on professional responsibilities and education. *European Educational Research Journal, 15*(1), 117–131.

Fairlie, P. (2011). Meaningful work, employee engagement, and other key employee outcomes: Implications for human resource development. *Advances in Developing Human Resources, 13*(4), 508–525.

Ferris, G. R., Jordan, S. L., Hochwarter, W. A., & Wright, T. A. (2019). Toward a work motivation conceptualization of grit in organizations. *Group and Organization Management, 44*(2), 320–360.

Formica, S., & Sfodera, F. (2022). The Great Resignation and Quiet Quitting paradigm shifts: An overview of current situation and future research directions. *Journal of Hospitality Marketing and Management, 31*(8), 899–907.

Galanis, P., Katsiroumpa, A., Vraka, I., Siskou, O., Konstantakopoulou, O., Moisoglou, I., ... Kaitelidou, D. (2023). The "Quiet Quitting" Scale: Development and Initial Validation. *AIMS Public Health, 10*(4), 828–848.

Gkinko, L., & Elbanna, A. (2022). Hope, tolerance and empathy: Employees' emotions when using an AI-enabled chatbot in a digitalised workplace. *Information Technology and People, 35*(6), 1714–1743.

Grant, A. M. (2020). An integrated model of goal-focused coaching: an evidence-based framework for teaching and practice. *Coaching Researched: A Coaching Psychology Reader,* 115–139.

Grazer, B., & Fishman, C. (2016). *A Curious Mind: The Secret to a Bigger Life.* New York: Simon and Schuster.

Grant, A. (2023). Proactivity: Taking initiative. Available at: https://characterlab.org/playbooks/proactivity/. Accessed on: 28 May 2024.

Hackman, J. R., & Oldham, G. R. (1976). Motivation through the design of work: Test of a theory. *Organizational Behavior and Human Performance, 16*(2), 250–279.

Hammedi, W., Leclercq, T., Poncin, I., & Alkire, L. (2021). Uncovering the dark side of gamification at work: Impacts on engagement and well-being. *Journal of Business Research, 122,* 256–269.

Heslin, P. A., & Keating, L. A. (2017). In learning mode? The role of mindsets in derailing and enabling experiential leadership development. *The Leadership Quarterly, 28*(3), 367–384.

Ho, T. C., Ng, S. M., Teo, P. C., & Hee, O. C. (2022). Presenteeism in the workplace and the effect on employees' well-being. *International Journal of Academic Research in Business and Social Sciences, 12*(6), 932–943.

Jackson, S. (2020). Present and correct? *Occupational Health & Wellbeing, 72*(3), 20–23.

Jacob, Y., & Steger, M. F. (2021). Meaning-centred coaching in the workplace. In D. W. A. Smith, I. Boniwell, & S. Green (Eds.), *Positive Psychology Coaching in the Workplace* (pp. 555–574). Springer Nature Switzerland AG. https://doi-org.biblioproxy.uqtr.ca/10.1007/978-3-030-79952-6_29.

Kashdan, T. B., Disabato, D., Goodman, F., & McKnight, P. (2018). Curiosity Has Comprehensive Benefits in the Workplace: Developing and Validating the

Multidimensional Work Related Curiosity Scale in United States and German Employees. *Personality and Individual Differences, 155*(1), 109–717.

Kerns, C. D. (2013). Clarity of purpose and meaningfulness at work: Key leadership practices. *International Leadership Journal, 5*(1), 27–44.

Kinman, G. (2019). Sickness presenteeism at work: Prevalence, costs and management. *British Medical Bulletin, 129*(1), 69–78.

Kuruveettissery, S., Gupta, S., & Rajan, S. K. (2023). Development and psychometric validation of the three dimensional grit scale. *Current Psychology, 42*(7), 5280–5289.

Lyons, P., & Bandura, R. (2023). Reciprocal action learning: Manager and employee development. *Journal of Workplace Learning, 35*(4), 371–385.

Malin, H., Reilly, T. S., Quinn, B., & Moran, S. (2014). Adolescent purpose development: Exploring empathy, discovering roles, shifting priorities, and creating pathways. *Journal of Research on Adolescence, 24*(1), 186–199.

Mantravadi, S., Jansson, A. D., & Møller, C. (2020). User-friendly mes interfaces: Recommendations for an ai-based chatbot assistance in industry 4.0 shop floors. In ACIIDS, *Asian Conference on Intelligent Information and Database Systems* (pp. 189–201). Cham: Springer International Publishing.

McLaughlin, M., & Cox, E. (2022). Challenging mindsets. In *Braver Leaders in Action: Personal and Professional Development for Principled Leadership* (pp. 51–66). Emerald Publishing Limited.

Mochon, D., Norton, M. I., & Ariely, D. (2012). Bolstering and restoring feelings of competence via the IKEA effect. *International Journal of Research in Marketing, 29*(4), 363–369.

Mostafa, A. M. S., & Abed El-Motalib, E. A. (2020). Ethical leadership, work meaningfulness, and work engagement in the public sector. *Review of Public Personnel Administration, 40*(1), 112–131.

Patil, R., & Gopalakrishnan, G. (2020). A study on employee experience with respect to remote working during the Covid 19-pandemic. *Journal of Critical Reviews, 7*(11), 3910–3918.

Pendell, R. & Wigert, B. (2022, June 14). The World's $7.8 trillion workplace problem. *Gallup Workplace.* Available at: The World's $7.8 Trillion Workplace Problem (gallup.com) Accessed on: 3 November 2022.

Pevec, N. (2023). The concept of identifying factors of quiet quitting in organizations: An integrative literature review. *Challenges of the Future, 2*, 128–147.

Prochaska, J. O., Evers, K. E., Johnson, J. L., Castle, P. H., Prochaska, J. M., Sears, L. E., ... Pope, J. E. (2011). The well-being assessment for productivity: A well-being approach to presenteeism. *Journal of Occupational and Environmental Medicine*, 735–742.

Rioux, S. M., & Penner, L. A. (2001). The causes of organisational citizenship behaviours: A motivational analysis. *Journal of Applied Psychology, 86*, 1306–1314.

Robson, K., Plangger, K., Kietzmann, J. H., McCarthy, I., & Pitt, L. (2016). Game on: Engaging customers and employees through gamification. *Business Horizons, 59*(1), 29–36.

Serenko, A. (2023). The human capital management perspective on quiet quitting: Recommendations for employees, managers, and national policymakers. *Journal of Knowledge Management, 3270,* 1367.

Shah, D., & Parekh, M. (2023). Understanding work-life balance: an analysis of quiet quitting and age dynamics using deep learning. *International Research Journal of Engineering Technology, 1*(06), 1230–1235.

Singh, J., & Chopra, V. G. (2016). Relationship among workplace spirituality, work engagement and grit. *IOSR Journal of Business and Management, 18*(11), 21–27.

Spinney, L. (2011). The secret of IKEA's success: We do the hard work. *New Scientist, 212*(2844), 80–81.

Spreitzer, G. M. (1995). Psychological empowerment in the workplace: Dimensions, measurement, and validation. *Academy of Management Journal, 38*(5), 1442–1465.

Steger, M. F., Dik, B. J., & Duffy, R. D. (2012). Measuring meaningful work: The work and meaning inventory (WAMI). *Journal of Career Assessment, 20*(3), 322–337.

Stein, M. K., Wagner, E. L., Tierney, P., Newell, S., & Galliers, R. D. (2019). Datification and the pursuit of meaningfulness in work. *Journal of Management Studies, 56*(3), 685–717.

Takano, Y., Iwano, S., Aoki, S., Nakano, N., & Sakano, Y. (2021). A systematic review of the effect of sleep interventions on presenteeism. *BioPsychoSocial Medicine, 15*(1), 1–10.

Ting, L. C., & Datu, J. A. D. (2020). Triarchic model of grit dimensions as predictors of career outcomes. *The Career Development Quarterly, 68*(4), 348-360.

Westman, S., Kauttonen, J., Klemetti, A., Korhonen, N., Manninen, M., Mononen, A., ... Paananen, H. (2021). Artificial intelligence for career guidance--Current requirements and prospects for the future. *IAFOR Journal of Education, 9*(4), 43–62.

Yun, J. J., Zhao, X., Kim, S. A., & Sadoi, Y. (2022). Open innovation dynamics of furniture design and function: The difference between IKEA and Nitori. *Science, Technology and Society, 27*(2), 172–190.

Chapter 6

Managing High-Intensity Workplaces

6.1 Employee Fatigue

A state of reduced physiological and psychological capacity marked by a sense of weariness, tiredness and lack of energy', employee fatigue is commonly associated with 'sleep loss or extended wakefulness, a disrupted circadian rhythm or an increased workload' (Bonetti, Campbell, & Lock, 2018). Distinguishing between acute, cumulative and circadian fatigue, Bonetti et al. (2018) define 'acute' fatigue as resulting from an extended period of wakefulness for more than 16 hours. On the other hand, 'cumulative' fatigue, also known as 'sleep debt', results from an accumulation of sub-optimal sleep times, which may be for days, weeks or months. 'Circadian' fatigue, also referred to as 'chrono-disruption' occurs as 'a consequence of shifting the sleep/wake cycle, either due to changes in working hours or following transmeridian travel' (Van Dongen, Maislin, Mullington & Dinges, 2003).

Individuals who expose themselves to light, during the biological night, disrupt the functioning of sleep-promoting hormones. Employees who expose themselves to artificial, indoor lighting, television, mobiles or laptops for prolonged periods of time suppress 'melatonin', which is detrimental to employee quality of sleep, thereby heightening levels of employee fatigue (Carriedo-Diez, Tosoratto-Venturi, Cantón-Manzano-Berghe, Sanz-Valero, 2022).

The occupational performance of fatigued individuals is highly likely to be impaired by slower reaction times, and ineffective decision-making, problem-solving, psychomotor skills, processing speed, memory and vigilance. Chronically fatigued employees are 62% more likely to cause or experience workplace accidents; evidence demonstrates how they have tendencies to overestimate their performances and create the potential for serious workplace harm. Further, higher probabilities of reporting dissatisfaction and low morale have been reported. This meant a poor tolerance to the organisation's environmental stressors, and slower career progression with relatively higher rates of early resignation and retirement (Coetzee, Maree & Smit, 2019). In addition to the 'years of available service lost', the training and financial investments made in the employee are wasted.

DOI: 10.4324/9781032705125-6

Employee Fatigue in the Aviation and Healthcare Industries

Research studies from the literature, whilst particularly analysing employee fatigue within safety-critical industries such as aviation and medicine, describe how 'long-haul international flights' and 'acute admission days' demand prolonged periods of employee wakefulness. Evidence from the US aviation context states that more than 25% of the most severe workplace accidents were caused by chronically fatigued individuals. Within the healthcare industry, employee fatigue was associated with a heightened risk of significant medical errors, adverse events and attentional failures (Garrubba & Joseph, 2019). Fatigued emergency doctors are known to have twice the risk of medical error, and three times the risk of safety-compromising behaviour whilst on shift, compared with non-fatigued doctors. Reducing doctor fatigue could address the current 850,000 adverse events and 12,000 associated deaths a year reported by the NHS (Bonetti et al., 2018).

Other employee fatigue physiological and psychological outcomes (such as increasing prevalence of heightened employee anxiety and depression, gastrointestinal, neurological and chronic pain sequelae) can lead to restrictions on driving, flying and operating heavy machinery (Ozel & Hacioglu, 2021).

Employee Fatigue Risk Mitigation Interventions

Investigators within the domains of workplace psychology propose a number of interventions for better employee fatigue risk forecasting and mitigation. Investing informationally, financially and socially in training line managers, propagating the significance of addressing employee fatigue and evaluating specific strategies to combat this within the workplace are imperative. (Caldwell, Caldwell & Lieberman, 2019).

In this light, some organisations invest in occupational health psychologists to assist with addressing factors attributable to employee fatigue, via symptom reporting and monitoring activities. Noting employee sleep histories and employing medical fitness checklists alongside employee social history is recommended. Employers may implement temporary employment restrictions until sleep deprivation has been minimised. Occupational psychologists recognised fatigued employees with medical conditions during the course of this review activity and flagged them as being at risk of physical/mental health deterioration and potentially to be considered for redeployment – away from work with chrono-disruption (Burgess, Brough, Biggs & Hawkes, 2020). Additionally, employees may be advised to enrol themselves at a local sleep clinic, an option that has been relatively underutilised and not recommended very often to combat employee fatigue.

Supporting studies that particularly address employee fatigue-related challenges in the aviation industry and medicine strongly recommend in-flight, prophylactic napping and the use of caffeine gum (Wingelaar-Jagt, Wingelaar, Riedel & Ramaekers, 2021). Further, there are a number of software tools (such as FAST, Crew Alert, 2-b alert, SAFE) administered in the aviation industry, which, by employing biomathematical modelling of fatigue, indicate the employee's risk of being challenged with acute, cumulative or circadian fatigue. This software is implemented for employee scheduling or for the long-term monitoring of an employee's fatigue (health) risk. The systems rely on accurate sleep data, which are easily obtained via the widespread use of actigraphy watches and sleep-tracking functions on smart phones (Shin, Kim, Yoon, Joo & Jung, 2019).

At the end of the work period, occupational psychologists, health psychologists or medical doctors may choose to advise the use of 'pharmacological stimulants such as Modafinil and various hypnotics and antihistamines' in order to foster and enhance employee sleep quality, subsequently mitigating workplace fatigue (Caldwell, Caldwell, Thompson & Lieberman, 2019).

Other researchers, however, argue that in order to address employee fatigue, 'a workplace cultural shift' and 'an acknowledgement of the health risks from employers' is crucial, although this continues to remain a challenge. In this light, aviation and occupational analysts recommend considering the timing of public holidays in the calendar year. Safety-critical occupational personnel, in the southern hemispheres specifically, report higher levels of fatigue between public holidays (this is because the longest public holiday period for the Christmas break coincides with summer, meaning there is no additional mid-year break as occurs in most northern hemisphere countries. In order to address this, researchers recommend 'that rostered work hours are selectively decreased between public holidays, to increase time away from work and enhance opportunities for adequate sleep' (Bonetti et al., 2018). Other recommendations include introducing late morning starts during winter to help facilitate quality sleep – this initiative means altering normal working hours to suit seasonal circadian rhythms. Further, given technological advancements, there persists a heightened pressure for employees to continually stay connected and updated. In this light, in order to address employee fatigue, employers must respect an employee/colleague's wish to not take work home. This is especially the case in global multi-national organisations, which communicate across different time zones (Caldwell, et al., 2019).

6.2 Employee Burnout

Employee burnout was identified in the 1970s and has received considerable attention within the workplace and subsequently within the domains of scientific research ever since (Demerouti, Bakker, Peeters, & Breevaart, 2021). Commonly understood as 'a psychological process, "burnout" refers to a series of attitudinal and emotional reactions – that an employee experiences, as a result of job related and personal experiences' (Demerouti et al., 2021). At the level of the individual, workplace burnout has been shown to result in a greater number of employee hospital admissions for cardiovascular illnesses and has been proven to bring a greater risk of mental health challenges. Supporting evidence appraise how 'emotional exhaustion', feeling drained or used up, accounts for one of the first symptoms of employee burnout. Additionally, victims of burnout cope with this prolonged, psychologically exhausted state by 'depersonalising' relationships with their employers and with their colleagues (Arrogante & Aparicio-Zaldivar, 2020). At the level of the organisation, research studies establish how burnout can decrease levels of organisational productivity, overall workforce satisfaction and commitment, and increase employee absenteeism, presenteeism, quiet quitting tendencies at a large scale, as well as intention to leave and actual personnel turnover (Prentice & Thaichon, 2019).

Employee 'Sleep Hygiene'

Poor employee sleep hygiene has been shown to be expensive for both businesses and societies. Findings from the Center for Disease Control and Prevention and the Institute of Medicine highlighted that 50–70 million American adults are battling chronic sleep disorders or sleep deficiencies, and as a result are more prone to cardiovascular illnesses, obesity, hypertension, stomach problems, menstrual irregularities, and excessive alcohol and tobacco use (Redeker, Caruso, Hashmi, Mullington, Grandner, & Morgenthaler, 2019). Being detrimental to cognitive functioning including 'attention, reaction time, verbal function and motivation', poor sleep quality, poorly timed sleep and short sleep durations consequently had a detrimental impact on memory, presenteeism, absenteeism, employee productivity and overall health and wellbeing (Redekar et al., 2019). Further, studies have recorded a 'decrease in immune system functioning', where immune stimulating hormones were affected, poorly serving physiological health. Lastly, poor sleep hygiene heightened levels of anxiety and the likelihood of experiencing depression and early mortality (Robbins, Jackson, Underwood, Vieira, Jean-Louis & Buxton, 2019). This subsequently deteriorated organisational performance.

Other evidence has detailed how a lack of sleep has cost developed nations approximately 2% of their GDP (approximately £40 billion pounds in the UK), and there are claims that today's employees are in the midst of a global sleep-loss epidemic (Barnes & Watson, 2019). In the United States, sleep-related work absence has been estimated to cost approximately 10 million working hours a year, with the numbers being 4.8 million in Japan and 1.7 million in Germany. Strenuous work schedules and long hours of commuting have had a serious detrimental impact on sleep schedules (Barnes et al., 2019).

'Sleep Hygiene' Employer Interventions

Formulation and Implementation of 'Sleep Hygiene' Practices

Research by Dam and Helm (2016) at McKinsey shows how practices encouraging flexibility, for instance permitting employees to book for an earlier flight (rather than an overnight 'red eye' flight) to invest in quality sleep before an important meeting and reinforcing mandatory work-free vacations, can contribute to enabling employee sleep management. The creation of 'tag teams' (where a group of employees hand over phone and home-based video conference responsibilities to colleagues from different time zones at the end of their duty shift for the business to continue to be increasingly responsive 24/7) can account for an additional strategy. Mindfully scheduling calls, taking local times and participant preferences into consideration, fosters a sleep-friendly organisational culture.

Using Employee Behavioural Data

To effectively address employee sleep hygiene, employers could consider the use of technology and 'wearable' devices to learn about sleeping behaviours (for instance, whether employees have regular times for waking and sleeping, and whether they have longer sleeping hours during weekends). Employers are then able to recognise employee intercultural behaviours and gender differences, whilst learning more about the influence of light, temperature, noise and humidity. It becomes easier for leaders to intervene and advise employees regarding shift work or flexible working hours, jet lag, employee training and engagement in competitive environments (de Clercq, Papalambros, & Silberzahn, 2021; Perez-Pozuelo, Zhai, Palotti, Mall, Aupetit, Garcia-Gomez, & Fernandez-Luque, 2020).

Sleep/Nap Pods

The effective designing of evidence-based, sleep management workshops/seminars, investing in sleep consultants, napping booths, sleeping pods, and spaces with couches, recliners and even massage chairs in the workplace can prove to be beneficial (Redekar et al., 2019). For instance, when *Google* introduced 'nap pods', the leadership team claimed was beneficial. 'The high-tech beds, which look like hibernation chambers, include a privacy visor (to prevent identity theft), a pre-programmed 20-minute nap setting and subsequently, timed waking, built-in sound system for those who like to drift off to relaxing music' (Autumn, Monica, Jitendra, & Bharat, 2016). Findings from Landis, Novo and Vick (2015) confirm a positive correlation between this sleep hygiene initiative, job involvement and employee psychological empowerment (involving the 'level at which people believe they can affect their environment, their understanding, and the value they bring to an organization'. The sleeping pod had an additional positive impact on employee attention, vigilance, mood, alertness and overall employee sleep hygiene.

In resonance with Google's initiatives, *Proctor & Gamble* introduced lighting systems within the organisation that regulated melatonin (the sleep hormone) to facilitate employee rest during the evenings. Other firms such as *Ben & Jerry's* and a London-based online marketing agency, *Reboot*, initiated and propagated the use of 'nap rooms' as part of their wellbeing strategy, letting employees know they were cared for (Baxter & Kroll-Smith, 2005; Soprovich, Bottorff, Wozniak, Oliffe, Seaton, Duncan, & Johnson, 2022).

'Nap room' services benefit employee sleep when the ambience is optimised. The use of blackout curtains, noise-blocking sound machines, humidifiers and thermostats automatically cool the room to match the typical drop in core body temperature during sleep (Goldman, 2017). Encouraging the workforce to employ sleep monitors, smart alarm clocks, sleep apparel, proactively make dietary considerations, engage in reading books/other reading devices can further foster sleep hygiene (Goldman, 2017). With relatively more severe sleep health challenges, analysts recommend advising employees to turn to medicinal sleep aids, electrotherapy-based stimulations, therapeutic interventions such as homoeopathic remedies, apnoea treatment devices, over-the-counter sleep devices, prescription sleep aids and diagnostic devices.

Nap Gadget Industry

Further research within the nap gadget industry has been increasingly propagated, including the use of devices to detect sleep quality, motion signals and bio-helpers, devices to prevent snoring, nap helpers, wrap-a-nap devices, 'nap anywhere' pillows, ostrich pillows and emergency nap kits. Although there has not been considerable evidence for whether these count as effective methods to foster sleep hygiene within workplaces, these sleep aids could be further tested, analysed and implemented by researchers and practitioners (Barnes et al., 2019; Kaushik & Guleria, 2020).

The Challenge with Managing and Implementing Employee Sleep Hygiene Interventions

Despite some of the proven benefits of these sleep hygiene initiatives, few organisations have embraced them proactively. The design and implementation of sleep management interventions within workplaces are challenged with 'sleep stigmatisation' (Soprovich et al., 2022). Seldom acknowledged and celebrated, senior management teams places 'just enough' importance on the 'sleep' theme. Employees availing of a restful nap are often not respected by their co-workers or may be perceived as being relatively less passionate, incompetent or persevering in their jobs (Alger et al., 2019). Being sleep-deprived is perceived as a 'source of pride' or a 'badge of honour' in corporate culture (Kaushik & Guleria, 2020). As a consequence of 'sleep stigma', employees resort to discretely heading towards their cars, a park bench or a coffee shop for a 'work-day' snooze. Destigmatising the 'need to rest', propagating its significance and its contribution to individual and organisational performance, and wellbeing, and subsequently initiating sleep interventions would be useful, especially in high-intensity workplaces (Baxter & Kroll-Smith, 2005; Soprovich et al., 2022).

Employing an 'In-House' Masseuse and 'At-Desk' Massage Interventions

One of the earliest and simplest tools, massage or massage therapy at work not only relieves pain but also reduces swelling or mobilisation of adhesive tissues. An investigation of the administration of massage interventions and consequential work-related outcomes demonstrated how 'pain interfering with normal work, days cut down on doing things and days off from work' were significantly lower in the intervention group (Imamura, Furlan, Dryden, & Irvin, 2008). Cady and Jones (1997) and Day, Gillan, Francis, Kelloway and Natarajan (2009) analysed whether a 15-minute 'on-site'/'at-desk' massage had an influence on physiological and psychological health-related outcomes of employees. Measuring employee blood pressure 15 minutes before and after the intervention, findings illustrated a significant decrease in blood pressure and workplace strain.

This is in addition to in-house masseuse services that have been evidenced to increase blood flow and circulation, and relieve tension in neck, back and shoulder muscles. This treatment can also increase flexibility and reduce the likelihood of workplace injuries, reduce irritability, and improve the productivity of employees who work for long hours. Previously offered as an attractive perk by organisations such as Google, the service proved to be a significant expense for the company, especially during times of recession (Cady & Jones, 1997; Day et al., 2009).

Ergonomics for Employee Musco-Skeletal Health and Wellbeing

Baydur, Ergör, Demiral and Akalın (2016) and Sundstrup, Seeberg, Bengtsen and Andersen (2020) report how musculoskeletal pains and injuries such as tendon disorders, chronic neck pains, lower back pains, ligament sprains, muscle strains, and injuries of the shoulder, elbow and wrist are highly prevalent amongst employees, with global reports suggesting an increase of more than 50% in similar incidences since 1990. Workers engaging in physically demanding such as 'lifting, pulling, pushing, standing, walking, bending, forceful or fast and repetitive tasks' are relatively more vulnerable to musculoskeletal injuries and, subsequently, a poor ability to perform at work and the likelihood of taking sick leave or pre-mature exit from the labour market.

Office workers who spend long hours on the computer and employees within the healthcare sector were deemed as equally vulnerable (Oakman, Macdonald, & Wells, 2014). This was particularly the case during COVID-19 when the global workforce witnessed an increased reliability on technology and the healthcare sectors.

Investigating further, Kilbom and Perrson (1987) highlight how the prevalence of musculoskeletal injuries varied less significantly across sectors. In contrast, they reaffirm the role of individual differences in working techniques, adopting the right posture, opting for appropriate postural support, physical capacity, and medical and working history as playing a greater role in the disability narrative. For instance, employees who worked with a 'forward flexion of the neck and raised arms' were perceived as at 'high risk' of musculoskeletal issues in contrast to those who were more relaxed and 'moved' more, who strained their shoulder and neck muscles less by avoiding 'long lasting' static postures, and who supported their arms as much as possible.

Other evidence from Woods (2005) indicate a strong correlation between the provision of social support (such as organisational communication channels, employee, work relationships and organisational culture) and musculoskeletal ill health. Strong social support systems decrease risks of musculoskeletal morbidities, protect against musculoskeletal issues, and promote pro-social behaviours that enable employees to cope more effectively in the face of an injury.

Lastly, Faez, Zakerian, Azam, Hancock and Rosecrance (2021) suggest that 'organisational ergonomic climate' ('the extent to which an employee believes his/her organisation to be emphasising and supporting the design and modification of work, such that operational performance and employee wellbeing are maximised') significantly influences both physical and psychological wellbeing. Survey findings from more than 100 employees in Iran illustrated how self-reporting was considerably lower when employees perceived their employers as 'ergonomically' aware and compassionate (Faez et al., 2021). These findings had implications for employees and their families, organisational policy makers and practitioners (who designed prevention programmes and organised social events for employees), and leadership teams that analysed sickness absences, early retirement and succession planning.

Why Must an Employer Invest in Ergonomics for Musculoskeletal Health and Wellbeing?

In addition to building and sustaining the reputation of the organisation as one that is compassionate if their employees become injured, in addition to a consideration of recruitment and training costs following the injury of the employee because of their resignation/termination, Peter (1990) explains how investing in employee musculoskeletal health is crucial to employer-employee relationship building. Employees quickly realise how much they are valued within the organisation by their employer's attitudes and actions when they are challenged with injury and ill health. A lack of trust and an employer's tendency to perceive an 'injured' or 'challenged' employee as a 'malingerer' can make the relationship, vulnerable. The employer's lack of 'good will' can significantly deteriorate employee morale and the quality of their relationship, 'even more than the financial cost of the injury' (Peter, 1990).

Evidence-Based Ergonomic Interventions for Musculoskeletal Wellbeing

In this light, the effectiveness of organisational ergonomic interventions to further foster musculoskeletal health has been analysed. For example, Baydur et al. (2016) tested the effect of a two-stage participatory ergonomic intervention programme on a sample of 116 office employees. In the first stage, employees were required to attend a training programme with the objective of building and developing basic office ergonomic and individual risk assessment skills. The content of the two-hour training session included an 'introduction to ergonomics and musculoskeletal disorders, adaptation of the work environment to avoid musculoskeletal disorders, implementation of exercises and relaxation programmes to avoid musculoskeletal disorders and gaining ergonomic risk assessment skills'.

Further, at the second stage of the intervention, each participant was visited at work and was required to use the hazard identification risk assessment checklist to assess their own risks and offer solutions for the same. This was later discussed with the researchers and implemented within the workplace. Findings firmly established how the implementation of the intervention significantly decreased the risk of developing wrist, hand, neck and other musculoskeletal symptoms or impairments of participants in contrast to the control group.

Within the Australian healthcare sector, Oakman et al. (2014) discuss how nurses – the largest occupational group within the healthcare sector – are most vulnerable to musculoskeletal issues. Because of this, traditional practitioners implemented 'no lift' programmes, reducing the exposure of nurses to physical hazards involving the 'handling of patients'. Consequently, a significantly lower number of workers (particularly older employees) reported lower back pain experiences, and absenteeism – sickness absence, more specifically – decreased. Supporting evidence from Ferguson (1992) describes how nursing staff are highly vulnerable to 'needle stick' injuries and the subsequent transmission of human immunodeficiency virus (HIV) and other infectious diseases. In this light, 'needle-less' systems that minimise exposure to needles, have been proposed within healthcare settings.

Contemporary researchers suggest that investing 'hazard management' interventions within the workplace, offers greater value. This entails identifying hazards, assessing risk from each identified hazard, and taking any necessary steps to control risk from each hazard separately (Oakman et al., 2014).

Other authors argue that physical exercise interventions were relatively more effective in managing musculoskeletal ill health. For instance, administering strength training, muscle strengthening interventions and endurance exercises were particularly beneficial in addressing neck pain and other long-term musculoskeletal disorders in office workers, industry and hospital workers, and individuals engaging in physically demanding work (Tersa-Miralles, Bravo, Bellon, Pastells-Peiro, Arnaldo & Rubi-Carnacea, 2022).

In addition to this, 'participatory ergonomics', meaning 'actively involving workers in developing and implementing workplace changes', improved productivity and decreased the risks to health and safety. It is crucial to note that participatory ergonomics is based on the assumption that employees are the experts, possessing appropriate knowledge, skill sets, tools, facilitation and resources and are best placed to identify and analyse problems, to develop and implement solutions which foster musculo-skeletal wellbeing (Sundstrup et al., 2020).

Further testing this with workers in the healthcare sectors, investigators implemented a 'spine care for nurses' programme entailing didactic education, spine-strengthening exercises, education on safe patient-handling techniques, physical, cognitive and mindfulness group-based training, participatory ergonomics, and physical and cognitive behavioural training. This was deemed an effective intervention for musculoskeletal health; researchers, however, recommend further investigations on diverse participant samples (Járomi, Kukla, Simon-Ugron, Bobály, Makai A, 2018).

Lastly, aerobics training and stretching exercises, in addition to offering rest breaks and reduced working hours, have been proposed as supplementary interventions, although their effectiveness will need to be further tested with greater rigour within diverse research contexts and with varied participant groups (Muñoz-Poblete, Bascour-Sandoval, Inostroza-Quiroz, Solano-López & Soto-Rodríguez, 2019).

6.3 Employee Dehumanisation

Drawing from the sociological sciences, 'organisational dehumanisation' has been described as 'the experience of an employee who feels objectified by his/her organisation, denied personal subjectivity, and made to feel like a tool or an instrument, for the organisation's ends' (Bell & Khoury, 2011). Facilitating moral disengagement, dehumanisation is a psychological phenomenon, and a consequence of a process, experience or attitude where the employee feels less human and more like an animal or a machine, with reduced capacities for reasoning, will and sentiment (Haslam, 2006).

This is in contrast to 'organisational humanisation', which refers to the employee's experience of having their experiences, desires and feelings recognised by the organisation and the opportunity for personal agency and self-actualisation, through creative and instrumental participation, in organisational processes (Bell & Khoury, 2011). The extent to which employees perceive their psychological experiences within their workplace to be humanising versus dehumanising influences employee perceptions of team and organisational fairness, justice and ethicality. The 'bureaucratisation of work' embraces an 'ends focused rationality, efficiency, control and calculative behaviours' (Weber, 1976). This workplace social order 'dehumanizes by orienting individual behaviour towards the organisation's goals regardless of personal goals, thus separating the individual from his/her own actions' (Weber, 1976).

Given that the pandemic was marked by a globally crippling healthcare system, significantly increasing workloads, insufficient resources (such as personal protective equipment, informational and financial resources and time), frequently changing teams, increasing health risks and feelings of powerlessness, particularly within the healthcare sector, studies such as Riedel, Kreh, Kulcar, Lieber and Juen (2022) highlight how employees within this industry often felt objectified by their organisation. Often having to invest double the number of hours at work serving patients, healthcare workers were often denied the expression of personal characteristics/personal subjectivity (Riedel et al., 2022). This constraint acted as a severe physiological and psychological deplete, and was detrimental to wellbeing.

Assessing Employee Perceived Dehumanisation

Deemed as robust and demonstrating strong reliability properties, Bell and Khoury (2011) propagate the use of an eight-item research instrument, with a seven-point semantic differential scale to measure perceived employee dehumanisation. The questionnaire comprised of statements such as 'does the organisation treat you as a person or just another part of a big machine?' and 'is the organisation concerned about your experiences, desires, plans and feelings, or does it think of you as a tool to use for its own goals?'.

The literature advises employers to informationally and financially invest in employee training and development interventions – consequentially making employees feel valued. Their personal growth must be prioritised (Riedel et al., 2022). Additionally, high levels of job autonomy and the exercising of procedural justice were found to be negatively correlated with employee dehumanisation (Riedel et al., 2022).

6.4 Employee Deindividuation

Festinger, Pepitone and Newcomb (1952), in their early studies, recognised 'deindividuation' as 'the situations in which employees engage in anti-normative behaviours, due to them not being paid attention to as individuals'. The definition of the terminology later evolved – employee deindividuation was described as 'an internal deindividuated, psychological state, in which an employee loses recognition of himself/herself, as a unique individual, within an organizational group dynamic' (Simonson, Bender, Fetherolf, Hancock,

Krodel, Reistad, & Bertsch, 2017). Situational inputs such as 'anonymity, arousal, sensory overload, novel or unstructured situations and intoxicants', although identified as accounting for some of the many causal factors, have been under-researched in the workplace literature (Ganegoda, 2012).

Decreased levels of self-awareness and self-evaluation, and a lower level of concern for negative consequences imposed by external parties are related to inconsistencies in the ways in which an employee perceives his/her own identity and in the beliefs that the organisation holds of the employee's identity. Employees who perceive themselves as 'unique' but believe that the employer does not perceive them as such will have a strong desire to resign from employment, thus resolving the dissonance and consequential psychological tension. When resignation becomes challenging or is not an option for the employee, deindividuation either results in further fostering of ethical, pro-social behaviours (such as donating to a charity anonymously) or results in employees reducing their commitment to the organisation and increasing engagement in anti-social, unethical behaviours (such as corporate theft) (Simonson et al., 2017).

Prentice-Dunn and Rogers (1982) formulated an eight-item deindividuation scale, consisting of items such as 'to what extent did you feel a sense of togetherness with the company?'. The scale was affirmed as 'psychometrically robust' by the instrument's formulators. Responses on the scale were rated on a seven-point Likert scale.

In this light, in order to ensure that employees do not lose their sense of self/identity when immersing themselves in a group, there must exist optimal balance between the natural outcomes of an employee, acknowledging him/her as part of a larger group and recognising his/her identity, as being different from the group (Lai, Chan, & Lam, 2013).

6.5 Building Collective Resilience with Employee Resource Groups (ERGs)

Firmly grounded in the identity theory (which is concerned with how employees perceive themselves), employee resource groups (ERGs) were initiated in the 1960s to address employee needs to be socially connected, and additionally fostering diversity and inclusion (Welbourne & McLaughlin, 2013). Also referred to as 'affinity groups', 'business resource groups' or 'employee network groups', Welbourne & McLaughlin (2013) describe how employee resource groups are formulated on the basis of five identities that employees may occupy at work. These include i) the employee's 'core job identity' (the core 'job' the employee has been recruited and selected for, the description of which is on job descriptions, ii) team member identity (concerns the teams that an employee is a member of), iii) innovator identity (relates to whether the employee is an individual who is a member of a group that initiates/implements new ideas), iv) career identity ('concerns specific career-related skills that are needed to advance in a particular field'), and v) organisation member identity ('concerns the employee's organisational commitment/loyalty, whether he/she has been identified as a member that does things that are 'good' for the company and/or undertakes additional tasks that are not contributing to his/her own job or career development).

To explain their significance, researchers elucidate how ERGs can be particularly useful for discussing sensitive matters with the organisation, and supporting staff with extenuating/challenging circumstances or those belonging to vulnerable groups such as the Black or other ethnic minority groups or the LGBTQ+ community (Green, 2018). Research further illustrates the case of Capital One, one of the UK's top credit card providers and its initiative to launch employee mental health resource groups in 2019. Its launch embraced peer support sessions and online events, where talks were held talks by speakers on positive mental health and wellbeing, resilience, daily mindfulness sessions, online yoga, internal blogs on kindness and a fireside chat about mental health with two leaders (CIPD, 2021).

Moreover, an open 'slack' channel – 'a messaging platform' that divided themes of the wellbeing conversation into distinct channels – was initialised. Employees shared advice, guidance, resources and encouraging messages to support each other with the challenges of working remotely during COVID-19 (Green, 2018). The interventions effectively addressed mental health stigma, and fostered employee wellbeing and organisational decision-making and development, consequentially noting and reaffirming the importance of ERGs (Schlachter, Rolf, & Welbourne, 2023).

Further studies demonstrate how the initiation and propagation of the Black Asian and Minority Ethic (BAME) networks within 'Network Homes' – an independent, charitable organisation in the UK – was crucial for diversity, inclusion and equality. The resource group aimed to increase the proportion of women and individuals hailing from BAME origins on the leadership board. The initiative was expected to enhance the quality of customer service, foster employee trust and encourage members within the organisation to continually reflect on the inclusivity of minority groups (Colgan & McKearney, 2012; Green, 2018; Schlachter et al., 2023).

Cross-Generational Employee Resource Groups

Authors such as Christopher Ardueser and Garza (2021) distinguish between five distinct groups of employees within workforces: the 'traditionalist generation' (born between 1922 and 1943), the 'baby boomer' generation (born between 1946 and 1964), 'Generation X' (born between 1965 and 1980), 'Millennials' (born between 1981 and 2000) and 'Generation Z' (born between 2000 and 2020). Employees belonging to the 'traditionalist generation' highly respected authority, valued top-down decision-making, displayed strength in working collaboratively with others, delayed rewards and struggled to gracefully adapt to technological advancements and value diversity. In this light, the 'baby boomers' were byproducts of the traditionalist generation. They were self-driven, respected authority and hierarchy, and were hardworking and competitive. This was in contrast with 'Generation X', who valued collaboration significantly more than competitiveness. They were brutally honest and thrived during change. Research on the 'Millennials' indicated that these employees were characterised by relatively higher levels of self-esteem, assertiveness and graceful acceptance of diversity. This was in stark contrast to 'Gen Z' employees, who were relatively less team-oriented/more individualistic, valued freedom and had significantly higher expectations of employer's ethical behaviours (Christopher et al., 2021).

In this light, evidence from Browne (2021) indicates how cross-generational employee resource groups offer more opportunities for 'reverse mentoring'. Junior employees offer experienced leaders new knowledge and skills. Additionally, they were found to value the stability and earned self-confidence and trustworthiness of senior leaders. The increasing adoption of reverse mentoring has significantly increased the speed of knowledge distribution across organisations and borders, enhancing the relevance of generational diversity within the workplace.

6.6 Problem Versus Strength-Based Approaches

Representing an individual's natural talents and skills, 'strengths', and its assessment and significance in work and positive psychology literature has been extensively researched and analysed. Although, fluctuating and continually developing during the course of an employee's life course, employee behaviours guided by their strengths 'may be anchored in neural networks, which explain the ease with which they are used by the individual, in addition to a sense of authenticity and energy, resulting from their use' (Miglianico, Dubreil, Miquelon, Bakker, & Martin-Krumm, 2020).

Evidence from the literature, in this light, elucidates how exercising individual/team/organisational strengths or employing a 'strengths-based approach' within workplaces has a significantly positive influence on employee performance (Miglianco et al., 2020). Reporting an enhanced ability to manage their workload more effectively and less likely to be susceptible to burnout, presenteeism and absenteeism, employees experience higher levels of flow, vitality, passion and overall wellbeing (Miglianco et al., 2020). This is in contrast to the traditional, 'deficit model', a problem-focused approach that emphasises defining the problems of individuals, families and communities (Russell – Bennett, Kelly, Letheren, & Chell, 2023).

Recognising and managing deficits, employers seek to amend employee dysfunctional skills, abilities, attitudes and behaviours by encouraging participation in training and development sessions, and providing proactive feedback and coaching. Although having the potential to enhance employee skill and performance, focusing on weaknesses demoralises employees. Further, using terms such as 'lacking', 'less' or 'unable', the use of a 'deficit lens' heightens the likelihood of employee frustration and anxiety, work or domestic violence, and obesity (Russell-Bennett et al., 2023).

Critics argue that the 'strengths' approach contains a 'dark side'. Recruiting fairly large samples from China, researchers analysed the relationship between a strengths-based human resource system (i.e. strengths-based recruitment practices, task assignment, job autonomy, performance management system, motivation, training and development) and employee thriving at work (Ding & Liu, 2022). Having a positive influence on levels of self-esteem and decreasing levels of emotional exhaustion, the practice to fostered knowledge-sharing and pro-social behaviours in more than 990 employees in the Chinese context (Ding & Liu, 2022). Many studies within the 'workplace strengths' realms of research were conducted in China; future research, therefore, could investigate this in other contexts.

Employing a Strengths-Based Approach for Performance Management

Performance management systems, being positioned at the core of human resources, have always attempted to 'maximise the values that employees create'. The general activities of the system include establishing objectives and goals for the employee, and enhancing their performance – assessing their contribution individually, to their team and to the organisation. Further, the system holds them accountable for their performance by positively and negatively reinforcing behaviours, rewarding employees appropriately and in a timely manner, and managing career progression and termination of contracts fairly.

Heavily criticised for being time-consuming, problem-focused, demotivating, divisive, and failing to foster individual and team motivation and performance, analysts propose the implementation of strengths-based approaches, or strengths-based conversations more specifically. Professional bodies, in placing importance on 'training the employer' to conduct strengths-based meetings, provide information of the possible interventions that could be administered within the workplace.

Adopting an 'Appreciative Inquiry'

'A counter-intuitive process, that facilitates the replacement of negative, reinforcing loops, with positive, optimistic loops, resulting in the identification of new values and associated positive actions', 'appreciative inquiry' has recently been investigated and propagated in the organisational psychology literature. An action research methodology, this fosters a collaborative and participative inquiry, and places importance on the discovery of what works, resulting in greater tendencies to engage in creative and innovative behaviours and sustainable high levels of organisational function and growth (Calabrese, Cohen, & Miller, 2013).

Gordon (2008), interestingly, highlights the difference between problem-solving questions (PSQs) and appreciative inquiry questions. The author recommends replacing problem-solving questions or requests such as 'tell me what the problem is' with 'what gives you energy?' (an appreciative inquiry question); 'tell me what's wrong' with 'what do you most value about yourself?'; 'what are you worried about?' with 'what do you want more of?'; and 'what do you need help with?' with 'what worked well for you before?'. Further, other PSQs that could be possibly replaced include 'what's bothering you?' and replacing it with 'what's working well now?'; 'what's working? what isn't working?' with 'what first attracted you to...?'; 'what are you going to do about...?' with 'what did you do to contribute?' or 'how are you going to contribute?'; 'how are you going to fix this?' with 'what does it look like when you...?'; and 'what do you think caused this to happen?' with 'how do you want to keep moving forward for yourself?' (Gordon, 2008).

Orem et al. (2007), in this light, recommend the use of appreciative language. Decreasing the use of problem-solving phrases from the world of business such as 'goals', 'action plans', 'skills gap' and the 'status quo', leaders could replace this with words/phrases such as 'affirmations', 'images', 'dreams' and 'potential'.

Interventions to Foster an 'Appreciative Inquiry'

In this light, the Appreciative Inquiry 4-D cycle has received prominence within a significant number of studies. It comprises four stages. The first is the 'discovery stage'. This entails recognising the 'best of what is' and engaging in appreciation. During the discovery stage intervention, employees can be encouraged to engage in participatory activities and were encouraged to brainstorm their own strengths and values whilst combining this with storytelling methodologies. Participants are advised to focus on positive experiences, optimistic possibilities and a desired future (Dal Corso, De Carlo, Carluccio, Piccirelli, Scarcella, Ghersetti & Falco, 2021).

Employing a 'Coach' for Appreciative Inquiry Interventions

In this light, Naca-Abell (2020) describes the role of the 'coach' at the discovery stage (which explores 'what has been?'). Being responsible for nurturing a positive connection between the coach and the client, the focus of the mentor is to lead the client to a more empowered perspective. There is a significant emphasis on affirming a 'sense of the possible', fostering the client's belief in a positive future during employee coaching sessions.

With these objectives at the core of the discovery stage, the following questions can be employed by organisational psychologists/coaches 'Describe what you consider stress at work to be. Can you offer a definition, phrase or quote to describe it and provide an example?', 'When have you recently displayed the ability to cope with stress at work? What was the situation that required coping behaviours?', 'What attitude(s) did you adopt at that time? What were you thinking?', etc.

Moving on to the second stage, the 'dream' stage (which entails 'what might be', what the world is calling for or the 'envisioning of results' stage), the coach's focus is on 'encouraging the client to create images of possibilities, inviting the client to give voice to his/her preferred future', and subsequently affirming the client's dream. In this light, the possible questions that could be employed include 'Imagine one night whilst you were asleep a miracle occurred, and when you woke up your coping behaviour was just as you've described, in all stressful situations. How would you know you were handling stress well?, What would be different?, What changed in your habits?, Who would be the first to notice these changes?, What will they say or do, and how will you respond?' (Gordon, 2008). Progressing into the third stage, the 'design' stage (this stage urges the client to reflect on 'what the ideal should be' and co-constructing), the coach focuses on enabling the client's dream to be brought into focus, further 'affirming the reality of the dream', and fostering mindful choices and actions (Gordon, 2008). Considering these objectives, the mentor may choose to seek answers to the methods or the ways in which the employee chooses to behave differently to make the dream work/manifest itself, the specific techniques that the employee believes as influencing their ability to cope with stress and whether the client was aware of anyone of being able to manage stress – how does the client believe this individual copes with stress? (Gordon, 2008).

Furthermore, at the fourth stage, the 'destiny' stage (here, the client seeks to comprehend 'what will be?'; this means empowering, learning, adjusting/improving or 'sustaining'), the coach helps the client to expand his/her capacity to create the dream and hold faith when the 'going gets tough'. Whilst taking these goals of coaching into consideration, the coach may choose to ask the client questions such as 'What one small change could you make right now, no matter how small, that would improve your ability to handle stress? The change does not have to be a physical action – it could be a shift in thinking or attitude' (Whitney, Trosten-Bloom & Vianello, 2019).

The 'Feed Forward' Interview Technique

'The feed forward' interview technique for performance management, for instance, has recently been discussed in the workplace literature. Whilst 'employee feedback' focuses on information from the past and might involve a discussion of employee deficits and developmental needs, 'the feedforward' approach embraces the 'future focus', resting on the employee to open up and share their positive work experiences and achievements at work.

The process requires the employee to first recall a specific success story from their course of work. Further, employing probing questions about the employee's experiences at work that made them feel at their best, full of life and in flow, and whether they were content even before their actions were rewarded, will enable the employer to learn more about the employee's strengths. In addition, employees should be encouraged to reflect on the peak moments of their success story, the contribution of others to their success narrative and the conditions (physical or temporal) of the organisation that facilitated the success (Whitney & Trosten-Bloom, 2010). Researchers strongly advise engaging in 'active listening' during the 'feed forward' interview process. By 'placing one's attitudes, beliefs and values aside' and attempting to fully understand the other individual, employers are able to employ a 'win – win approach' with their employee, thereby engaging in good business practice and building and strengthening their rapport (Drollinger, Comer, & Warrington, 2006).

Additionally, encouraging employees to reflect and articulate their own code for success fosters a sense of employee self-awareness and self-efficacy, and enhances the line manager's knowledge about their employee. Finally, when encouraging employees to reflect, employers could ask feed forward questions, probing into how the employee wishes to apply their own secret code for success in the future. Kluger and Nir (2010), whilst describing how the interview technique is based on the principles of 'appreciative inquiry', investigated its effectiveness with 30 high school principles. Findings demonstrated how new knowledge of strengths shared between employer and employee led to better alignment between employee needs and the organisation's objectives. This further elicited positive emotions and employee self-esteem, fostered bonding and psychological safety, and ultimately enhanced employee wellbeing.

Challenges with Employing a 'Strengths-Based' Practice

Critics argue that transitioning from traditional methods, investing in strengths-based performance appraisals, and subsequent strength-based training and development workshops for leaders can consume considerable time, money and energy. Additionally, in order to ensure the effectiveness of strengths-based performance management systems, the organisational context – the culture, values and goals of the organisation – must be taken into account. Lastly, the implementation of a strengths-based practice demands that employers continually invest in repeated follow-up sessions and strength-based exercises for leaders, and ensure there are reminders of possible interventions/messages that could be reinforced for their employees. Challenging work demands hinder the timely initiation of lengthy strengths-based conversations. Creating space for reflection and persistence were deemed as necessary to embed learning and change behaviour.

6.7 Mindfulness Interventions for Organisations

'A psychological state in which one focuses attention on events occurring in the present moment, with an attitude of curiosity and kindness', the practice of 'mindfulness' has increasingly been discussed in the workplace literature. Allowing employees to perceive workplace experiences and events more objectively and 'dispassionately', 'mindfulness' enables effective regulation of thought, emotion and subsequent physiological reactions.

Authors such as Dane and Brummel (2014), and Glomb, Duffy, Bono and Yang (2011), in this light, investigated the influence that mindfulness practices have within work settings. Findings demonstrated a strong positive correlation between judgement accuracy, insight-related problem-solving, employee work performance and wellbeing. A negative correlation was firmly established between the employee's likelihood of being challenged with poor quality work relationships, experiences of anxiety, depression and turnover intentions (Glomb et al., 2011).

Deible, Fioravanti, Tarantino, & Cohen (2015), recruiting healthcare sector employees for their investigation, found that employee training in a variety of complementary and alternative medicine techniques, such as reiki, prana yoga, musical toning for relaxation, meditation, guided imagery, intuitive body scanning and creative expression, if implemented continually for a period of eight weeks, could significantly improve employee coping mechanisms, levels of self-efficacy and overall wellbeing. This consequently enhanced work-related outcomes such as employee performance and commitment (Tarantino et al., 2014). Duncan et al. (2011) described a dedicated complementary and alternative medicine wellness clinic for more than 2,500 healthcare sector employees. The interventions at the clinic included ear acupuncture, clinical acupressure and a form of osteopathy known as zero-balancing. Findings post-intervention indicated that more than 97% of employees felt more relaxed, more than 94% perceived themselves as experiencing less stress, more than 84% felt more energised and more than 78% reported less pain.

The onset of the pandemic witnessed most individuals working from home. Subsequently, many employees experienced workplace ostracism – a sense of being left out of main conversations or meaningful interactions within the organisation (Al Riyami, Razzak, & Al-Busaidi, 2023). Although illustrating that a fair number of employees reported a sense of isolation and social exclusion, further findings from McKinsey & Company highlighted how employees who practised mindfulness coped emotionally more effectively in contrast to others. Having greater sensitivity to the environment, mindful individuals were able to keep an open mind and consider alternative perspectives. This impacted the ways in which they perceived and appraised their workplace circumstances and the quality of relationships (Al Riyami et al., 2023).

Claimed to possess strong psychometric properties, the Mindfulness Attention Awareness Scale (MAAS) was recently formulated by Brown and Ryan (2003) and administered in numerous studies after the onset of the pandemic. The 15-item reversely-coded research instrument investigated an individual's dispositional tendency for attention and awareness of what was happening at that moment. Sample statements included 'I could be experiencing some emotion and not be conscious of it, until sometime later' (Al Riyami et al., 2023).

6.8 Mental Toughness for High-Intensity Workplaces

To gain momentum within the domains of workplace psychology, 'mental toughness' was conceptualised within the sports sciences. The psychological construct of 'mental toughness' is described as an 'individual's capacity to work in the direction of self-defined goals, dealing with demands, adversities and challenges and sustaining employee performance levels' (Ruparel, Choubisa, & Seth, 2022). The construct comprised performing optimally, possessing control over one's emotions, and being aware of one's potentialities, thereby enhancing employee levels of optimism, honing coping skills and overall employee effectiveness. Identified as an employee's personal resource, 'mental toughness' is considered highly relevant to enhancing levels of employee performance in challenging circumstances – these included high-intensity workplaces or constantly transforming organisations. Levels of employee mental toughness determine whether the individual's personal resources are adequate to manage person-environment exchanges (Ruparel, 2020).

Research studies conducted by Ruparel et al. (2022), in analysing the importance of 'employee mental toughness' in 496 employees in India, confirmed how mental toughness was crucial for the experience of 'authentic happiness', especially when job demands were challenging. Employees who systematically worked towards self-defined goals and dealt effectively with adversities recurrently experienced joy, serenity and contentment. Further, these individuals were often reported to experience a 'state of flow' and sustain interest in their jobs. On a similar note, Lee and Kim (2023) investigated the variable amongst more than 500 employees; findings here established a negative correlation between employee fatigue and burnout, demonstrating a positive correlation with job satisfaction and organisational commitment. This meant that employers were able to save on employee recruitment, and training and development costs, retaining a skilled workforce who were more likely to participate in organisational citizenship behaviours, less likely to engage in counter-productive work behaviours and embody relatively greater abilities to cope with workplace challenges.

Other contemporary analysts, in investigating mental toughness amongst more than 500 employees in the UK, argue how seniority on the organisational hierarchy and age moderated employee mental toughness. Mental toughness has been evidenced as being significantly higher in those in managerial roles. Further, 'mental toughness' was found to increase as employees grew older (Ruparel, 2020). Other supporting studies, such as Tham, Kong, Yung and Lee (2015), employing a large sample (N= 275 employees), reported age as similarly influencing employee mental toughness. However, they did not find that gender significantly moderated employee mental toughness.

Clough et al. (2002) designed a 48-item, 'Mental Toughness Questionnaire', comprising four sub-components: 'challenge', 'commitment', 'confidence' (interpersonal and in one's own abilities) and 'control'. Here, items included 'I usually find something to motivate me' (commitment), challenges usually bring out the best in me (challenge), 'I generally find it hard to relax' (control) and 'I generally feel I am a worthwhile person' (confidence), etc. Each statement is rated on a five-point Likert scale, with 1 point being 'strongly disagree' and 5 'strongly agree'.

More recently, a moderately altered version was designed by Ruparel et al. (2022). The analysts developed a 'mental toughness' questionnaire, analysing the construct against four factors – perseverance, control, resilience and confidence. The instrument comprised 10–12 items for each of the sub-dimensions. Deemed as possessing strong psychometric properties, the instrument comprised of statements such as 'I normally go the extra mile for my work', 'I believe that I can achieve anything', 'I can handle difficult things that come my way' and 'I keep myself engaged on a task until I achieve it', etc.

Interventions

The literature describes how recruiters, in building on and affirming the importance of employee mental toughness during the course of their human resource practice, can screen, assess and recruit candidates who demonstrate mental toughness. Further, during the course of work, in order to achieve optimal levels of employee performance, employers/leaders could consider adequately and appropriately challenging the knowledge and skills of employees. Employees are productive, possess high levels of self-efficacy, and perceive greater meaning/purpose and engagement (are enthusiastic, interested and engaged) in life when they perceive their workload to be adequate and have a set deadline for the completion of tasks assigned to them (Turkington, Tinlin-Dixon & St Clair-Thompson, 2023). These ingredients have been evidenced as imperative to the fostering of employee wellbeing and authentic happiness within workplaces.

Other research further recommends encouraging employees to engage in training and learning regimes, which cultivate mental toughness. These include team training, outdoor training, sensitivity training, management games, role play and stimulus-based training (Ruparel et al., 2022).

6.9 Summary

In summary, this chapter, with the objective of analysing high-intensity work-places, discussed employee dehumanisation, fatigue and burnout as consequences of prolonged workplace stress. In this light, the author drew the reader's attention to the aviation and healthcare industries, highlighting how long international flights and acute admission days significantly increased the risk of attentional failures and medical errors. In-flight, prophylactic napping and the use of caffeine gum were particularly recommended. A number of software tools (such as FAST, Crew Alert, 2-b alert, SAFE) further assisted with recognising an employee's risk of being challenged with acute fatigue (Bonetti et al., 2018).

Although large-scale companies such as Google additionally chose to employ at-desk interventions and in-house masseuse services, post-recession the organisation concluded this to be an 'expensive' workplace proposition. These interventions, however, did improve employee blood circulation and lower blood pressure levels – making employees less susceptible to cardiac ailments. The chapter later explored a number of recommendations to foster employee sleep hygiene. Investing in employee resource groups, particularly cross-generational resource groups, promoted inclusion, collective resilience and consequentially physiological and psychological wellbeing in employees. To conclude, the author advises employing evidence-based, strengths-based interventions such as embracing an appreciative inquiry and utilising feed forward interviewing techniques to enhance employee experiences and thereby levels of positive affect.

6.10 Further Readings

Buxton, O. M., Lee, S., Beverly, C., Berkman, L. F., Moen, P., Kelly, E. L., & Almeida, D. M. (2016). Work-family conflict and employee sleep: evidence from IT workers in the work, family and health study. Sleep, 39(10), 1911–1918.

Sajjad, A., & Shahbaz, W. (2020). Mindfulness and social sustainability: An integrative review. Social Indicators Research, 150(1), 73–94.

Sianoja, M., Crain, T. L., Hammer, L. B., Bodner, T., Brockwood, K. J., LoPresti, M., & Shea, S. A. (2020). The relationship between leadership support and employee sleep. Journal of Occupational Health Psychology, 25(3), 187.

Williams, B. K. (2010). The Influence of a Strengths-Based Intervention on the Performance-Appraisal Process. USA: University of Phoenix.

6.11 Suggested Websites

Abramson (2022). *Burnout and Stress are Everywhere.* American Psychological Association. Available at: https://www.apa.org/monitor/2022/01/special-burnout-stress Accessed on: 7 November 2023

American Psychological Association (2023). Employers need to focus on workplace burnout: Here's why. Available at: https://www.apa.org/topics/healthy-workplaces/workplace-burnout Accessed on: 7 November 2023

Dingfelder (2006). Control over day to day tasks can reduce fatigue. Available at: https://www.apa.org/monitor/apr06/fatigue Accessed on: 7 November 2023

NHS Employers (2023). Improving staff mental health through mindfulness. Available at: https://www.apa.org/monitor/apr06/fatigue Accessed on: 7 November 2023

NHS Employers (2023). Sleep, fatigue and the workplace. Available at: https://www.nhsemployers.org/articles/sleep-fatigue-and-workplace Accessed on: 7 November 2023

6.12 Reflective Questions – for Learners

From your reading and research

1. Explicate the key differences between employing a problem- versus a strengths-based approach to employee work performance management. What are the benefits and potential pitfalls of adopting the latter approach?
2. What do you understand by 'organisational humanisation'? What are the specific ways in which employers can foster this within the workplace?
3. What evidence-based interventions can organisations employ to effectively manage employee fatigue and burnout? Elucidate a few challenges that they might be faced with when administering the intervention, and reflect on how the challenge/s can be addressed.

6.13 Reflective Questions – for Researchers/Practitioners

1. What specific strategies does your organisation employ to combat employee fatigue and burnout?
2. Design and conduct a pre- and post-intervention study to test the effectiveness of treadmill desks/an in-house masseuse on employee physical/mental health and wellbeing.
3. Conduct an EBSCOhost/Psychinfo search covering the literature published in the past couple of years using the terms 'appreciative inquiry', 'strengths-based approach', 'feed forward interview', individually or in combination. Identify a study that resonates with your interests and that is feasible to replicate and extend. Conduct the replication.

References

Alger, S. E., Brager, A. J., Andrews, M., Prindle, N. E., Ratcliffe, R. H., Balkin, T. J., ... & Doty, T. J. (2019). 0182 The role of sleep extension and deprivation in processing threat-related information. *Sleep, 42*, A74–A75.

Al Riyami, S., Razzak, M. R., & Al-Busaidi, A. S. (2023, August). Mindfulness and workplace ostracism in the post-pandemic work from home arrangement: Moderating the effect of perceived organizational support. *Evidence-Based HRM: A Global Forum for Empirical Scholarship, 12*(2), 353–370.

Arrogante, O., & Aparicio-Zaldivar, E. G. (2020). Burnout syndrome in intensive care professionals: Relationships with health status and wellbeing. *Enfermería Intensiva* (English ed.), *31*(2), 60–70.

Autumn, M., Monica, H., Jitendra, M., & Bharat, M. (2016). The perfect nap. *Advances in Management; Indore, 9*(4), 1–8.

Barnes, C. M., & Watson, N. F. (2019). Why healthy sleep is good for business. *Sleep Medicine Reviews, 47*, 112–118.

Baxter, V., & Kroll Smith, S. (2005) Normalizing the workplace nap: Blurring the boundaries between public and private space and time. *International Sociological Association, 53*(1), 33–55.

Baydur, H., Ergör, A., Demiral, Y., & Akalın, E. (2016). Effects of participatory ergonomic intervention on the development of upper extremity musculoskeletal disorders and disability in office employees using a computer. *Journal of Occupational Health, 58*(3), 297–309.

Bell, C. M., & Khoury, C. (2011). Dehumanization, deindividuation, anomie and organizational justice. In S. W. Gilliland, D. D. Steiner & D. P. Skarlicki, *Emerging Perspectives on Organizational Justice and Ethics, Research in Social Issues in Management* (pp. 169–200). USA: Information Age Publishing.

Bonetti, D. M., Campbell, A. D. K., & Lock, A. M. (2008). The psychological and physiological effects of fatigue. *Occupational Medicine, 68*(8), 502–511.

Brown, K. W., & Ryan, R. M. (2003). The benefits of being present: mindfulness and its role in psychological well-being. *Journal of Personality and Social Psychology, 84*(4), 822.

Browne, I. (2021). Exploring reverse mentoring; "win-win" relationships in the multi-generational workplace. *International Journal of Evidence Based Coaching & Mentoring, 15*, 246–259.

Burgess, M. G., Brough, P., Biggs, A., & Hawkes, A. J. (2020). Why interventions fail: A systematic review of occupational health psychology interventions. *International Journal of Stress Management, 27*(2), 195.

Cady, S. H. & Jones, G. E. (1997). Massage therapy as a workplace intervention for reduction of stress. *Perceptual and Motor Skills, 84*(1), 157–158.

Calabrese, R., Cohen, E., & Miller, D. (2013). Creating a healthy workplace culture using an appreciative inquiry 4-D cycle. *Organization Management Journal, 10*(3), 196–207.

Carriedo-Diez, B., Tosoratto-Venturi, J. L., Cantón-Manzano, C., Wanden-Berghe, C., & Sanz-Valero, J. (2022). The effects of the exogenous melatonin on shift work sleep in health personnel: A systematic review. *International Journal of Environmental Research and Public Health, 19*(16), 10199.

Caldwell, J. A., Caldwell, J. L., Thompson, L. A., & Lieberman, H. R. (2019). Fatigue and its management in the workplace. *Neuroscience & Biobehavioral Reviews, 96*, 272–289.

Christopher Ardueser, M. B. A., & Garza, D. (2021). Exploring cross-generational traits and management across generations in the workforce: A theoretical literature review. *Research Association for Inter-Disciplinary Studies, 1*, 1–8.

Clough, P., Earle, K., & Sewell, D. (2002). Mental toughness: The concept and its measurement. In I. Cockerill (Ed.), *Solutions in Sport Psychology* (pp. 32–45). London: Thomson.

Coetzee, N., Maree, D. J., & Smit, B. N. (2019). The relationship between chronic fatigue syndrome, burnout, job satisfaction, social support and age among academics at a tertiary institution. *International Journal of Occupational Medicine and Environmental Health, 32*(1), 75–85.

Colgan, F. & McKearney, A. (2012). Visibility and voice in organisations: Lesbian, gay, bisexual and transgendered employee networks. *Equality, Diversity and inclusion: an International Journal, 31*(4), 359–378.

Dal Corso, L., De Carlo, A., Carluccio, F., Piccirelli, A., Scarcella, M., Ghersetti, E., & Falco, A. (2021). "Make your organization more positive!": The power of appreciative inquiry. *TPM: Testing, Psychometrics, Methodology in Applied Psychology, 28*(1), 47–63.

Dam, N., & Helm, E. (2016). The organisational cost of insufficient sleep. Available at: https://www.mckinsey.com/capabilities/people-and-organizational-performance/our -insights/the-organizational-cost-of-insufficient-sleep Accessed on: 18 March 2024.

Dane, E., & Brummel, B. J. (2014). Examining workplace mindfulness and its relations to job performance and turnover intention. *Human Relations, 67*(1), 105–128.

Daniels, K., Gedikli, C., Watson, D., Semkina, A., & Vaughn, O. (2017). Job design, employment practices and well-being: A systematic review of intervention studies. *Ergonomics, 60*(9), 1177–1196.

Day, A. L., Gillan, L., Francis, L., Kelloway, E. K., & Natarajan, M. (2009). Massage therapy in the workplace: Reducing employee strain and blood pressure. *Giornale Italiano di Medicina del Lavoro ed Ergonomia, 31*(3 Suppl B), B25–B30.

De Clercq, D., Papalambros, N., & Silberzahn, T. (2021). Sleep on it: Addressing the sleeploss epidemic through technology. Available at: https://www.mckinsey.com/ industries/life-sciences/our-insights/sleep-on-it-addressing-the-sleep-loss-epidemic -through-technology. Accessed on: 28 May 2024.

Deible, S., Fioravanti, M., Tarantino, B., & Cohen, S. (2015). Implementation of an integrative coping and resiliency program for nurses. *Global Advances in Health and Medicine, 4*(1), 28–33.

Demerouti, E., Bakker, A. B., Peeters, M. C., & Breevaart, K. (2021). New directions in burnout research. *European Journal of Work and Organizational Psychology, 30*(5), 686–691.

Ding, H. & Liu, J. (2022). Perceived strengths-based human resource system and thriving at work: The roles of general self-esteem and emotional exhaustion. *The Journal of Psychology, 157*(2), 71–94.

Drollinger, T., Comer, L. B., & Warrington, P. T. (2006). Development and validation of the active empathetic listening scale. *Psychology and Marketing, 23*(2), 161–180.

Duncan, A. D., Liechty, J. M., Miller, C., Chinoy, G., & Ricciardi, R. (2011). Employee use and perceived benefit of a complementary and alternative medicine wellness clinic at a major military hospital: evaluation of a pilot program. *The Journal of Alternative and Complementary Medicine*, 17(9), 809–815.

Faez, E., Zakerian, S. A., Azam, K., Hancock, K., & Rosecrance, J. (2021). An assessment of ergonomics climate and its association with self-reported pain, organizational performance and employee well-being. *International Journal of Environmental Research and Public Health*, 18(5), 2610.

Festinger, L., Gerard, H. B., Hymovitch, B., Kelley, H. H., & Raven, B. (1952). The influence process in the presence of extreme deviates. *Human Relations*, 5(4), 327–346.

Ferguson, T. J. (1992). Needle-stick injuries among health care professionals. *Western Journal of Medicine*, 156(4), 409.

Ganegoda, D. B. (2012). Why Do Individuals Act Fairly or Unfairly? An Examination of Psychological and Situational Antecedents of Organizational Justice. *Academy of Management Proceedings*, 2013(1), 14710–14710.

Garrubba, M., & Joseph, C. (2019). *The Impact of Fatigue in the Healthcare Setting: A Scoping Review*. Melbourne, Australia: Centre for Clinical Effectiveness, Monash Health.

Glomb, T. M., Duffy, M. K., Bono, J. E., & Yang, T. (2011). Mindfulness at work. *Research in Personnel and Human Resources Management*, 30, 115–157.

Goldman, D. (2017). Investing in the growing sleep health economy. Available at: https://www.mckinsey.com/industries/private-equity-and-principal-investors/our -insights/investing-in-the-growing-sleep-health-economy. Accessed on: 17 March 2024.

Gordon, S. (2008). Appreciative inquiry coaching. *International Coaching Psychology Review*, 3(1), 8.

Green, W. M. (2018). Employee resource groups as learning communities. Equality, Diversity and Inclusion: An International Journal, 37(7), 634–648.

Haslam, N. (2006). Dehumanization: An integrative review. *Personality and Social Psychology Review*, 10(3), 252–264.

Imamura, M., Furlan, A. D., Dryden, T., & Irvin, E. (2008). Evidence-informed management of chronic low back pain with massage. *The Spine Journal*, 8(1), 121–133.

Járomi, M., Kukla, A., Simon-Ugron, A., Bobály, V. K., & Makai, A (2018). Back school programme for nurses has reduced low back pain levels: A randomised controlled trial. *Journal of Clinical Nursing*, 27(5–6), e895–e902.

Kamure, B. (2014). Job design characteristics and their effects on employee wellbeing. *The Strategic Journal of Business and Change Management*, 2(6), 93–111.

Kaushik, M. & Guleria, N. (2020). The impact of pandemic COVID-19 in workplace. *European Journal of Business and Management*, 12(15), 1–10.

Kilbom, Å., & Persson, J. A. N. (1987). Work technique and its consequences for musculoskeletal disorders. *Ergonomics*, 30(2), 273–279.

Kluger, A., & Nir, D. (2010). The feedforward interview. *Human Resource Management Review*, 20(1), 235–246.

Lai, J. Y. M., Chan, K. W., & Lam, L. W. (2013). Defining who you are not: The roles of moral dirtiness and occupational and organizational disidentification in affecting casino employee turnover intention. *Journal of Business Research*, 66(9), 1659–1666.

Landis, Eric A., Vick, Courtney L., & Novo, Bianca N. (2015). Employee Attitudes and Job Satisfaction. *Journal of Leadership, Accountability and Ethics; Lighthouse Point, 12*(5), 37–42.

Lee, M., & Kim, B. (2023). Effect of the employees' mental toughness on organizational commitment and job satisfaction: Mediating psychological well-being. *Administrative Sciences, 13*(5), 133.

Miglianico, M., Dubreuil, P., Miquelon, P., Bakker, A. B., & Martin-Krumm, C. (2020). Strength use in the workplace: A literature review. *Journal of Happiness Studies, 21*(2), 737–764.

Muñoz-Poblete, C., Bascour-Sandoval, C., Inostroza-Quiroz, J., Solano-López, R., & Soto-Rodríguez, F. (2019). Effectiveness of workplace-based muscle resistance training exercise program in preventing musculoskeletal dysfunction of the upper limbs in manufacturing workers. *Journal of Occupational Rehabilitation, 29,* 810–821.

Naca-Abell, K. J. (2020). Appreciative inquiry: Building teamwork and leadership. *American Nurse Journal,* 15(11).

Oakman, J., Macdonald, W., & Wells, Y. (2014). Developing a comprehensive approach to risk management of musculoskeletal disorders in non-nursing health care sector employees. *Applied Ergonomics, 45*(6), 1634–1640.

Orem, S. L., Binkert, J., & Clancy, A. L. (2007). *Appreciative coaching: A positive process for change.* USA: John Wiley & Sons.

Ozel, E., & Hacioglu, U. (2021). Examining the relationship between burnout and job satisfaction of flight crew: An analysis on the critical fatigue risk factors in the aviation industry. *International Journal of Business Ecosystem & Strategy (2687-2293), 3*(1), 01–20.

Perez-Pozuelo, I., Zhai, B., Palotti, J., Mall, R., Aupetit, M., Garcia-Gomez, J. M., ... Fernandez-Luque, L. (2020). The future of sleep health: A data-driven revolution in sleep science and medicine. *NPJ Digital Medicine, 3*(1), 42.

Poulsen, K. B., Jensen, S. H., Bach, E., & Schostak, J. F. (2007). Using action research to improve health and the work environment for 3500 municipal bus drivers. *Educational Action Research, 15*(1), 75–106.

Prentice-Dunn, S., & Rogers, R. W. (1982). Effects of public and private self-awareness on deindividuation and aggression. *Journal of Personality and Social Psychology, 43*(3), 503.

Prentice, C., & Thaichon, P. (2019). Revisiting the job performance–burnout relationship. *Journal of Hospitality Marketing & Management,* 28(7), 807–832.

Redeker, N. S., Caruso, C. C., Hashmi, S. D., Mullington, J. M., Grandner, M., & Morgenthaler, T. I. (2019). Workplace interventions to promote sleep health and an alert, healthy workforce. *Journal of Clinical Sleep Medicine, 15*(4), 649–657.

Riedel, P. L., Kreh, A., Kulcar, V., Lieber, A., & Juen, B. (2022). A scoping review of moral stressors, moral distress and moral injury in healthcare workers during COVID-19. *International Journal of Environmental Research and Public Health, 19*(3), 1666.

Robbins, R., Jackson, C. L., Underwood, P., Vieira, D., Jean-Louis, G., & Buxton, O. M. (2019). Employee sleep and workplace health promotion: A systematic review. *American Journal of Health Promotion, 33*(7), 1009–1019.

Ruparel, N. (2020). Mental toughness: Promising new paradigms for the workplace. *Cogent Psychology, 7*(1), 1722354.

Ruparel, N., Choubisa, R., & Seth, H. (2022). Imagining positive workplaces: Extrapolating relationships between job crafting, mental toughness and authentic happiness in millennial employees. *Management Research Review, 45*(5), 599–618.

Russell-Bennett, R., Kelly, N., Letheren, K., & Chell, K. (2023). The 5R Guidelines for a strengths-based approach to co-design with customers experiencing vulnerability. *International Journal of Market Research, 65*(2–3), 167–182.

Schlachter, S., Rolf, S., & Welbourne, T. M. (2024). Dynamics of employee resource groups: Leader experiences driving mutual benefits for employees and employers. *Compensation & Benefits Review, 56*(3), 119–137.

Shin, J., Kim, S., Yoon, T., Joo, C., & Jung, H. I. (2019). Smart fatigue phone: Real-time estimation of driver fatigue using smartphone-based cortisol detection. *Biosensors and Bioelectronics, 136*, 106–111.

Simonson, A., Bender, A., Fetherolf, O., Hancock, S., Krodel, K., Reistad, K., ... Bertsch, A. (2017). Exploring relationships between work ethic and organizational commitment. *International Research Journal of Human Resources and Social Sciences, 4*(1), 53–84.

Soprovich, A. L., Bottorff, J. L., Wozniak, L. A., Oliffe, J. L., Seaton, C. L., Duncan, M. J., & Johnson, S. T. (2022). Sleep health in male-dominated workplaces: a qualitative study examining the perspectives of male employees. *Behavioral Sleep Medicine, 20*(2), 224–240.

Sundstrup, E., Seeberg, K. G. V., Bengtsen, E., & Andersen, L. L. (2020). A systematic review of workplace interventions to rehabilitate musculoskeletal disorders among employees with physical demanding work. *Journal of Occupational Rehabilitation, 30*(4), 588–612.

Tersa-Miralles, C., Bravo, C., Bellon, F., Pastells-Peiro, R., Arnaldo, E. R., & Rubi-Carnacea, F. (2022). Effectiveness of workplace exercise interventions in the treatment of musculoskeletal disorders in office workers: A systematic review. *BMJ Open, 12*(1), e054288.

Tham, E. K., Kong, M., Yung, N., & Lee, C. (2015). Mental Toughness and Workplace Stress: An Exploratory Study. *Sport Psych Mental Toughness Research Series, 2*(1), 2329–4269.

Turkington, G. D., Tinlin-Dixon, R., & St Clair-Thompson, H. (2023). A mixed-method exploration of mental toughness, perceived stress and quality of life in mental health workers. *Journal of Psychiatric and Mental Health Nursing, 30*(6), 1152–1169.

Van Dongen, H. P., Maislin, G., Mullington, J. M., & Dinges, D. F. (2003). The cumulative cost of additional wakefulness: dose-response effects on neurobehavioral functions and sleep physiology from chronic sleep restriction and total sleep deprivation. *Sleep, 26*(2), 117–126.

Wang, B., Liu, Y., Qian, J., & Parker, S. K. (2021). Achieving effective remote working during the COVID-19 pandemic: A work design perspective. *Applied Psychology, 70*(1), 16–59.

Welbourne, T. M. & McLaughlin, L. L. (2013). Making the business case for employee resource groups. *Employment Relations Today, 40*(2), 35–44.

Weber, M. (1905, 1976). *The Protestant Ethic and the Spirit of Capitalism* (T. Parsons, Trans.). New York: Scribner.

Whitney, D. D., & Trosten-Bloom, A. (2010). *The Power of Appreciative Inquiry: A Practical Guide to Positive Change*. California: Berrett-Koehler Publishers.

Whitney, D., Trosten-Bloom, A., & Vianello, M. G. (2019). Appreciative inquiry: Positive action research. In *Action Learning and Action Research: Genres and Approaches* (pp. 163–177). Emerald Publishing Limited.

Wingelaar-Jagt, Y. Q., Wingelaar, T. T., Riedel, W. J., & Ramaekers, J. G. (2021). Fatigue in aviation: safety risks, preventive strategies and pharmacological interventions. *Frontiers in Physiology, 12*, 712628.

Woods, V. (2005). Work-related musculoskeletal health and social support. *Occupational Medicine, 55*(3), 177–189.

Chapter 7

Employee Social Capital, Diversity and Inclusion

7.1 Fostering Psychological Safety within Teams

Broadly concerning an organisational climate in which individuals feel free to express and be themselves, without negative consequences to self-image, status or career, 'psychological safety' addresses learning anxiety. The theme elucidates the reason and the extent to which employees disseminate information and knowledge, 'speak up' with recommendations to foster improvements within the organisation and take initiatives to build on new products and services (Edmondson & Lei, 2014).

Often misunderstood as synonymous with 'trust', researchers have clarified how although both terminologies concern 'psychological states involving perceptions of risk or vulnerability', 'trust' meant 'giving others the benefit of doubt – indicating a focus on other's potential actions or trustworthiness'. Psychological safety, in contrast, questioned whether 'others will give *you* the benefit of the doubt when, for instance, *you* have made a mistake' (Edmondson et al., 2014). Psychological safety is also mistaken for the 'removal of consequences for lack of performance' (Siemsen et al., 2009). Researchers clarify how the theme simplistically refers to 'not being punished or humiliated for errors, questions or requests for help' (Edmondson et al., 2014).

Lee (2021) explained how employee psychological needs and emotions were acute during the COVID-19 health crisis. The consequential labour market fluctuations, the significant number of furloughs and widespread unemployment resulted in employee emotions being triggered by insecurities, social comparisons and critical socio-emotional resources (including flexibility, communication, social support, etc.). The author identified a positive correlation between psychological safety and EW. Employers who exercised equity when allocating resources and managing their relationships with employees and those who seldom engaged in micro-management and control of their employees fostered greater psychological safety, with lower levels of employee frustration and anxiety, and subsequent employee wellness (Lee, 2020).

DOI: 10.4324/9781032705125-7

Analysts advise propagating 'psychological safety' amongst leaders – urging them to be more available and approachable. Leaders who were accessible were more likely to be appraised as fostering a safe team environment. Further, framing work as a 'learning problem' rather than an execution problem was crucial. This conveyed 'high uncertainty' and 'high task interdependence' and continually encouraged stakeholders to ask meaningful questions, inviting and sustaining engagement (Siemsen et al., 2009). In addition, explicitly acknowledging and demonstrating fallibility can help reduce counterproductive barriers created by status differences (Kark & Carmelli, 2009).

The 'Marshmallow' Intervention

Further, Parker and Plooy (2021) elucidated the implementation of the 'marshmallow challenge'. Developed by the product designer Peter Skillman in 2002, the game required a team of four individuals to build a structure using raw materials (such as spaghetti) with a marshmallow on the top. The task had to be completed within a specific number of minutes and involved no competition, and hence was evidenced as successful at fostering psychological safety, creative behaviours and, consequentially, positive affect amongst employees.

The 'CENTRE' Tool

Standing for 'Confidentiality' (with standard limits), 'Equal airtime', 'Non-judgemental' (respectful) listening, Timeliness, the 'Right to Pass' and 'Engagement', this tool was proposed to consider clinical team functioning (Chen & Tan, 2023). The tool has been employed and found to be useful in a wide range of circumstances – teaching, clinical family meetings, and meetings with mentors and professionals. The tool can be modified; for instance, it can be simplified when confidentiality is not a concern. Altering the tool to 'CENTRE+', where additional regulations were necessary to resolve ambiguity, was deemed possible (Cave, Jamal, Pearson, & Whitehead, 2016; Chen et al., 2023). Although not comprehensively researched, developers claim that this facilitates group formation and addresses challenges with relationships, diversity, inclusion and interpersonal trust between family members. It can also reduce the possibilities and 'risk of undeclared assumptions and expectations of how groups function' and consequential interpersonal discord (Cave et al., 2016).

The 'TeamGAINS' Intervention

Kolbe, Weiss, Grote, Knauth, Dambach, Spahn and Grande (2013), during the course of their research, developed the 'TeamGAINS' intervention – 'a hybrid, structured debriefing tool for simulation-based team trainings in healthcare that integrates three different approaches: guided team self-correction, advocacy-inquiry and systemic-constructivist techniques'. The 'guided, team self-correction' approach aims at team self-correction. The trainer asks the team to reflect on positive and negative instances of their performance during simulations. For example, he/she may ask, 'Give me an instance of when priorities were clearly and appropriately stated'. The participants are encouraged to employ a critical and systematic self-analysis. The trainer, on the other hand, is taught to adopt a non-judgemental and neutral stance, and offer their opinions and observations only after each team member has offered their input (Kolbe et al., 2013).

Moving on, during the 'advocacy-inquiry' approach, the feedback and reflective practices are combined. In contrast to the guided, team self-correction approach, this methodology is instructor-led. Placing significance on expert judgement, the trainer must voice performance gaps and question the trainee's assumptions and beliefs (Frake & Dogra, 2006).

The 'systemic-constructivist' approach employs the principles used in systemic therapy. Whilst focussing on individuals within their systems, the technique helps analyse patterns and dynamics of interactions and relationships, rather than on isolated human behaviour (Kriz, 2010).

The 'TeamGAINS' intervention, comprising of all these three approaches, aimed at honing clinical, behavioural and team-working skills and leader inclusiveness – particularly of significance and relevance during medical emergencies. Employing four anaesthetists, 28 residents and 29 nurses, the developers established and propagated a significant difference in pre-measure and post-measure perceived psychological safety assessments (Kolbe et al., 2013; Kolbe, Grande, & Spahn, 2015).

The 'TeamUP' Intervention

Mayer (2018) informs readers of a 'multi-player, three-dimensional game', available under a commercial licence. The game consists of five puzzle levels, Door Puzzle, Tile Puzzle, Maze Puzzle, Pile Puzzle, Bridge Puzzle and Pillar Puzzle, and requires players to self-organise, communicate, collaborate and arrange team communication, coordination and leadership in order to find solutions to the five levels of puzzles/team challenges. Requiring players to demonstrate different and alternative forms of leadership styles, the game assesses team quality and team performance. Whilst investigating 106 sets of gaming data, Mayer (2018) reported this intervention as a valid methodology for team research and assessment, making a significant difference in psychological safety, team cohesiveness and in-game team performance.

The 'Art of Teamwork' Toolkit

With an objective of urging employees to think and work differently and effectively within teams, specialists at Microsoft designed the 'Art of Teamwork'

Toolkit, comprising two well-designed interventions – the 'persona swap' and 'casting call' intervention.

The 'Persona Swap' Intervention from Microsoft

This 60–90-minute intervention needed team members to draft and distribute 'persona' swap cards to participants of a team. The activity required participants to take on 'new personas' – such as that of an 'examiner', who encourages the team to think critically and go deeper into topics (urging the participant to ask themselves 'what are we missing?'), the 'doer', who encourages the team to be practical and find an actionable way forward (urging the participant to ask themselves 'what actions do we need to take?') and the 'mediator', who helps the team understand their common objectives and navigate tension (urging the participant to ask themselves 'what are our common objectives?'). Other cards include the personas of the 'dreamer', 'decider', 'leader', 'coach', 'operator' and 'critic'. Urging individuals to reflect and synthesise their perspectives, this intervention empowered team members to demonstrate understanding, and respect and embody different points of view (Microsoft, 2019).

The 'Casting Call' Intervention from Microsoft

The 'Casting Call', a 30–45 minute intervention, on the other hand, urges the team leader to choose a project that he/she wishes to examine with the team. Whilst inviting the team to reflect on and establish what they are trying to accomplish and what success looks like, the leader and the team, together, take note of what personas they need to achieve their goals. Employing 'persona required' cards, on which participants determine the 'persona type' and potential team members, was evidenced as useful (Microsoft, 2019).

Suggested Activity

Team building and team cohesiveness interventions significantly deteriorates employee loneliness, fosters social health and wellbeing. This justifies the employer's financial investment in the proposition. Reflect and discuss.

7.2 Discrimination and Inclusion – Cancer Survivors

Pre-pandemic studies from Stergiou-Kita, Pritlove and Kirsh (2016) elucidate how a significant number of cancer survivors are faced with stigma and discrimination, counting as a prominent and rising challenge in contemporary workplaces. Employer discrimination manifests in the form of hiring discrimination (due to a history of cancer), harassment and hostility from colleagues when survivors return to work and the employer denying workplace support and the implementation of workplace accommodations. Employers demonstrate discriminatory behaviours when employees are faced with a loss in job responsibilities, a reassignment of job tasks or demotion. Denying an employee a deserved promotion or a wage increase, reducing their salary or requesting the survivor to step down from their position (job termination/dismissal) due to the ailment count as employer discriminatory behaviours (Stergiou-Kita et al., 2016).

Stigma and related behaviours, in particular, have been reported by employees battling lung cancer, or head and neck cancer during the course of which facial disfigurement has occurred. Furthermore, women challenged with cervical cancer and men faced with colorectal cancer experience relatively greater blame, shame and stigma because the illnesses are associated with sexually transmitted diseases or changes in sexual functioning (Peterson, Silva, Goben, Ongtengco, Hu, Khanna & Dykens, 2021).

Moreover, individuals with metastatic cancer and visible, physiological changes may be further stigmatised and discriminated against. This is given the increasing prevalence of 'death anxiety' amongst both cancer survivors and the public. Recognised as 'an unpleasant emotion, which is existential in nature and includes thoughts about both, one's and other's death', 'death anxiety' is a significant contributor to workplace and societal stigmatisation, more generally (Sliter, Sinclair, Yuan, & Mohr, 2014). Lastly, cancer survivors with compromised work abilities, productivity and reliability, and individuals needing appropriate workplace accommodations are faced with relatively greater differentiation (Stergiou-Kita et al., 2016).

The onset of the pandemic left cancer survivors in a particularly vulnerable situation. They were hit with an increased likelihood of contracting the virus, a poor immune system making them susceptible to multiple health ailments, changes in physical activity and weight, 'the possibility of additional disease burden from treatment delay or interruptions', costs of cancer care and other health conditions, prolonged unemployment for them and their caregivers, changes in the quality of familial relationships, changes in routine follow-ups and diets, and the financial strain imposed by the pandemic (Baddour, Kudrick, Neopaney, Sabik, Peddada, Nilsen, & Mady, 2020). Additionally, this deteriorating health-related quality of life, increasing symptom burden, elevated risk of admission to intensive care units and invasive ventilation, emotional distress, and mortality left employers with heavy burdens of employee healthcare insurance costs (Baddour et al., 2020).

Why Employers Must Invest in Interventions for Cancer Survivors

Soldano (2016) discusses how the rates of chronic ailments and subsequent healthcare costs are rising. Qualified, skilled and trained employees challenged with cancer often struggle to cope with their workloads or manage medical and family commitments. Evidence from De Rijk, Amir, Cohen, Furlan, Godderis, Knezevic & De Boer (2020) illustrates a significant difference in the number of employees considering reducing working hours, quitting a job, turning down (or not applying) for a promotion, taking sick or unpaid leave or reporting difficulties in concentrating when they experienced a lack of support from their employer. The initiation of workplace interventions enabled employers to effectively tackle employee health-related anxieties, burnout, depression, absenteeism, presenteeism and overall lack of productivity in the workplace.

Employer Interventions

Stergiou-Kita, Pritlove, Van Eerd, Holness, Kirsh, Duncan and Jones (2016), having conducted interviews with cancer survivors, health/vocational service providers and employer representatives, advise drafting clear policies that elucidate 'return to work plans and flexible work scheduling' for survivors (including the accommodation of medical appointments and rehabilitation needs) and modification of work responsibilities (including the elimination of non-essential job tasks and duties) and 'performance expectations'. In this light, designing a five-step model, the researchers propose a process and specific strategies to ensure the effectiveness of workplace accommodations for cancer survivors.

First, before initiating and implementing any intervention, employers had to acquire adequate knowledge about the role, responsibilities and the challenge the employee was faced with. Interview findings additionally establish the significance of effective communication so that employees can gauge the employer's ability to make necessary accommodations in the workplace, and negotiate and customise reasonable adjustments. This was crucial in order for both parties to understand the 'employee's restrictions and how to assist the employee to compensate for impairments, rather than expecting the employee to fit within the workplace' (Stergiou-Kita et al., 2016).

Further, they recommend the initiation of physical work-space modifications (for instance, barrier-free building designs, workspaces free of distractions and ergonomically designed workstations) and making provisions for adaptive aids and technologies (Alleaume, Bendiane, Peretti-Watel & Bouhnik, 2020).

Critics argue that despite being offered reasonable accommodations, employees may not avail of useful services. Their anxieties about 'appearing different', managing changing perceptions of their ability to perform on the job, coping with potential job loss, refraining from disclosure about their illness and attempting to protect their privacy often deteriorated their likelihood of engaging in employee cancer support interventions within the workplace (Feuerstein, Luff, Harrington, & Olsen, 2007). Further, poor quality pre-cancer working relationships, physically demanding or high-risk jobs, battling psycho-vegetative exhaustion, decreasing muscular strength, reactive depression and adjustment disorder related to the malignancy were deemed additional challenges to the effective implementation of interventions (Feuerstein et al., 2007; Rick, Kalusche, Dauelsberg, König, Korsukéwitz, & Seifart, 2012; Stergiou-Kita et al., 2016).

Evidence from the literature, however, shows how employer collaboration with the relevant healthcare specialists (such as oncologists, physiotherapists, rehabilitation therapists, physicians and nurses) and the quality of support, advice and provision of services (for instance – employee counselling services, opportunities for employee training and development, job replacement, job search assistance and maintenance) positively influenced employment outcomes for individuals challenged with cancer (Stergiou-Kita, Grigorovich, & Tseung, 2014).

Making a more specific proposition, Ilic (2013) recommends the implementation of workplace health education and promotion initiatives. Having conducted in-depth interviews with men, the researcher's findings established workplace educational campaigns and interventions enhanced employee's knowledge and awareness pertaining to cancer. For instance, delivering cancer-related educational material via the internet, video or in written format fostered timely health screening and health-fostering behaviours (Ilic, 2013).

Offering more specific instances, the author describes the implementation of the 'help a mate' education campaign in Victoria, Australia, where a calendar, pamphlet and website were created that offered detailed information about the epidemiology, physiology and anatomy (where applicable), the risk factors, diagnosis and treatment options for prostate cancer and six other health conditions. Participants were receptive to the initiative, and positive modifications in health behaviours were reported. On a similar note, administering a 'mobile health unit', which enabled employees to 'seek health advice' or 'use medical services' at their workplace is an example of a multi-faceted, workplace intervention that can enhance 'awareness, knowledge and uptake of health services' offered within the workplace (Ilic, 2012).

7.3 Discrimination and Inclusion – Workplace Wellbeing for Caregivers

'Caregivers' or 'family members and other significant people, who provide care and assistance to individuals (i.e. parent, spouse or life partner, adult child, sibling and/or friend) living with debilitating physical, mental and cognitive conditions, whilst also working in paid employment' (Ireson, Sethi, & Williams, 2018) play a crucial role within families and broader society.

Supporting and enhancing the quality of life for those challenged with ill health, carers are often vulnerable to high levels of stress. Gordon, Pruchno, Wilson-Genderson, Murphy and Rose (2012) appraise how the 'financial resilience' of households can deteriorate if carers have to work fewer hours or have to resign from their jobs. Further, carers who have other jobs find it challenging to invest sufficiently in social relationships, including relationships with those at work and those whom they care for. Poor social health, as a consequence, heightens perceived carer isolation.

In addition, gender differences have been evidenced to influence overall caregiver health and wellbeing – a greater number of women have reported 'experiencing difficulty' in combining work and care responsibilities. However, this was only the case with women who additionally had to balance childcare responsibilities with work and caregiving responsibilities. When comparing the perceived difficulty or stress levels of other women with men, no significant difference was reported. Additionally, a survey of working carers (2019) that investigated the influence of caregiving on line managerial responsibilities illustrated how 'manager-carers' claimed that their caregiving circumstances enhanced their levels of empathy for the needs of their team members. This is particularly of significance since some employers have reported 'lacking the emotional capacity to assist team members with their development' or that 'they did not have the time to help them' (CIPD, 2020).

Significance of Investing in Employees who are 'Carers'

There are both organisational and social benefits to investing in employees who are caregivers. With significant increases in the ageing population, overall participation and engagement within the workforce (the percentage of working individuals who are either employed or unemployed but actively looking for work) have been adversely influenced. For instance, in the UK, 3.7 million people have identified themselves as carers, with a significant number reporting that caregiving responsibilities had a detrimental impact on their levels of concentration and work performance.

A lack of workplace support has a number of health and financial consequences. These include increased or unplanned absenteeism, increasing prevalence of presenteeism, employee quiet quitting behaviours and employee turnover, plans to retire early, and deteriorating employee performance or health. Caregiver employees are approximately three times more challenged with poor health in contrast to non-caregivers.

By creating a carer-friendly workplace, organisations are able to better attract and retain a skilled workforce. Further, the employer can build on a reputation of being a 'caregiver' friendly employer, given how physically, psychologically, emotionally and financially challenging this can potentially be.

Suggested Activity

Conduct interviews with line managers/human resource managers of an organisation that you have access to and have implemented care giver work policies and interventions. Discuss the benefits and pitfalls appraised by the stakeholders.

Challenges with the Implementation of Workplace Initiatives

Research evidence elucidates how a lack of awareness of workplace informational, financial, social and emotional support can act as a barrier to employees reporting their role as a caregiver or making use of caregiver support interventions. Further, knowledge of how, when and why to access these services and how the services could potentially be useful to a caregiver may be lacking or not adequately reinforced within the workplace. This is a reason why a significant number of surveyed employees believed that they could cope with work and caregiving responsibilities without workplace caregiving interventions.

In addition, a lack of a 'sense of autonomy' or a 'perceived sense of control' about how their working hours are scheduled and a fear of detrimental consequences to their job or career prospects can be an additional challenge to engaging with caregiver support interventions. This explains why a fair number of employees in the Survey of Working Carers (2019) reported that 'the ways in which their work was organised made it too difficult' to avail of workplace resources/interventions. Others believed that their line manager would not positively perceive or support their engagement with these initiatives.

Employer Interventions

Having recognised the significance of retaining trained and skilled employees, contemporary workplaces are initiating proactive interventions to accommodate caregiver needs, subsequently investing in their wellbeing. Research studies, including that of Ireson et al. (2018), suggest that it is important to define who a 'caregiver' is and for the organisation to offer organisational stakeholders clarity on the theme. Many employees may incorrectly identify themselves as carers or not categorise themselves as such, meaning the latter group will not seek line manager support when needed. Defining who a caregiver is and making note of their needs can prove to be a beneficial starting point during employee induction programmes, employee performance appraisal meetings and employee surveys.

The formulation of caregiver-friendly workplace policies or work-family 'initiatives' and the deliberate creation of organisational changes targeting the culture can minimise the likelihood of work-family conflict and thus reduce caregiver levels of stress. Most organisations have been shown to lack or not offer any support to caregivers, but many stakeholders report employers to be granting 'carer employees' permission to use the telephone or with private time to make/receive phone calls. Others refer their employees to 'external services' of support (Arieli & Yassour-Borochowitz, 2024).

Research evidence from the literature describes the usefulness of administering formal records or a 'carer's register' – this states that the employee is a carer and enables them with access to leave and other carer benefits. Employers could additionally adopt a 'voluntary carer's passport scheme', which states the employee's individual plan detailing their needs and working arrangements as a 'carer'. Whilst refraining from collecting/recording any caregiver data, any information given should be regularly updated, although caregivers must never be forced to share any information (Khan-Shah, 2020).

Other findings suggest that organisational policies could offer employees 'drop in lunch time carer support sessions, information on career breaks, access to wellbeing services, access to external carer's support line and carer's support networks' (Jegermalm & Torgé, 2023). Making provisions for occupational health and employee assistance programmes, access to a telephone to be able to contact people in case of emergencies and counselling interventions can further foster the wellbeing of working carers (Meyer, Zachmeyer, Paccione, Cardenas, Zernial & Smith, 2024).

Additionally, human resource departments are encouraged to manage caregiver's data confidentially, only releasing this at the discretion of the caregiver. Further, taking initiatives to destigmatise 'caregiving' will allow more employees within workplaces to identify themselves as caregivers, when appropriate, report this and seek support from their line manager and the organisation more broadly. Despite initiatives to destigmatise, employees who choose not to disclose their circumstances must be respected.

Flexible Working Schedules

Caregiver policies and practices can include the provision of flexible working hours, a change of work mode, from full-time to part-time, job sharing, working from home or telework, compressed work weeks and customising employee working hours. Further, unpaid leave and support services ('resource and referral services, information services, counselling, support groups, workshops and seminars addressing challenges faced by caregivers') should be offered to caregivers (Lorenz, Whittaker, Tazzeo & Williams, 2021).

A number of financially affluent organisations have chosen to offer extensive employee support in the forms of 'case management' services, discounted provision for caregiving services, adult daycare facilities, emergency short-term care, dependant care, flexible spending accounts and 'dependant care' car parks (a car parking slot for those less able of self-care) (Ireson et al., 2018).

Investing in Training Line Managers

Critics argue that the effective implementation of caregiving policies and practices are only possible if employers invest in training line managers about the significance and specific methods by which caregivers can be included within the workplace. In addition to training workshops and workplace awareness-raising sessions, conducting or participating in campaigns such as 'Carer's Rights Day' has been evidenced as beneficial (Mofidi, Tompa, Williams, Yazdani, Lero & Mortazavi, 2019).

Researchers from the domains of workplace psychology advise governmental bodies/policy-makers to informationally, socially and financially support professional bodies to invest in creating evidenced-based practices to change workplace cultures to foster inclusion and acceptance to accommodate the needs of caregivers. Whilst investing in and calling for the formulation of caregiver policies, governments must ensure that differences in age, gender, class, immigration status, family structures, caregiving responsibilities, etc. are comprehensively accounted for. Similar investments should be made when considering the 'propagation' of 'carer-employee' evidence-based practices (Larkin, Henwood & Milne, 2019).

On another note, nurturing opportunities for policy-makers to collaborate with employers and carer employees to formulate the best carer policies and practices, including recommendations to effectively integrate paid work and unpaid caregiving, was perceived as crucial. Lastly, socially and financially advocating for destigmatising 'employee caregiving' through local, national and international campaigns were recommended by contemporary workplace analysts (Larkin et al., 2019).

7.4 Discrimination and Inclusion – Accommodating Women's Menstrual Health, Menopause Transition and Subsequent Wellbeing Challenges

Women's menstrual health, although a public global health concern, is relatively under-researched in the workplace literature (Sang, Remnant, Calvard, & Myhill, 2021). Similar to other public health issues such as obesity and mental health, menstrual health and related workplace policies and practices are challenged with stigmatisation. Despite this, evidence from the literature draws attention to an organisation in Bristol, UK, which was the first in the country to formalise 'period leave' in 2016. This was important because gynaecological health conditions are associated with negative employment outcomes – employees have been evidenced as being more prone to experiencing fatigue and burnout, heightened levels of presenteeism, leavism, and quiet quitting behaviours, and therefore detrimental to overall employee engagement and wellbeing.

Employee Fertility Policies

Experiencing difficulties with starting or growing a family can be emotionally exhausting, socially demanding and financially crippling. Recent reports from the CIPD (2023) define fertility challenges, investigations or treatments as referring to 'any employee experiencing difficulties in conceiving or undergoing any investigations or type of fertility treatment or supporting a partner who is undergoing investigations or treatment'. This includes homosexual and heterosexual couples, individuals who have chosen single parenthood or to delay parenthood (through egg freezing) and those challenged with 'secondary infertility' ('have a child or children but have difficulties conceiving again').

Managing physiological and psychological challenges alongside the demands of employment can prove to be stressful without 'compassionate' organisational policies and interventions. Being required to attend several clinic appointments (sometimes scheduled with little notice), storing medication in the office refrigerator, finding clean and private spaces to inject the medication, taking sensitive phone calls at work and coping with the subsequent cycles of hope and grief significantly strain an employee's relationships inside and outside work, and thereby their physical and mental health (Colussi, Hill & Baird, 2024).

A pre-pandemic study by Zoll, Mertes and Gupta (2015) discusses how organisations such as Apple and Facebook in the United States – two, well-recognised and valuable brands – initiated and implemented fertility policies. In addition to an 'extended maternity leave policy', Apple offered their female employees 'egg freezing' services. This was similar to organisations such as ICICI Bank, Godrej and Salesforce, in the Indian context, which supplemented employee health and wellbeing benefits with traditional fertility medical procedures, diagnostic testing, egg harvesting and freezing costs, and IVF consultations (Rami, 2013).

Initially implemented for cancer patients (given that chemotherapy can damage a woman's eggs), egg freezing services remove and fertilise a woman's eggs in her 20s. Given that women are relatively less likely to conceive in the later years of their lives, 'fertility preservation' enables pregnancy in a woman's 30s or 40s. Facebook offers up to $20,000 for egg freezing. 'A typical round of egg freezing costs about $10,000, with $500 or more in fees each year for storage. Two rounds are usually necessary to harvest about 20 eggs, which is considered ideal' (Mertes, 2015). In addition to a host of other fertility services, the organisation offers employees adoption and surrogacy assistance. Supporting arguments reinstate how these benefits are particularly advantageous for women considering 'delayed pregnancy'. Diversity and inclusion reports from the United States reaffirm how the initiative addresses gender inequality within the labour market. Apple and Facebook, for instance, reported more than 70% of its workforce to be male-dominated (Mertes, 2015).

Critics argue that high failure rates and risks associated with using in vitro fertilisation (IVF) or elective egg freezing processes have not been taken into consideration, jeopardising instead of safeguarding an employee's fertility. The lack of medical evidence, the organisation's inadequate knowledge on the subject or the lack of consideration given to the safety and efficacy of such processes could act as detrimental to employee physical health and wellbeing. Further, there is evidence that establishes a correlation between using IVF treatments for pregnancy and the probability of 'pre-term birth' or 'neo-natal death', increased likelihood of birth defects, and prevalence of autism and mental retardation (Mertes, 2015; Zoll et al., 2015).

Researchers, in this light, state that fertility interventions such as IVF 'lead to an inescapable paradox' (Zoll et al., 2015). If organisations begin offering 'egg freezing' services, some female employees may be susceptible to subtle, social pressures to avail of the service – inexplicitly having to demonstrate their commitment and loyalty towards the company. Secondly, some employees may 'naively assume that they are insured against natural fertility decline'. Lastly, fertility policies or propagating the use of the elective egg freezing processes, whilst postponing parenthood and increasing the probability of gestational diabetes, delays addressing social problems – the consequences of competing and challenging demands of parenthood, family and career. Rather than exposing women to artificial and potentially harmful procedures, leaders could consider investing in more contemporary workplace benefits that encourage both men and women to plan their families during their safest, biological window whilst retaining job security (Rami, 2013; Zoll et al., 2015).

The onset of the pandemic not only witnessed a tremendous change in the nature of work but, as a consequence, changes in the quality of marital relationships, financial stressors within families, increasing work-family conflicts and postponing pregnancies/family planning due to the vaccination (Peng, Mou, & Xu, 2023). Although enhancing reproductive desires amongst couples, mass vaccinations induced 'pregnancy' phobia amongst most women, significantly influencing their family planning intentions and behaviours. These conflicting moderators increased the need to raise awareness about changing work and familial dynamics and challenges, the prevalence and consequences of fertility treatments, making an argument for effective workplace support and exploring what this must embrace. Organisations were required to place greater emphasis on organisational and familial commitment, planning and operability in the face of uncertainty and unforeseen stressors (Peng et al., 2023).

The Case for Why Employers Must Invest in Employee Fertility Policies

In this light, authors such as Duan, Xu and Cai, (2022) reinstate the rationale for why organisations must communicate and intervene in matters of employee fertility. From an employer's perspective, this is firstly reputational. Making employee support accessible communicates to internal and external stakeholders that the organisation values the 'health and wellbeing' of its employees (Duan et al., 2022). Similar to any other employee wellbeing challenge or intervention, employer support and carefully drafted policies and practices can enable individuals to stay at work and perform relatively more productively (Wilkinson & Mumford, 2024). Conversely, a lack of support may lead to skilled, capable and talented individuals leaving the workforce. Adding to the human resource department's workload, this further means costs in terms of recruitment and training. This additionally has a detrimental impact on co-worker workload, motivation, engagement and levels of wellbeing.

Employee Support Services

The several support services that can potentially be offered to employees undergoing fertility investigations, challenges and treatment include flexibility of working hours to accommodate fertility treatment, paid time off to attend medical consultations and treatments, and access to counselling services (Steyn, Sizer & Pericleous-Smith, 2022). Moreover, educational workshops and training for employees and line managers on how to include and support staff faced with fertility challenges, creating and participating in employee support groups, and financial aid that contributes to the cost of the fertility treatment count as some of the many ways by which employers could offer assistance (Wilkinson & Mumford, 2024).

Researchers and specialists within the domains of human resources further advise three principles of good practice when designing support that may prove to be useful to employees. First, the use of carefully considered sensitive language and approach is crucial when educating and raising awareness amongst employees; hence, drawing from reliable sources/expert advice is beneficial. For instance, seeking knowledge or guidance from professional accredited bodies will inform and enable leaders and employees within the field to acquaint themselves and adhere to appropriate social norms and legal guidelines.

Second, in order to address stigmatisation concerning employee fertility, propagating the significance of an inclusive and supportive culture is crucial. This means positively communicating about the support services offered whilst reaffirming the significance of being empathetic and understanding. Human resource analysts further recommend considering how leave/absences should be managed compassionately, clearly and flexibly. Absence/leave management policies must be inclusive of both men and women. Third, studies in the literature elucidate the significance of building trust-based relationships – enabling employees to communicate and confide sensitive familial challenges with their line manager/employer (Payne, Seenan & Van Den Akker, 2019).

Lactation Rooms/'Breastfeeding' Pods

Lactation, or infant feeding behaviours (direct and expressed), where the child is fed breast milk', has been relatively under-researched within the workplace literature.

The Case for Why Employers Must Invest in Lactation Rooms/ Breastfeeding Pods

Given the increasing prevalence of young working mothers with infants, there is an increasing importance of the theme within the domains of occupational psychology has suggested that employers may be able to significantly reduce absenteeism, and improve workplace performance, commitment and employee retention in their skilled female employees (Litwan, Tran, Nyhan, & Pérez-Escamilla, 2021). The organisation, additionally, benefits reputationally from being inclusive of women, addressing familial and wellbeing challenges and gender disparities within the organisation and the global workforce. Lastly, the employer significantly saves on any time and money invested in recruitment and training (Litwan et al., 2021). Despite continuing to be considered a 'taboo' topic, social and justice movements, in the recent past, have made calls to improve equity, diversity and inclusion in the workplace (Thomas, Murphy, Mills, Zhang, Fisher, & Clancy, 2022).

The Theoretical Underpinnings for the Provision of Lactation Services

Lactation provisions within workplaces must be grounded and align with two fundamental theoretical frameworks – first, the 'role' theory, which considers 'how work and family role demands compete for employee resources (such as time, energy and effort) and that such competition (work-family conflict) can result in strain'. Second, the 'stigma' theoretical framework embraces how women are faced with unique workplace experiences, due to stigmatisation of their own identity, whilst engaging in lactation behaviours. Lactating employees can be relatively more susceptible to harassment and/or ostracism consequentially, which can be detrimental to gender ratios and organisational culture (Thomas et al., 2022).

Burns and Triandafilidis (2019), in their analysis of return-to-work experiences of breastfeeding mothers, highlighted how women were challenged with inappropriate private and unsafe office spaces (toilet stalls and storage closets) to breastfeed – threatening the employee's sense of dignity, and making them feel exposed and more vulnerable. In addition, there is an inherent fear of being perceived as 'unprofessional', further necessitating being 'thick skinned', 'resilient to judgement' and building on the capacity to not be 'offended easily' (Burns et al., 2019).

In this light, lactation rooms or breastfeeding pods when at a convenient location within the organisation, possessing necessary amenities (such as power, storage and sink), 'private and secure' and fostering relaxation' can significantly enhance the wellbeing of young mothers. Occupational breast-feeding pod designers such as Mamava (refer to mamava.com) offer office pods (small to large) that, in addition to featuring compact refrigerators for storing breast milk, ventilation fans and app-enabled access (permitting access whilst minimising exposure to microbes), are wheel-chair accessible with a 60-degree turnaround and 'grab bars' for mothers with a disability.

Critics describe how employers are often challenged with making provisions for an appropriate space for the pod within the workplace and financial resources to invest in and maintain the facility. In this light, therefore, it is advisable for employers to conduct a 'needs' analysis – evaluating the number of female employees likely to potentially benefit from the service, their job and occupation conditions, and challenges and needs for organisational social and psychological support. Creative, outsourced/rented, breastfeeding pods account for some of the many viable options to offer support with limited organisational funds (Burns et al., 2019; Scott, Taylor, Basquin, & Venkitsubramanian, 2019; Thomas et al., 2022).

Litwan et al. (2021) elucidates how the effectiveness of any workplace breastfeeding intervention, such as the initiation of a 'breastfeeding' pod, is moderated by whether the intervention has been positively propagated amongst working mothers as well as their working environment, whether workplace culture has been appropriately altered, whether manager/supervisor/co-worker support has been offered, and whether there is provision for enough time, adequate space and facilities for women to express their milk and feed their infants every day.

'Leaning in' versus the 'Lazy Girl Jobs' Phenomenon for 'Gen Z'

Kennedy (2018) in her study discusses 'Lean In' – a premise and a community introduced by Sheryl Sandberg, Chief Operating Officer of Meta Platforms. Observing few women holding leadership roles in either government agencies or within the business domains, Sandberg appraised the paradox of women being challenged with family and child-caring responsibilities and taking and keeping a seat at the leadership table. This had profound implications for their physiological and psychological wellbeing. They were more prone to sexism, discrimination and sexual harassment, and consequentially were more likely to experience anxiety or fear (fear of not being liked), and they could 'internalise systematic discrimination and societal gender roles'.

Chrobot-Mason, Hoobler and Burno (2019) whilst analysing propositions made by Sandberg, appraised propositions made by the 'Lean In' community (Leanin, 2024) (see leanin.org). This included -

Creating Network Circles for Women within Outside Organisations

Enabling women to find connections, uniting women and fostering cohesiveness within the gender group (in small numbers) offered them opportunities to talk about their challenges/experiences, engage in collective learning, hone skills (particularly leadership skills), share advice and celebrate each other's wins. 'Circles' enabled women to forge broad and deeper connections that led to new opportunities and made a 'valuable addition' to the individual's CV, given that this was a self-led leadership initiative. The evidence established how the implementation of this 'no-cost' intervention resulted in '73% of women feeling more equipped to being better leaders, embracing new challenges and making positive changes in their lives, as a result of being part of "circles"' (Chrobot-Mason et al., 2019; Leanin, 2024).

Sandberg suggests the implementation of 'connection activities' – by employing a deck of cards and tabling topics for the circle, participants answer questions and get to know one another quickly. The sharing of deep information through the answering of a series of questions has proven to foster cohesiveness. This intervention has been criticised for having a relatively temporary effect and employees resisting participation. Ice-breaking and team-building activities, however, must be continually invested in to sustain high-quality work relationships (Leanin, 2024).

Urging Men to Mentor Women

When men commit to mentoring and supporting women at work, women are less likely to be challenged with anxiety, depression, harassment, sexual harassment or the likelihood of being overlooked or undermined. Men not harassing women was 'not enough'. Women who are guided, given actionable advice (rather than vague feedback) and supported by their seniors and colleagues, alongside their female peers, are more likely to embrace challenges, perform well in their job roles (particularly leadership roles) and more likely to receive a promotion, consequentially contributing to a stronger and safer workplace (Bickel, 2014; Madsen, Townsend & Scribner, 2020).

Fostering Allyship

Foster-Gimbel, Ganegoda, Oh, Ponce de Leon and Tedder-King (2022) and Leanin (2024) appraise 'allyship' as 'an active and consistent effort to use your privilege and power to support and advocate for people, with less privilege'. Organisational analysts recommend the implementation of workplace workshops – engaging female employees, urging them to reflect on 50 ways to combat biases (due to their race, sexuality and other aspects of their identity) within the workplace. Further, educating employees about the biases that women of colour face and learning more about their experiences is crucial (Leanin, 2024). Subsequently, appraising and implementing specific strategies to combat biases, such as speaking up for someone in the moment, asking a probing question (for instance 'what makes you say that?') recognising biases in their own thinking, sticking to factual information (concrete and neutral information) to minimise biases, explaining how and when biases are at play within the workplace, and advocating for policy and practice change prove to be beneficial.

Fossil Group, an American fashion design and manufacturing company, implemented the '50 ways to combat bias' intervention in a small and large group discussion, their 'Lean In' Circles and a Deck of Cards activity. They reported that 94% of their employees reported 'knowing what to do' when they witnessed a bias, a 92% increase in men and a 119% increase in women feeling more confident and equipped with discussing biases within their teams (Leanin, 2024). This interactive and scalable intervention, therefore, was effective at combatting biases that limit the potential, contribution and wellbeing of women at work.

The 'Lazy Girl Job' Phenomenon

Fast-paced living, an increasing obsession with women achieving their professional goals and their need to be productive whilst balancing family and caregiving responsibilities, and the onset of the pandemic (which brought work-from-home and flexible working benefits to the business to the fore) led to the emergence of the 'lazy girl job' phenomenon. The phenomenon was coined by TikTok influencer Gabrielle Judge, in 2023, in an attempt to challenge the hustle culture and over-work norms, promoting a transformation in work culture, and promoting work-life balance, employee health and wellbeing, equilibrium and employee dignity.

Promising good pay, demanding minimal effort, avoiding the need to invest in extensive training or traditional working hours and being done from the comfort of the couch, 'lazy girl' roles fall into the categories of social media management, freelance writing, virtual assistance, online surveys, market research, e-commerce, YouTube and blogging. Organisations such as the *Deep Nova Network*, although offering enticing benefits such as flexibility, independence and relatively few entry barriers, have garnered scepticism in the phenomenon, that it fosters unrealistic expectations of candidates and variable income.

This, practitioners advise, can be combatted by emphasising the importance of having realistic expectations, adaptability, networking, continuous learning and financial planning.

The phenomenon on social media is being challenged – women being lazy/laid back, the gender group just wanting to have fun (and a good job), lacking ambition and this being a privilege is only offered to affluent women.

'Lazy jobs' are not thought of as being a 'choice' for the poor or the middle-class sections of society – demanding jobs are a necessity 'driven by economic circumstances, societal pressures and lack of opportunities'. Critics, whilst drawing attention to how this is a likely trend in the 'new normal', point out 'lazy girl job blues', highlighting women's constant battle with pursuing their dream job (which offers flexibility, enables the 'breaking of the glass ceiling' and the making of meaningful contributions to society) and drawing a decent pay.

There is however a lack of scientific evidence that has analysed the significance of 'lazy girl' jobs, its potential influence on employee physical and mental health and wellbeing, and its demand amongst women and its prevalence/trends within diverse labour markets and contexts.

7.5 Discrimination and Inclusion – Men's Health and Wellbeing Challenges

When proposing and evaluating interventions for the wellbeing of men, the research suggests that this must be initiated in 'male friendly' settings whilst being 'culturally sensitive'. Employer initiatives and interventions for men must take style and language into consideration – this means employing 'male-oriented' terminologies (such as 'activity' rather than 'health', 'regaining control' rather than 'help-seeking'). Research evidence has elucidated how the 'virtual' or the 'arms-length' approaches such as online settings or telephonic wellbeing services prove to be beneficial given the element of anonymity. Further, activity or social-based interventions such as the 'Men's Sheds' approach and gender-specific, tailored social activities have proven to make a significant, positive contribution to the wellbeing of men. This is in addition to music and art therapy interventions.

Although relatively few, there has been some evidence demonstrating the effectiveness of exercise-based interventions for addressing anxiety and depression symptoms amongst men. On a similar note, studies highlight the designing and implementation of programmes such as 'Real Men', 'Real Depression Public Health Campaign' developed and propagated by the National Institute of Mental Health (NIMH), the 'MATES in Construction' programme in Australia and the 'HeadsUpGuys', an online intervention for men with depression in Canada (Milner, King, Scovelle, Batterham, Kelly, LaMontagne, Harvey, Gullestrup, & Lockwood, 2019; Ogrodniczuk, Oliffe, & Beharry, 2018).

Further investigations in the men's health and wellbeing literature have drawn attention to an online provocative 'man therapy' mental health intervention, a mental health campaign that employed 'dark humour' or 'maladaptive ideas of masculinity' to address mental health and wellbeing challenges amongst men 'head on' (Frey, Osteen, Sharpe, Mosby, Joiner, Ahmedani, & Gilgoff, 2023). The objectives of the intervention, in this light, included i) urging 'men to reflect and explore how gender socialisation influences their relationships and mental health, ii) reducing stigma pertaining to mental health and suicide, iii) empowering men to seek help and iv) reducing suicide risks (Frey et al., 2023). 'Humour' was evidenced as a beneficial nuance to this wellbeing intervention for men and has been identified as an important tool for the fostering of men's mental health. The intervention makes efforts to reduce stigma and alters the lens through which men's 'mental health and wellbeing' is perceived. It encourages men to view help-seeking as a sign of 'strength' rather than as a sign of 'weakness'.

When analysing suicide prevention, researchers place significance on the importance of peer emotional support systems, given that men prefer to seek support from informal rather than formal sources of assistance. Single element interventions (such as awareness-raising) and multi-dimensional approaches have also proven to be beneficial to reduce stigma, influence attitudes and change behaviours (particularly increasing talking and help-seeking behaviours) (although relatively less effective to peer support groups) (Kelly et al., 2019).

The literature has established the importance of creating an awareness that men, similar to women, can experience emotional and mental health challenges. In this light, investing in 'pre-crisis' management or mental health first aid, tailored specifically for men, is crucial. Any mental health and wellbeing programmes must recognise and demonstrate a comprehensive understanding of the social determinants of health and the impact of socio-economic factors, moderating the wellbeing narrative (Sagar-Ouriaghli, I., Godfrey, E., Bridge, L., Meade, L., & Brown, J. S., 2019).

Further, 'building trust' with male employees, through gender-aware and male-sensitive provisions, is important. Additionally 'creating safe spaces' where targeted groups of men are likely to engage in fun activities that facilitate talk, employ attractive media and language and encourage dialogue and reflection in modes acceptable to men. Moreover, developing and implementing initiatives that foster strong partnerships is evidenced to enable men to easily access informational and social resources and services such as early health intervention). Partnership interventions, particularly, can assist men with voicing concerns regarding challenging gender-insensitive practices (Waling, 2019).

Contemporary research has established how policy-makers, governments and those employed within professional bodies must challenge negative stereotypes and false portrayals of men in the media. 'Speak out' programmes, supported by significant leadership figures, which elicit the scale of the mental health and wellbeing concerns and the prevalence of suicide amongst men, will further fuel the propagation of wellbeing (Oliffe, Rossnagel, Bottorff, Chambers, Caperchione & Rice, 2020; Kelly, Steiner, Mason & Teasdale, 2019).

On another note, if individuals in power and authority insist that informational and social resources, access to funding opportunities and specialist services commissioned for men (such as support for fathers) be extensively offered, 'wellbeing' concerns for men would then be perceived as 'important'.

More robust research needs to be conducted to reaffirm the effectiveness of the virtual or the arms-length approach. Further investigations pertaining to gender-sensitive approaches for training programmes, the effectiveness of activity-based interventions, individual – 'talking therapy' – interventions, Men's Sheds (discussed in the paragraphs below) and the impact of workplace policies formulated for fostering mental health and wellbeing in men are recommended (Kelly at al., 2019; Oliffe, et al., 2020.).

'Men's Sheds'

Globally, the social and subsequent mental health and wellbeing of men have been overlooked and relatively under-researched. Specific groups of men such as those from rural and remote areas, those who are chronically ill, men who are unemployed, those with limited education or from cultural minority groups, or men from the lower end of the social strata are more prone to experiencing social isolation and loneliness (Cordier & Wilson, 2013). Employees with low-quantity and low-quality social relationships are more prone to experiencing mood or cognitive challenges and are at a higher risk of disability, demonstrate poor recovery from illness and die earlier. In addition, men are less likely to engage in help and health-seeking behaviours in contrast to women. Recognising the prevalence of social isolation, perceived loneliness, and its individual and societal consequences, especially amongst older men, the Men's Sheds movement was initiated in Australia and gained momentum there and in the UK and Ireland in the 1990s (Kelly, Steiner, Mason, & Teasdale, 2019; Milligan, Neary, Hanratty, Payne & Dowrick, 2016).

Having attracted funding of approximately $7 million, more than 550 Men's Sheds exist in Australia, with more than 550,000 older men participating in the initiative. Offering a space and an opportunity for older men to socialise, learn new skills and engage in activities with other men, Men's Sheds encourages men to engage in informal, adult learning activities, offers health-related information, and refers men to relevant services. Men standing 'shoulder to shoulder' enables them to effectively cope with unemployment, difficult past lives (including separation from their spouse), the stresses of ageing and substance abuse issues. In essence, the initiative does not solely alleviate men from social isolation and loneliness but also enhances physical, mental and spiritual wellbeing (Cordier et al., 2013).

7.6 Discrimination and Inclusion – Age

'Age discrimination', also understood as synonymous with 'ageism', has been described as 'the differential treatment, stereotyping, prejudice and discrimination against people, based on their age' (Mishra & Mishra, 2015). Ageism has been found to persist predominantly in two groups: younger employees, and older employees. Middle-aged employees have been evidenced as being less prone to biases or different treatment within the workplace. Contemporary researchers draw attention to three pertinent issues that must be addressed in older workers: direct and indirect discrimination, victimisation and harassment (Campbell & Smith, 2023).

Findings from a series of audit studies illustrate how recruiter callbacks significantly decline as employees age, subsequently influencing the duration of unemployment. Further, the decline has been found to be steeper for female employees (Francioli & North, 2021). Further studies, which examined exposure, participation, engagement and learning from training and development sessions/opportunities, identified that older employees were less likely to social support, opportunities for educational development, mentoring and feedback. Allocated to roles that are familiar, they are encouraged to adhere to fixed schedules, offering little prospects for growth (Francioli et al., 2021). Lastly, employers were less likely to invest in retention initiatives (including socialisation and organisational climate interventions, job design and personnel policy amendments) for older employees.

Further to having conducted field experiments during the course of which '6,000 fictitious resumes, with randomly assigned information about age (35–70 years) were sent to Swedish employers, with vacancies in low and medium skilled occupations', researchers elucidate a number of reasons for age-related stigmatisation and discriminatory behaviours (Carlsson & Eriksson, 2019). Firstly, older workers are assumed to be less likely to adapt to changes or to possess a lower ability to acquire any new skills. They are also perceived as 'less ambitious' or 'less persevering'. Employer discriminatory behaviours may also be 'taste-based'; i.e. driven by ageism, a dislike of older workers. Critics argue that older workers are not always less preferred or valued; within industries such as academia, for instance, older employees with extensive experience are highly sought after (Chou & Choi, 2011).

The literature has also established how age interacts with gender; employers prefer recruiting and retaining older women given that they are, on average, in better health than men. Older male employees, generally, are more likely to be faced with health concerns and retire relatively earlier (Carlsson et al., 2019).

The literature elucidates a wide range of benefits of being an age-inclusive employer. Whilst boosting reputation by initiating and implementing age-inclusive interventions, employers mitigate stigmatisation and the discrimination experienced by younger and older job seekers alike (Zacher, Kooij, & Beier, 2018). Additionally, they enhance productivity and knowledge-sharing behaviours within the workplace. Lastly, investing in age-inclusive practices meant that the employer was taking steps to prepare for an ageing workforce (Zacher et al., 2018).

In this light, analysts such as Marchiondo, Gonzales and Ran (2016) propagate the use of the Workplace Age Discrimination Scale (WADS). Measuring perceived covert and overt workplace age discrimination, the psychometrically robust instrument comprised of statements such as 'I have been passed over for a work role/task due to my age', 'my contributions are not valued as much, due to my age', 'I receive less social support due to my age' and 'I have been treated as though I am less capable, due to my age'.

Employer Interventions

When recruiting and retaining older candidates/employees, professional bodies such as the CIPD recommend that employers employ age-inclusive practices to eliminate biases. This, for instance, meant drafting age-inclusive job descriptions, person specifications and job advertisements. Circulating job adverts as widely as possible, using multiple platforms that are relatively frequently accessed by older people, and regularly drawing and scrutinising age-related data from the recruitment process count as some of the many diverse age-embracing initiatives that an employer can potentially adopt.

Further, organisational and national implementation of physical and mental occupational healthcare screenings and interventions is expected to increase the likelihood of employees experiencing a relatively healthier and enhanced quality of life. This is the case as economic inactivity is likely to rise after the age of 50. Lastly, combatting assumptions of older employees not being interested in or not being worth investing in is crucial. Employers must invest in the training, development and upskilling of older employees to the same level, if not more, than they do for the rest of the workforce (Burnes, Sheppard, Henderson, Wassel, Cope, Barber & Pillemer, 2019; Zacher et al., 2018).

7.7 Chronic Employee 'Pain' and Wellbeing

Crippling more than 100 million people in the United States and a significant number of individuals across other regions of the world, 'chronic pain in one or more anatomical regions, that persists or recurs for longer than 3 months', has a significant, detrimental influence on employee quality of life and wellbeing. Four employee pain diagnoses have been particularly analysed in the literature – musculoskeletal (such as rheumatoid arthritis and back pain), myofascial, neuropathic and visceral (Giladi, Scott, Shir, & Sullivan, 2015).

Pain challenges an individual's core sense of who they are by distorting their identity (Blanchflower & Bryson, 2022). 'One's identity can be enmeshed so closely with pain that it becomes difficult to think of any aspect of one's life as being free of pain, including one's idea about any future'. Research highlights the importance of personality characteristics in the pain experience, the likelihood of reporting pain experiences and the management of chronic pain at work. For instance, employees who score highly on neu-roticism are more likely to catastrophise pain and subsequently report more paiin experience, whilst engaging in maladaptive behaviours, more often, than those who scored low on the characteristic (Wong, Lam, Chen, Chow, Wong, Lim, & Fielding, 2015).

Irrespective of personality characteristics, employee chronic pain expe-riences were correlated with poor employee sleep hygiene. Evidence from the literature further describes how the relationship between employee pain and sleep was bi-directional, with pain having a sleep-interfering effect, and sleep deprivation or poor quality sleep having a pain-inducing effect (Tang, Fiecas, Afolalu, & Wolke, 2017). Research studies have also firmly confirmed a link between employee chronic pain and the likelihood of being challenged with clinical anxiety and depression. A similar strongly positive correlation was demonstrated with 'kinesiophobia' or 'the experience of an irrational and debilitating fear of movement or physical activity' (McFarland, Norrie, Atherton, Power, & Jones, 2008).

Employee chronic pain additionally means increasing the use of health-care insurance and related services offered by an employer. This further leads to decreased labour market participation. Those challenged with musculo-skeletal pain, for instance, were more likely to be faced with unemployment and economic inactivity (Giladi et al., 2015). Other consequential work outcomes included employees increasingly taking sickness absences, differ-ences in the individual's ability to work, changes in employment status (for instance work type and job status) and increasing occurrences of presentee-ism (McFarland et al., 2008).

'Employee pain (and its subsequent consequences) cannot be addressed if it cannot be assessed' (Karcioglu, Topacoglu, Dikme, & Dikme, 2018). In this light, Karcioglu et al. (2018) describe how an employee's self-report accounts for the most accurate and reliable measure of the existence and intensity of pain. For this, the Visual Analog Scale (VAS), the Numerical Rating Scale (NRS), the Verbal Rating Scale (VRS) or Verbal Descriptor Scale (VDS) and the Wong-Baker Faces Pain Rating Scale are some of the many research instru-ments that can be employed for the assessment of employee pain.

Employer Interventions

McParland, Andrews, Kidd, Williams, and Flowers (2021) discuss a number of propositions that organisations can choose to employ – these include offer-ing services for physiological rehabilitation or a rheumatology clinic, exercise or medication management.

Critics point out that employees crippled with chronic pain may have several other challenges. Thematic findings from Eccleston, Wainwright and Wainwright (2018) describe the importance of employers engaging in active listening. Employees were found to place importance on clear, regular, empathetic communication with their employers, where the employer not only asks the employee how they were but is genuinely interested in the response. Assessing employee track records to ascertain the extent to which the employees' reports of subjective conditions, such as pain, could be believed, was crucial. It was important to acquire holistic knowledge of employees to assess the authenticity of illness claims (Lennox Thompson, Gage & Kirk, 2020).

On another note, whilst emphasising the importance of employer-employee relationship trust, physical adjustments to workstations and flexi-time, participants also reported how provisions for taxis to work were appreciated. The service not only enabled employees to easily get to work but also was a 'symbolic' gesture of trust and value (Eccleston et al., 2018).

Employer initiatives could further address the psychological component by drawing upon cognitive behavioural therapy (CBT) approaches, interventions embracing other psychological and behavioural principles, counselling, acceptance and commitment therapy, motivational interviewing or mindfulness-based stress reduction (McParland et al., 2021).

7.8 Summary

In essence, this chapter aimed to clarify what 'psychological safety' signifies in the workplace literature and how this distinct from employee trust. Although, commonly misunderstood, 'psychological safety' concerned an organisational climate, within which employees felt free to express themselves, without any negative consequences to their image, status or their career. Employee 'trust' on the other hand, simplistically implied 'giving the other the benefit of doubt – indicating a focus on the other's trustworthiness. In this light, the chapter appraised the marshmallow intervention, the CENTRE tool, The TEAMGAINS intervention and a number of other evidence-based interventions to foster psychological safety within the workplace. High levels of within team and organisational psychological safety implied greater socio-emotional resources, lower levels of employee frustration and angst.

The chapter moved on to elucidating how cancer survivors are often challenged with stigma and discriminatory behaviours – including hiring discrimination and denial of workplace support. The section discusses how employer evidence-based policies including return to work plans, flexible work scheduling initiatives and employer collaboration with health care specialists positively influenced employment outcome and employee health care savings. Later, a relatively under-researched theme in the workplace literature, although a global health concern – women's menstrual health, was discussed, in the sections to follow. Organisations such as ICICI bank, Godrej and Salesforce implemented employee fertility policies. These initiatives in addition to lactation rooms and breast-feeding pods, were critically analysed. The latter proposition, although expensive and made women more prone to harassment and/or ostracism at work, enabled working mothers consider 'returning to work', post delivery.

Moreover, the chapter drew attention to men's physical and mental health. The author affirmed the significance of employing 'culturally sensitive' and 'male oriented' terminologies – such as – 'activity' rather than 'health', 'regaining control' rather than 'help seeking' with men. Embedding humour in wellbeing interventions was additionally found to benefit the group and further encouraged men to perceive 'seeking help' as a sign of 'strength', rather than a sign of 'weakness'. Recongising the prevalence of loneliness amongst men, the literature drew attention to the 'Men's Shed's movement. The initiative attempted to foster high quality relationships, encouraging men to participate in informal, adult learning activities. Offering health and employment related information, the initiative enabled men effectively cope with unemployment, separation from spouse/family and substance abuse. Lastly, the author appraised evidence-based interventions for older employees and those challenged with chronic pain. Employer active listening, flexible working propositions, physical adjustments to workstations, acceptance and commitment therapeutic interventions and motivational interviewing techniques were found to benefit these employee groups.

7.9 Suggested Readings

Guo, L. (2020). The effect of workplace loneliness on silence behavior. Psychology, 11(03), 467.

Shaw, W. S., Tveito, T. H., Geehern-Lavoie, M., Huang, Y. H., Nicholas, M. K., Reme, S. E., ... Pransky, G. (2012). Adapting principles of chronic pain self-management to the workplace. Disability and Rehabilitation, 34(8), 694–703.

Wright, S. L. (2015). Coping with loneliness at work. Ami & Ami, In Addressing Loneliness (pp. 123–134). New York: Psychology Press.

7.10 Suggested Websites

British Psychological Society (2023a). In vulnerable times we tend to remember the words said to Us. Available at: https://www.bps.org.uk/psychologist/vulnerable -times-we-tend-remember-words-said-us Accessed on: 7 November 2023

British Psychological Society (2023b). An honest and raw insight into baby loss. Available at: https://www.bps.org.uk/psychologist/honest-and-raw-insight-baby -loss Accessed on: 7 November 2023

NHS (2021a). Work and pregnancy. Available at: https://www.nhs.uk/pregnancy/ keeping-well/your-health-at-work/ Accessed on: 7 November 2023

NHS (2021b). Work and cancer. Available at: https://www.nhsinform.scot/illnesses -and-conditions/cancer/practical-issues/work-and-cancer/ Accessed on: 7 November 2023

NHS Employer (2023). Guidance on musculoskeletal health in the workplace. Available at: https://www.nhsemployers.org/publications/guidance-musculoskeletal-health -workplace Accessed on: 7 November 2023

7.11 Reflective Questions – for Learners

From your reading and research -

1. Why should employers invest in the wellbeing of employees challenged with cancer? What interventions could they employ to support this vulnerable group, particularly post-pandemic?
2. Elucidate the wellbeing benefits of investing in 'Men's Sheds'.
3. Critically analyse the factors that could potentially contribute to aggravating employee perceived loneliness.

7.12 Reflective Questions – for Researchers/Practitioners

1. Reflect and elucidate specific organisational practices/interventions at your workplace that combat employee perceived loneliness..
2. Design and conduct a pre- and post-intervention study to test the effectiveness of an exercise-based intervention on employee (men) physical/ mental health and wellbeing.
3. Conduct an EBSCOhost/Psychinfo search covering the literature published in the past couple of years using the terms 'music therapy', 'art therapy' and/or 'employee wellbeing', individually or in combination. Identify a study that resonates with your interests and that is feasible to replicate and extend. Conduct the replication.

References

Alleaume, C., Paraponaris, A., Bendiane, M. K., Peretti-Watel, P., & Bouhnik, A. D. (2020). The positive effect of workplace accommodations on the continued employment of cancer survivors five years after diagnosis. *Supportive Care in Cancer, 28*, 4435–4443.

Arieli, D., & Yassour-Borochowitz, D. (2024). Decent care and decent employment: Family caregivers, migrant care workers and moral dilemmas. *Ethics & Behavior, 34*(5), 314–326.

Baddour, K., Kudrick, L. D., Neopaney, A., Sabik, L. M., Peddada, S. D., Nilsen, M. L., ... Mady, L. J. (2020). Potential impact of the COVID-19 pandemic on financial toxicity in cancer survivors. *Head and Neck, 42*(6), 1332–1338.

Barry, J. E., & Cramer, K. M. (1999). Conceptualisations and measures of loneliness: A comparison of sub-scales. *Personality and Individual Differences, 27*(3), 491–502.

Bickel, J. (2014). How men can excel as mentors of women. *Academic Medicine, 89*(8), 1100–1102.

Blanchflower, D. G., & Bryson, A. (2022). Chronic pain: Evidence from the national child development study. *PLoS One, 17*(11), e0275095.

Buchanan, D. A., & Huczynski, A. (2010). *Organisational Behaviour*. Essex: Financial Times Prentice Hall.

Burnes, D., Sheppard, C., Henderson, C. R., Wassel, M., Cope, R., Barber, C., & Pillemer, K. (2019). Interventions to reduce ageism against older adults: A systematic review and meta-analysis. *American Journal of Public Health, 109*(8), e1–e9.

Burns, E., & Triandafilidis, Z. (2019). Taking the path of least resistance: A qualitative analysis of return to work or study while breastfeeding. *International Breastfeeding Journal, 14*, 1–13.

Campbell, C., & Smith, D. (2023). Distinguishing between direct and indirect discrimination. *Modern Law Review, 86*(2), 307–330.

Carlsson, M., & Eriksson, S. (2019). Age discrimination in hiring decisions: Evidence from a field experiment in the labor market. *Labour Economics, 59*, 173–183.

Cave, D., Pearson, H., Whitehead, P., & Rahim-Jamal, S. (2016). CENTRE: Creating psychological safety in groups. *The Clinical Teacher, 13*(6), 427–431.

Chen, K., & Tan, K. (2023). How video games saved me during the pandemic: A gamer's guide to psychological safety. *Journal of Medical Imaging and Radiation Sciences, 54*(2S), S10–S14.

Chou, R., & Choi, N. (2011). Prevalence and correlates of perceived workplace discrimination among older workers in the United States of America. *Ageing and Society, 31*(06), 1051–1070.

Chrobot-Mason, D., Hoobler, J. M., & Burno, J. (2019). Lean in versus the literature: An evidence-based examination. *Academy of Management Perspectives, 33*(1), 110–130.

CIPD (2020). Supporting Working Carers: How Employers and Employees Can Benefit. Available at: www.cipd.org, Accessed on: 20 July 2024.

Colussi, S., Hill, E., & Baird, M. (2024). *Reproductive policies: An expanding approach to work and care.* At a Turning Point: Work, care and family policies in Australia, 19.

Cordier, R., & Wilson, N. J. (2013). A narrative review of Men's sheds literature: Reducing social isolation and promoting Men's health and wellbeing. *Health and Social Care in the Community, 21*(5), 451–463.

Duan, J., Xu, T., & Cai, Y. (2022). To act or not to act? How do pregnant employees perform based on family-supportive supervisor behavior. *Applied Psychology, 71*(4), 1493–1512.

De Rijk, A., Amir, Z., Cohen, M., Furlan, T., Godderis, L., Knezevic, B. & De Boer, A. (2020). The challenge of return to work in workers with cancer: Employer priorities despite variation in social policies related to work and health. *Journal of Cancer Survivorship, 14*, 188–199.

Dutton, J. E. (2003). *Energize Your Workplace: How to Create and Sustain High-Quality Connections at Work.* USA: John Wiley & Sons.

Eccleston, Wainwright, Wainwright & Keogh (2013). Return to Work with Chronic Pain: Employers and Employees Views. *Occupational Medicine, 63*(7), 501–506.

Edmondson, A. C., & Lei, Z. (2014). Psychological safety: The history, renaissance, and future of an interpersonal construct. *Annual Review of Organizational Psychology and Organizational Behavior, 1*(1), 23–43.

Feuerstein, M., Luff, G. M., Harrington, C. B., & Olsen, C. H. (2007). Pattern of workplace disputes in cancer survivors: A population study of ADA claims. *Journal of Cancer Survivorship: Research and Practice, 1*(3), 185–192.

Frake, C., & Dogra, N. (2006). The use of reflecting teams in educational contexts. *Reflective Practice, 7*, 143–149.

Francioli, S. P., & North, M. S. (2021). Youngism: The content, causes, and consequences of prejudices toward younger adults. *Journal of Experimental Psychology: General, 150*(12), 2591.

Frey, J. J., Osteen, P. J., Sharpe, T. L., Mosby, A. O., Joiner, T., Ahmedani, B., & Gilgoff, J. N. (2023). Effectiveness of man therapy to reduce suicidal ideation and depression among working-age men: A randomized controlled trial. *Suicide and Life-Threatening Behavior, 53*(1), 137–153.

Foster-Gimbel, O., Ganegoda, D. B., Oh, S., Ponce de Leon, R., & Tedder-King, A. (2022). Allyship in the workplace: An examination of antecedents and consequences. *Academy of Management Proceedings, 2022*(1), 10857). Briarcliff Manor, NY: Academy of Management.

Giladi, H., Scott, W., Shir, Y., & Sullivan, M. J. L. (2015). Rates and correlates of unemployment across four chronic pain diagnostic categories. *Journal of Occupational Rehabilitation, 25*(3), 648–657.

Glaser, P., Liu, J. H., Hakim, M. A., et al. (2019). Is social media use for networking positive or negative? offline social capital and internet addiction as mediators for the relationship between social media use and mental health. *New Zealand Journal of Psychology, 47,* 12–18.

Gordon, J. R., Pruchno, R. A., Wilson-Genderson, M., Murphy, W. M., & Rose, M. (2012). Balancing caregiving and work: Role conflict and role strain dynamics. *Journal of Family Issues, 33*(5), 662–689.

Ha, N. T. T. (2021). Workplace isolation in the growth trend of remote working: A literature review. *Review of Economic and Business Studies, 27,* 97–113.

Ilic, D. (2013). Educating men about prostate cancer in the workplace. *American Journal of Men's Health, 7*(4), 285–294.

Ireson, R., Sethi, B., & Williams, A. (2018). Availability of care – Giver friendly workplace: An international scoping review, *28*(1), 1–14.

Jegermalm, M., & Torgé, C. J. (2023). Three caregiver profiles: Who are they, what do they do, and who are their co-carers?. *European Journal of Social Work, 26*(3), 466–479.

Karcioglu, O., Topacoglu, H., Dikme, O., & Dikme, O. (2018). A systematic review of the pain scales in adults: Which to use? *The American Journal of Emergency Medicine, 36*(4), 707–714.

Kark, R., & Carmeli, A. (2009). Alive and creating: The mediating role of vitality and aliveness in the relationship between psychological safety and creative work involvement. *Journal of Organizational Behavior: The International Journal of Industrial, Occupational and Organizational Psychology and Behavior, 30*(6), 785–804.

Kelly, D., Steiner, A., Mason, H., & Teasdale, S. (2019). Men's Sheds: A conceptual exploration of the causal pathways for health and well-being. *Health and Social Care in the Community, 27*(5), 1147–1157.

Kennedy, T. A. (2018). Lean in and tell me a (true) story: Sheryl Sandberg's revision of feminist history. In D. Letort and B. Lebdai (Eds.), *Women Activists and Civil Rights Leaders in Auto/Biographical Literature and Films,* Cham: Palgrave

Khan-Shah, F. (2020). Support for unpaid carers: The working carers' passport. *British Journal of Community Nursing, 25*(3), 144–147.

Kriz, W. C. (2010). A systemic-constructivist approach to the facilitation and debriefing of simulations and games. *Simulation Gaming, 41:* 663–680.

Larkin, M., Henwood, M., & Milne, A. (2019). Carer-related research and knowledge: Findings from a scoping review. *Health & Social Care in the Community, 27*(1), 55–67.

Leanin (2024). Available at: https://leanin.org/about Accessed on: 12 March 2024.

Lennox Thompson, B., Gage, J., & Kirk, R. (2020). Living well with chronic pain: A classical grounded theory. *Disability and Rehabilitation, 42*(8), 1141–1152.

Leung, K., Deng, H., Wang, J., & Zhou, F. (2015). Beyond risk-taking: Effects of psychological safety on cooperative goal interdependence and prosocial behavior. *Group and Organization Management, 40*(1), 88–115.

Litwan, K., Tran, V., Nyhan, K., & Pérez-Escamilla, R. (2021). How do breastfeeding workplace interventions work?: A realist review. *International Journal for Equity in Health, 20*(1), 148.

Lord, R. G., Brown, D. J., Harvey, J. L., & Hall, R. J. (2001). Contextual constraints on prototype generation and their multilevel consequences for leadership perceptions. *The Leadership Quarterly, 12*(3), 311–338.

Lorenz, F., Whittaker, L., Tazzeo, J., & Williams, A. (2021). Availability of caregiver-friendly workplace policies: an international scoping review follow-up study. *International Journal of Workplace Health Management, 14*(4), 459–476.

MacFarlane, G. J., Norrie, G., Atherton, K., Power, C., & Jones, G. T. (2008). The influence of socioeconomic status on the reporting of regional and widespread musculoskeletal pain: Results from the 1958 British Birth Cohort Study. *Annals of the Rheumatic Diseases, 68*(10), 1591–1595.

Madsen, S. R., Townsend, A., & Scribner, R. T. (2020). Strategies that male allies use to advance women in the workplace. *The Journal of Men's Studies, 28*(3), 239–259.

Marchiondo, L. A., Gonzales, E., & Ran, S. (2016). Development and validation of the workplace age discrimination scale. *Journal of Business and Psychology, 31*(4), 493–513.

Marshall, G. W., Michaels, C. E., & Mulki, J. P. (2007). Workplace isolation: Exploring the construct and its measurement. *Psychology and Marketing, 24*(3), 195–223.

Mayer, I. (2018). Assessment of teams in a digital game environment. *Simulation & Gaming, 49*(6), 602–619.

McParland, J. L., Andrews, P., Kidd, L., Williams, L., & Flowers, P. (2021). A scoping review to ascertain the parameters for an evidence synthesis of psychological interventions to improve work and wellbeing outcomes among employees with chronic pain. *Health Psychology and Behavioral Medicine, 9*(1), 25–47.

Mertes, H. (2015). Does company-sponsored egg freezing promote or confine women's reproductive autonomy?. *Journal of Assisted Reproduction and Genetics, 32*, 1205–1209.

Metcalfe, B., & Metcalfe, J. (2007). Development of a private sector version of the engaging transformational leadership questionnaire. *Leadership and Organization Development Journal, 28*(2), 104–121.

Microsoft (2019). Trust and vulnerability: Facilitator guide. Available at: www.microsoft.com, Accessed on: 21 July 2024.

Milligan, C., Neary, D., Hanratty, B., Payne, S., & Dowrick, C. (2016). Older men and social activity: A systematic review of Men's Sheds and other gendered interventions. *Ageing and Society Firstview*, Article, *36*(5), 1–29.

Milner, A., King, T. L., Scovelle, A. J., Batterham, P. J., Kelly, B., LaMontagne, A. D., Harvey, S. B., Gullestrup, J., & Lockwood, C. (2019). A blended face-to-face and smartphone intervention for suicide prevention in the construction industry: Protocol for a randomized control trial with MATES construction. *BMC Psychiatry, 19*(1), 146–154. https://doi.org/10.1186/s12888-019-2142-3.

Mishra, B., & Mishra, J. (2015). Discrimination in the workplace. *Journal of Higher Education Theory & Practice, 15*(4), 64–72.

Mofidi, A., Tompa, E., Williams, A., Yazdani, A., Lero, D., & Mortazavi, S. B. (2019). Impact of a caregiver-friendly workplace policies intervention: A prospective economic evaluation. *Journal of Occupational and Environmental Medicine, 61*(6), 461–468.

Munir, Y., Sadiq, M., Ali, I., Hamdan, Y., & Munir, E. (2016). Workplace isolation in pharmaceutical companies: Moderating role of self-efficacy. *Social Indicators Research, 126*(3), 1157–1174.

Norem, J. K., & Cantor, N. (1986). Defensive pessimism: Harnessing anxiety as motivation. *Journal of Personality and Social Psychology, 51*(6), 1208.

Ogrodniczuk, J., Oliffe, J., & Beharry, J. (2018). HeadsUpGuys: Canadian online resource for men with depression. *Canadian Family Physician Medecin de Famille Canadien, 64*(2), 93–94.

Oliffe, J. L., Rossnagel, E., Bottorff, J. L., Chambers, S. K., Caperchione, C., & Rice, S. M. (2020). Community-based men's health promotion programs: Eight lessons learnt and their caveats. *Health Promotion International, 35*(5), 1230–1240.

Parker, H., & du Plooy, E. (2021). Team-based games: Catalysts for developing psychological safety, learning and performance. *Journal of Business Research, 125*, 45–51.

Payne, N., Seenan, S., & van den Akker, O. (2019). Experiences and psychological distress of fertility treatment and employment. *Journal of Psychosomatic Obstetrics & Gynecology, 40*(2), 156–165.

Peng, R., Mou, W., & Xu, P. (2023). Factors associated with fertility intention among Chinese married youth during the COVID-19 pandemic. *Behavioral Sciences, 13*(2), 184.

Peterson, C. E., Silva, A., Goben, A. H., Ongtengco, N. P., Hu, E. Z. Khanna, D., & Dykens, J. A. (2021). Stigma and cervical cancer prevention: A scoping review of the US literature. *Preventive Medicine, 153*, 106–849.

Rick, O., Kalusche, E. M., Dauelsberg, T., König, V., Korsukéwitz, C., & Seifart, U. (2012). Reintegrating cancer patients into the workplace. *Deutsches Ärzteblatt International, 109*(42), 702.

Russell, D., Cutrona, C. E., Rose, J., & Yurko, K. (1984). Social and emotional loneliness: An examination of Weiss's typology of loneliness. *Journal of Personality and Social Psychology, 46*(6), 1313–1321.

Sahai, S., Ciby, M. A., & Kahwaji, A. T. (2020). Workplace isolation: A systematic review and synthesis. *International Journal of Management (IJM), 11*(12), 2745–2758.

Sang, K., Remnant, J., Calvard, T., & Myhill, K. (2021). Blood work: Managing menstruation, menopause and gynaecological health conditions in the workplace. *International Journal of Environmental Research and Public Health, 18*(4), 1951.

Scalise, J. J., Ginter, E. J., & Gerstein, L. H. (1984). A Multidimensional loneliness measure: The Loneliness Rating Scale (LRS). *Journal of Personality Assessment, 48*(5), 525–530.

Scott, V. C., Taylor, Y. J., Basquin, C., & Venkitsubramanian, K. (2019). Impact of key workplace breastfeeding support characteristics on job satisfaction, breastfeeding duration, and exclusive breastfeeding among health care employees. *Breastfeeding Medicine, 14*(6), 416–423.

Siemsen, E., Roth, A. V., Balasubramanian, S., & Anand, G. (2009). The influence of psychological safety and confidence in knowledge on employee knowledge sharing. *Manufacturing and Service Operations Management, 11*(3), 429–447.

Sliter, M. T., Sinclair, R. R., Yuan, Z., & Mohr, C. D. (2014). Don't fear the reaper: Trait death anxiety, mortality salience, and occupational health. *Journal of Applied Psychology, 99*(4), 759.

Soldano, S. (2016). Workplace wellness programs to promote cancer prevention. *Seminars in Oncology Nursing, 32*(3), 281–290.

Stergiou-Kita, G. A., & Tseung, V (2014). Qualitative meta-synthesis of survivors' work experiences and the development of strategies to facilitate return to work. *Journal of Cancer Survivorship: Research and Practice, 8*(4), 657–670.

Stergiou-Kita, M., Pritlove, C., & Kirsh, B. (2016). The "Big C"—Stigma, cancer, and workplace discrimination. *Journal of Cancer Survivorship: Research and Practice, 10*(6), 1035–1050.

Stergiou-Kita, M., Pritlove, C., van Eerd, D., Holness, L. D., Kirsh, B., Duncan, A., & Jones, J. (2016). The provision of workplace accommodations following cancer: Survivor, provider, and employer perspectives. *Journal of Cancer Survivorship: Research and Practice, 10*(3), 489–504.

Steyn, F., Sizer, A., & Pericleous-Smith, A. (2022). Fertility in the workplace: The emotional, physical and psychological impact of infertility in the workplace. *Human Reproduction, 37*, 104–127.

Tang, K. Y., Fiecas, M., Afolalu, E. F., & Wolke, D. (2017). Changes in sleep duration, quality, and medication use are prospectively associated with health and well-being: Analysis of the UK Household Longitudinal Study. *Sleep, 40*(3), zsw-079

Thomas, C. L., Murphy, L. D., Mills, M. J., Zhang, J., Fisher, G. G., & Clancy, R. L. (2022). Employee lactation: A review and recommendations for research, practice, and policy. *Human Resource Management Review, 32*(3), 100848.

Wainwright, E., Wainwright, D., & Keogh, E., (2013) Return to work with chronic pain: Employers and employees views. *Occupational Medicine, 63*(7), 501–506.

Waling, A. (2019). Problematising 'toxic' and 'healthy' masculinity for addressing gender inequalities. *Australian Feminist Studies, 34*(101), 362–375.

Wilkinson, K., & Mumford, C. (2024). Navigating fertility treatment alongside work and employment: The work-fertility interface. In *Work-Life Inclusion: Broadening Perspectives Across the Life-Course* (pp. 67–79). Emerald Publishing Limited.

Wittenberg, M. T. (1986). *Emotional and Social Loneliness: An Examination of Social Skills, Attributions, Sex Role, and Object Relations Perspectives.* Unpublished doctoral dissertation. University of Rochester.

Wong, W. S., Lam, H. M. J., Chen, P. P., Chow, Y. F., Wong, S., Lim, H. S., ... Fielding, R. (2015). The fear-avoidance model of chronic pain: Assessing the role of neuroticism and negative affect in pain catastrophizing using structural equation modeling. *International Journal of Behavioral Medicine, 22*(1), 118–131.

Zacher, H., Kooij, D. T. A. M., & Beier, M. E. (2018). Active aging at work. *Organizational Dynamics, 47*(1), 37–45.

Zoll, M., Mertes, H., & Gupta, J. (2015). Corporate giants provide fertility benefits: Have they got it wrong?. *European Journal of Obstetrics, Gynecology, and Reproductive Biology, 195*, A1–A2.

Index

Printed in the United States
by Baker & Taylor Publisher Services